The Origins of Modern Banking in Spain

This book analyses the formation of the Spanish banking system. It provides a general overview of European financial systems in operation during the mid-nineteenth century, followed by a detailed analysis of the economic and institutional changes that gave rise to a new form of banking in Spain.

The chapters analyse changes on banking regulation; study the social origin of banks' promoters; investigate the economic results of banks; and evaluate the interaction between banks and the economy as a whole. Finally, the causes, extent and consequences of monetary plurality in Spain and its European context are discussed. As such, this book covers the gap that exists in the Spanish banking historiography. Until now only the Bank of Spain and its predecessors had been adequately examined. As the Bank of Spain acted mostly as the state's financial agent, we know very little about private-sector financing. This text provides data and analysis for a more comprehensive view of early Spanish financial development in a comparative European framework.

The Origins of Modern Banking in Spain should be considered essential reading for financial history students and scholars, as well as anybody interested in long-view approaches to modern financial development.

Carles Sudrià is Professor of Economic History at the Universitat de Barcelona. He has published widely on financial history and the history of energy in Spain, and contributed to journals such as *Business History*, *Financial History Review*, *European Review of Economic History* and *Revista de Historia Económica*.

Yolanda Blasco-Martel is Associate Professor of Economic History at the Universitat de Barcelona. She has published on financial history, social history and business networks in Spain, and contributed to journals such as *Business History*, *Atlantic Studies*, *Investigaciones de Historia Económica* and *Revista de Historia Industrial*.

Financial History
Edited by Farley Grubb and Anne L. Murphy

The Globalization of Merchant Banking before 1850
The case of Huth & Co.
Manuel Llorca-Jaña

Monetary Statecraft in Brazil
1808–2014
Kurt Mettenheim

Banking Modern America
Studies in regulatory history
Edited by Jesse Stiller

Money, Politics and Power
Banking and Public Finance in Wartime England, 1694–96
Richard A. Kleer

Regulation of the London Stock Exchange
Share Trading, Fraud and Reform 1914–1945
Chris Swinson

Monetary Plurality in Local, Regional and Global Economies
Edited by Georgina M. Gómez

Share Trading, Fraud and the Crash of 1929
A Biography of Clarence Hatry
Chris Swinson

The Origins of Modern Banking in Spain
The Role of Monetary Plurality
Edited by Carles Sudrià and Yolanda Blasco-Martel

For more information about this series, please visit www.routledge.com/series/FINHIS

The Origins of Modern Banking in Spain

The Role of Monetary Plurality

Edited by Carles Sudrià and Yolanda Blasco-Martel

Routledge
Taylor & Francis Group
LONDON AND NEW YORK

First published in English 2019
by Routledge
2 Park Square, Milton Park, Abingdon, Oxon OX14 4RN

and by Routledge
605 Third Avenue, New York, NY 10017

First issued in paperback 2020

Routledge is an imprint of the Taylor & Francis Group, an informa business

Published in Spanish by Fundación BBVA 2016

British Library Cataloguing-in-Publication Data
A catalogue record for this book is available from the British Library

Library of Congress Cataloging-in-Publication Data
A catalog record for this book has been requested

ISBN 13: 978-0-367-72995-0 (pbk)
ISBN 13: 978-1-138-31655-3 (hbk)
ISBN 13: 978-0-429-45558-2 (ebk)

Typeset in Times New Roman
by Apex CoVantage, LLC

Contents

Figures

Tables

Contributors

Mercedes Bernal Lloréns (PhD, Economics, University of Murcia). Associate professor of accounting and finance at University of Murcia. Her research focuses on financial information and regulation, and on accounting history. She has recently published articles in *Explorations in Economic History, Accounting Historians Journal* and *Accounting History*.

Yolanda Blasco-Martel (PhD, Economic History, University of Barcelona). Associate professor of economic history at University of Barcelona. Her research focuses on banking and financial history, and in social history. She has published in *Business History, Revista de Historia Industrial, Investigaciones de Historia Económica* and *Historia Social*. She is co-author of *Banco de Barcelona 1844–1874. Historia de un banco emisor* (2010), and *Banco de Barcelona, 1874–1920. Decadencia y quiebra* (2016), with Carles Sudrià.

Lluís Castañeda (PhD, History and Civilization, European University Institute). Associate professor of economic history at University of Barcelona. He researches on Spanish financial history, with a focus on the development of the Bank of Spain in the nineteenth century. He has published in *Revista de Historia Económica, Revista de Historia Industrial* and on the *Economic History Studies* Series. *Bank of Spain*.

Juan Pedro Sánchez-Ballesta (PhD, Economics, University of Murcia). Associate professor of accounting and finance at University of Murcia. His research is centred on corporate finance and governance, and financial information. He has published in *Journal of Banking and Finance, Journal of Business Finance and Accounting, Explorations in Economic History* and *European Accounting Review*.

Carles Sudrià (PhD, Economics, Autonomous University of Barcelona). Professor of Economic History at University of Barcelona. He has published widely on industrial and energy history, and on financial history. He is the director of *Revista de Historia Industrial*. His articles have appeared in *Business History, Financial History Review, European Review of Economic History* and *Revista* *de Historia Económica*. He has recently contributed to *Immortal Banks: Strategies, Structures, and Performances of Major Banks* (M. Lescure, ed., Droz, 2016); and *The Book of Payments: Historical and Contemporary Views on the Cashless Society* (B. Bátiz-Lazo and L. Efthymiou, eds., 2016), with Y. Blasco-Martel.

Acknowledgements

The research that sustains this book has been funded at various stages by the Spanish Ministry of Education and Science, through the research project HAR2010–17482, and by the BBVA Foundation (research project: "Banks of issue and the formation of Spanish financial system"). The authors are also grateful for financial support received from the Ministry of the Economy and Competitiveness of the Spanish government (MINECO) and from the European Regional Development Fund of the European Union (FEDER) through the project HAR2015–64769-P, "Industrial crisis and productive recovery in the economic history of Spain, 1686–2018"; the consolidated research group of the Generalitat de Catalunya (2014 SGR 1345) and the Antoni de Capmany Research Centre in Economics and Economic History (University of Barcelona), with which the editors are affiliated. In addition, we would like to express our gratitude to the team at the Cañada Blanch Centre for Contemporary Spanish Studies (London School of Economics) for their warm hospitality and for providing us with an opportunity to complete part of our research there.

This book is the result of collaboration with a group of scholars who have prepared histories of local banking (see the Spanish edition). We are grateful to all of them for having shared their knowledge and for their patience in constructing a history of provincial banks of issue in Spain using homogeneous criteria. This body of knowledge has enabled us to draw the general conclusions that appear in the book. Similarly, we wish to acknowledge the support and assistance of our colleagues in the Department of Economic History, Institutions and Policy and World Economy at the University of Barcelona (UB). We must also recognise our students in the Inter-University Master in Economic History, taught jointly by the UB, the University of Zaragoza and the Autonomous University of Barcelona; they have played an active role in countless debates on the subjects addressed in the book. In addition, we have had an opportunity to present aspects of our conclusions at a variety of conferences and meetings, such as CLADHE (Latin American Congress of Economic History) in Bogotá, Colombia, on 23–25 July 2014; *Encuentro: La economía política de la España liberal* (a tribute to Pedro Tedde de Lorca) at the Bank of Spain in Madrid, 3 September 2014; the Conference of the Spanish Association for Economic History (AEHE) in Madrid, 4–5 September 2014; and the conference entitled "Origins of Banking Globalisation: The

Experience of Spain and Latin America" held in Santander, 17–19 February 2016, jointly organised by the Foundation UCEIF and the European Association for Banking History (EABH). We are very grateful for all criticisms and suggestions that we have received. They have served as incentives for us to sharpen our arguments and correct any errors. Those that remain are of our exclusive responsibility.

Carles Sudrià and Yolanda Blasco-Martel

The original work, published and partly funded by the BBVA Foundation (in accordance with Foundation Bosch i Gimpera of the University of Barcelona) can be found here: www.fbbva.es/publicaciones/la-pluralidad-de-emision-en-espana-1844-1874/

Fundación BBVA

Editors' note

This book is an extensively revised version of the general chapters of the book on issue plurality in Spain entitled ***La pluralidad de emisión en España, 1844–1874*** (Madrid, 2016), published by the BBVA Foundation in collaboration with the Bosch i Gimpera Foundation (University of Barcelona). We would like to thank both foundations for their permission to publish the present edition in English. The selected chapters analyse the development of Spanish banking as a whole, covering the period from 1844, the year in which the semi-official Bank of San Fernando was joined by newly authorised banks of issue, to 1874, the year in which the Bank of Spain, successor to the Bank of San Fernando, was granted a monopoly on banknote issue. The Spanish edition also featured 21 additional monographs on each of the provincial banks of issue and the Bank of Spain's branches. Any reader who is interested in the monographs can find the unabridged Spanish book and the detailed banks' statements at: www.fbbva.es/publicaciones/la-pluralidad-de-emision-en-espana-1844-1874/.

Introduction

Carles Sudrià and Yolanda Blasco-Martel

Two Spanish banks, Santander and the BBVA, rank among the top 20 banks in Europe according to the latest edition (2018) of the study "Top 1000 World Banks", which is published each year by the prestigious journal *The Banker*. Both banks maintain a strong presence in Latin America and hold leading positions in important foreign markets, such as the United Kingdom and Turkey. As a result, Spain ranks third in Europe in terms of outside resources attracted by its major banks, behind the UK and France. Spanish banks have earned this distinction in the past 25 years through a vigorous strategy of mergers and acquisitions both within and outside Spain.[1] Santander and the BBVA also share another important peculiarity: both were founded in the same year of 1857 in two burgeoning port cities in the north of Spain, Bilbao and Santander. This coincidence is not happenstance. In 1854–1856, the Spanish parliament enacted a set of laws that would profoundly transform the economic organisation of the country. One of the laws authorised the creation of banks of issue in Spain's most prominent cities and granted them the exclusive right to issue banknotes in their respective provinces. This was the starting point for the establishment of the Spanish banking system that has continued to the present day.

1. Aim and scope of the book

The aim of the book which readers hold in their hands is, precisely, to analyse the formation of the Spanish banking system in the middle decades of the nineteenth century, which was typified by issue plurality. The analysis focuses on the combination of economic and institutional changes that gave rise to roughly 20 banks of issue in Spain's various provinces. To this end, we take issue plurality to be the existence of multiple entities issuing banknotes within a country. The entities could circulate their banknotes in the same national or local territory under competitive conditions. However, if the entities obtained privileged conditions, their banknotes could circulate on a monopoly basis at a given territorial level, which is what occurred in Spain for the better part of the period under study.

The general hypothesis that guides our study is that issue plurality played a key role in the formation of Spain's modern banking system. Its disappearance in 1874 turned out to be premature, given the still very unequal levels that had been achieved by the process of banking modernisation and the spread of modern financial habits. Researchers have not addressed the subject in these terms, though there do exist important studies on the activities of the provincial banks of issue.

The role of issue plurality in the formative stages of modern financial systems has been underscored by several authors, foremost among them being Walter Bagehot, who wrote: "without the benefits of issue, it proves very difficult to extend the banking system as required."[2] One might say that, in a sense, the greater the delay in the process of financial modernisation, the more useful the decentralisation of banknote issue can prove. Spain officially instituted issue plurality on 25 January 1844, the day on which authorisation was given to found the Bank of Isabel II, in Madrid, and it came to an end formally on 19 March 1874, the day on which a decree was signed to unify monetary circulation and grant a monopoly to the Bank of Spain. Over the 30 intervening years, there were simultaneously as many as 21 independent banks of issue, which, as we shall see, contributed roughly half of all banknotes in circulation at given times. This 30-year period can be divided into two very distinct phases: before and after the law of 28 January 1856 on banks of issue. Before the law took effect, there were only four banks of issue in Spain: two in Madrid and two in the cities of Barcelona and Cádiz. The two established in Madrid, whose banknotes competed openly, were forced to merge in 1847 during a crisis that initiated a period governed by an extremely restrictive policy, which was brought to an end only when the progressive party took power in 1854.

The second phase began after the enactment of the aforementioned law of 1856, which was liberal in nature, and the phase was typified by the creation of new banks and by a general expansion of the system against a backdrop of economic growth. The crisis of 1866 marked the end of this expansionary period and landed the banking system in dire straits. Most of the banks of issue, however, remained in operation until 1874. In that year, in the midst of a political crisis and with the state's coffers severely depleted, the government decreed the unification of fiduciary issue. The reasons for the measure did not reflect the ideas of the politicians who adopted it, nor was it the result of political or economic debate. Simply put, it was an expedient way to secure resources to combat the various rebellions that threatened Spain's fragile institutional continuity at the time.

In 1874, the introduction of note-issue monopoly led to the disappearance of most of the existing banks of issue, which were absorbed by the Bank of Spain. However, the ones that had achieved greater size and deeper roots decided to carry on with their commercial activities, renouncing their right to issue banknotes. This included the banks in Santander and Bilbao, the direct forerunners of the two major banking groups to which we referred at the outset.

2. "The old is dying and the new cannot be born", Spain 1790–1840

In order to analyse the formation process of any banking system we need to address the social, economic and political environment in which it was taking place. Our purpose in the remainder of this introduction is to provide the reader with summary information about the political conditions under which the new Spanish banking system emerged.

One of the most prominent factors in modern Spanish history was, doubtless, the almost unbroken sequence of armed conflicts that assailed the country from 1793 to 1840. The most serious of these conflicts were fought on home soil and had effects on assets, people and economic activity. Wars against France, first, and Great Britain, later, were disastrous for Spain, which lost effective control of its mainland colonies in the Americas and all of its naval power. In 1808, the invasion of the country by Napoleonic forces spurred a popular uprising that escalated into war. This time again, the costs were enormous, not only economically but also in terms of population.

After six years of war and with the help of British forces (Peninsular War) French troops were expelled, and King Ferdinand VII was set free by Napoleon and came back to Spain. His return to the throne could not have been more unfortunate. Once he was back on Spanish soil, he ordered the abolition of the constitutional regime approved in 1812 and restored the absolute monarchy with all its powers. His actions initiated a long conflict that gave rise to two civil wars and a steady stream of mutinies and uprisings throughout the whole century. At the king's death, in 1833, Charles, his younger brother, claimed the crown with the support of absolutists (known as Carlists), meanwhile the widowed queen and regent defended the legitimacy of her daughter Isabella, who was still a young girl at the time, and found herself forced to accept the support of the liberals. Open warfare broke out at once. The conflict, known as the First Carlist War, dragged on for six years, though the liberal forces had more men and resources. Only in 1839 did they gain a decisive advantage and were able to compel their adversaries to surrender. A treaty known as the Convention of Vergara (in Spanish, the *Convenio de Vergara*) was signed in August of that year and brought the war to an end in most of Spain's territory.

It must be noted that it was in the years 1835–1840 when Spain, despite the warfare and hardships of all kinds, laid out the institutional foundations of the liberal state that would function in the country until the revolution of 1868 and, in some sense, until the proclamation of the dictatorship of Primo de Rivera in 1923. The Constitution of 1812 was restored and replaced in 1837 by another one more in step with the times. In addition, a series of measures were taken to put an end to Spain's ancien régime: the abolition of the feudal system (1811; 1837); the elimination of primogeniture and tithes (1820; 1836); the suppression of the convents and the disentailment of church property (1835); and the freedom of trade and industry (1829; 1834; 1836). The birth of a new political system took longer and was more painful in Spain than in other European countries. According to Juan Pro, "[. . .] the peninsular kingdoms of the Spanish monarchy wrested their independence from it and started down a new path as a nation-state when the absolute monarchy came to an end. After the collapse of the monarchy and the loss of its empire, it was necessary to set up a completely new apparatus of power, both in its legal definition and in its material implementation: it was necessary to build a state at the same time as a nation" (Pro, 2001, p. 450).

The years of political renewal were also a period of moderate economic growth. In the agricultural sector, some wasted land from church charities and municipalities was put under cultivation, and the production grew. Foreign trade experienced too significant changes in the routes and goods transported. Spain's loss of control over its mainland colonies in the Americas prompted a concentration in trade with Cuba and Puerto Rico and spurred the predominance of wine as an export product and of raw cotton and other colonial goods as imports. There were also new developments on the Atlantic routes to northern Europe, where Spain's growing exports of metallic minerals (i.e., lead and iron) encountered their necessary counterpart in coal. As a consequence, some of the innovations typical of the Industrial Revolution were introduced. Steelworks employing coal only were launched in Málaga in 1826; and the country's first steam-powered cotton mill began operations in 1833 in Barcelona, a traditional textile centre.

3. The financial distress of the monarchy and the birth of a state's bank

While the effects of warfare and political instability hit all sectors of the economy, the area that suffered the most severe impact was naturally the public finances. The first serious financial difficulties to strike the Bourbon monarchy appeared in 1780 as a consequence of its support for the insurgents in the American Revolution against Great Britain. As the conflict itself impeded the arrival of silver from the Spanish colonies, the government of Charles III began to face trouble meeting its payment commitments.

One of the formulas adopted to confront the situation was to issue so-called *vales reales*, which were public debt securities that could be used as banknotes and were accepted in payments to the state. The securities were issued in very high denominations and, therefore, only circulated among large merchants and state lenders. The persistent imbalance in the public finances compelled the government to increase its issue of *vales* sharply and they began to depreciate. In response to the need to forestall the loss of value and to maintain the monarchy's debt capacity, the first modern bank in Spain was founded in Madrid in 1782: the Bank of San Carlos. The idea to create the bank was presented to the king by a French merchant residing in Spain, François Cabarrus, who had already advised the government on its first issues of *vales reales*. The new bank was allowed to issue banknotes – though only in Madrid – and to engage in discounting and lending to the state and individuals.

In reality, the Bank of San Carlos had a rather erratic performance, which ended with its practical capture by the state (Tedde, 1988). Until 1790, its most important activity was procurement for the Spanish army and navy. This business, which was seemingly sound, became a nightmare when the rising prices of provisions were not recognised by the state, which demanded enforcement of the existing contracts on the terms agreed. In the aforementioned year of 1790, irregularities were detected in Cabarrus's management, the Frenchman was sent to prison and a new team took over the bank's leadership. In the years that followed, the meticulousness and parsimony that prevailed in the management of lending and discounting resulted in the bank's keeping a very large portion of its available resources in its coffers. From 1793, however, the bank's resources were employed to meet the ongoing demands of the government, which as noted earlier became embroiled in new wars. The bank faced mounting difficulties because of the credit it had granted to the state as any real possibilities of recouping the loans dwindled almost to nothing. The bank came practically to a standstill and only maintained a small line of discounting that enabled it to stagger on for some years, though in a near-lethargic state.

In 1829, the government tried to remedy the bank's anomalous situation by completely re-establishing the entity. The government reached an agreement with the shareholders of the Bank of San Carlos that entailed the bank's acceptance of a payment of 40 million *reales* (10 million pesetas) in cash to write off all the state's debts. With this money, the shareholders undertook to form a new bank that would operate under the name of the Bank of San Fernando (Banco Español de San Fernando). In order to avoid problems, the new bank's statutes were very strict as to its potential operations and required reserves. This partly explains why its activities were very modest at first. Only from 1833 did its operations begin to increase and the reason once again was the outbreak of an armed conflict, this time the First Carlist War. At the end of 1834, the bank had 67.5 million *reales* in assets, of which 6.6 million *reales* corresponded to loans to the public sector. By 1840, at the end of the war, assets stood at 100.4 million *reales*, of which 61.0 million *reales* corresponded to operations with the state. In six years, the state multiplied its demands on the bank tenfold and the bank had been forced to limit its operations with individuals in order to meet the state's growing demand. This would become a defining feature of the activities of the Bank of San Fernando and later Bank of Spain until well into the twentieth century (Tedde, 1999).

In short, we could say that Spain had started down the path toward the consolidation of a liberal society at the beginning of the 1840s, while the country's still essentially agricultural economy was showing glimpses of modernisation in various sectors. However, getting to this point had proved extraordinarily costly, which can be seen not only in Spain's institutional and economic backwardness relative to neighbouring countries, but also in the state's heavy indebtedness, which increasingly became one of the key challenges in recovering the levels of GDP and growth that had been lost.

4. Political swings and alternative economic policies, 1840–1874

The liberal's victory of 1840 allowed for a more normal functioning of the political system. During this period, two groups alternated power: the moderate party and the progressive party. The first, despite its name, was conservative in nature and highly resistant to innovations in the economic sphere. The progressive party, by contrast, was more genuinely liberal, defending tariff reductions, non-intervention by the government in the economy and the separation of church and state.

The operation of the political system in the Spanish case was marked by the rotation of power between the country's two leading parties, but not as a result of elections, but rather through interventions by the armed forces. Typically, one or several high-ranking officers issued a public proclamation (in Spanish, a *pronunciamiento*) asking for the queen to replace the government. If the proclamation garnered enough support and the sitting government proved unable to stifle or stymie it, a change in government would proceed, elections would be called and the new executive would be the one that obtained a parliamentary majority. The political swings produced by this system appear in Table I.1.

As Table I.1 shows, the so-called moderate party was in power for most of the period, but it was when the progressive party ruled the country that most important regulatory changes to ensure continued growth were adopted. Particularly noteworthy is the major overhaul of the economic framework that took place during the Progressive Biennium (1854–1856). The laws enacted in those years were not repealed afterwards and, as a result, they played a crucial role in the country's economic transformation. Less fortunate were the reforms introduced by the progressive party after the 'Glorious Revolution' of 1868. The political instability of the period made it impossible for the new legal framework, largely inspired by doctrinaire liberalism, to have any effect.

5. Economic backwardness and growth

Taken globally, the period 1850–1875 was one of moderate economic growth, similar to that of France and a little less than Germany or Great Britain, in terms of per capita income. This result was much better than that experienced in the prior and post periods, but was not enough to reduce more than slightly the distance between Spanish GDP per capita and those of major European countries. In 1875 Spain's income per inhabitant was similar to Italy's, but around 50% lower than that of France and Germany and less than half that of Britain's (Table I.2).

Spain's economic backwardness has been a recurring theme of Spanish historiography. The classic studies of Gabriel Tortella (Tortella, 1973) and Jordi Nadal (Nadal, 1975) have explored the country's economic performance in the nineteenth century from different perspectives, but they both point to similar factors to explain Spain's persistent unability to approach European leaders. On the one hand, the country's climate, soil and topography resulted in lower agricultural yields and higher transport costs. On the other hand, rigidity and extreme social inequality led to a greatly weakened domestic market and an inadequate and unfair taxation system. Ultimately, Spain's agricultural backwardness and inequality would lead to the "failure of the Industrial Revolution" (Nadal), while the inadequacy of the tax system made it impossible for the state to take the necessary economic action and posed serious finance problems for the private sector (Tortella).

In short, there is still much debate between those who argue that the inability or unwillingness of the Spanish ruling classes to modernise the country and alleviate

Table I.1 Political and banking timeline for Spain, 1833–1875

Year	Political period/events	Banking events
1833	Death of Ferdinand VII First Carlist War begins	
1840	End of the First Carlist War	
1841	Espartero regency	
1842		
1843	Transitional governments	
1844		Bank of Isabel II (Madrid) and Bank of Barcelona are founded
1845	Conservative Decade	
1846		Bank of Cádiz is founded
1847		Banks of Isabel II and San Fernando are merged
1848		Law on joint-stock companies (Ley de Sociedades Anónimas)
1849		Law reorganising the Bank of San Fernando (Ley de Reorganización del Banco de San Fernando)
1850		
1851		Banking reorganisation act (Ley de Reorganización Bancaria)
1852		
1853		
1854	Progressive Biennium	
1855		Liberal proposals debated in Parliament Legislation on banks of issue, credit companies and railways approved Bank of San Fernando renamed Bank of Spain
1856		Bank of Málaga is founded
1857	"Moderate" (conservative) governments	Bank of Valladolid, Bank of Santander, Bank of Bilbao, Bank of Seville, Bank of A Coruña and Bank of Zaragoza are founded
1858		Bank of Spain branches opened in Valencia and Alicante
1859		
1860		Bank of Jerez de la Frontera is founded
1861		
1862		Bank of San Sebastián is founded
1863		Bank of Burgos and Bank of Reus are founded
1864		Bank of Pamplona, Bank of Oviedo, Bank of Tarragona, Bank of Palencia, Bank of Vitoria, Bank Balear and Bank of Santiago are founded
1865		
1866		Financial crisis
1867		

(*Continued*)

Table I.1 (Continued)

1868 1869 1870 1871 1872 1873		"Glorious" Progressive Revolution Amadeo I, king First Republic	Law on banking freedom enacted
1874		Provisional government	Note-issue monopoly granted to Bank of Spain
1875		Bourbon Restoration Alfonso XII, king	Monopoly decree ratified

	Progressive government
	Transitional government
	Conservative government

Source: Own elaboration

Table I.2 Estimates of GDP per capita and economic growth. Europe, 1820–1913

	France	*Germany*	*Italy*	*Great Britain*	*Spain*
GDP per capita (1990 Int. GK$)					
1820	1,135	1,077	1,511	2,074	1,025
1850	1,597	1,428	1,481	2,330	1,079
1875	2,219	2,112	1,550	3,434	1,496
1913	3,485	3,648	2,305	4,921	2,056
GDP per capita annual growth (%)					
1820–1850	1.14	0.94	–0.07	0.39	0.17
1850–1875	1.33	1.58	0.18	1.56	1.32
1875–1913	1.19	1.45	1.05	0.95	0.84
1820–1875	1.23	1.23	0.05	0.92	0.69
1875–1913	1.21	1.32	0.45	0.93	0.75

Sources: Maddison Project Database, version 2013; Alvarez-Nogal and Prados (2013)

its inequalities lies at the origin of the country's economic backwardness and those who hold that the course of Spain's economy could not have been more successful than it was, given the political circumstances and the limitations imposed by the natural environment (Prados, 1988).

These considerations lead us to conclude that economic development in nineteenth-century Spain was marked by a persistent tension between the economic dynamics themselves and the legal framework in which productive activities occurred. The growth and transformation of the economy repeatedly ran into the inadequacy of the existing regulatory measures. When these situations became more acute, the pressure on the government escalated and unrest spread until the conditions were created for a change of executive, whether by military "proclamation" or by replacing the ministers with other members of the same party that would be more willing to remove the legal barriers that hindered economic activity.

The governments of the period, whether moderate or progressive, were severely constrained by an inadequate taxation system that neither party proved able to reform. As a consequence, they sometimes had to take steps that were not in their party programmes, went against their political leanings and had undesired effects, but that proved indispensable to meeting the state's inescapable financial obligations. As the reader will observe throughout the book, the financial burdens of the state hover over the formation of the Spanish banking system that was built on the basis of issue plurality. Similarly, the government's financial emergencies contributed to the elimination of issue plurality and the granting of a monopoly on banknote issue to the Bank of Spain. The ultimate result was a banking system in which the Bank of Spain held a strong position of dominance, even though it did not assume the functions proper to a central bank. This decision marked the end of an experience that had brought about the spread of banknotes and modern credit across the length and breadth of Spain.

* * *

The book is laid out in seven chapters. The first gives an overview of the origins and organisational forms of banks of issue in the leading European countries up to the end of the nineteenth century. The second chapter examines the changes that occurred in the legal framework of banking in Spain in the period under study, focusing on the causes of the changes and the debates that arose on the subject of banking regulation. The third chapter turns its attention to the social environment in which the banks of issue appeared and looks too at the characteristics of the local bourgeoisies who were their driving force. The fourth chapter delves into the performance of the banks of issue as private companies, analysing their profitability and solvency. The fifth chapter seeks to situate the dynamics of banking within the framework of the development of the Spanish and European economies, while the sixth chapter focuses on a detailed analysis of the process of winding up banking plurality and the decisions taken by each of the banks of issue still in existence at the time. Finally, the book closes with some general conclusions that pull together the results from preceding chapters, including a review of the case of Spain in the context of European banking development in the nineteenth century.

Notes

1 For additional information on the long-term trajectory of Spanish banking, see Sudrià (2016). For an overview of Spain's financial and monetary evolution, see Tortella and García Ruiz (2013).
2 Enquête (1867, I, p. 25).

Source

Maddison Project Database, ed. 2013.

Bibliography

Alvarez-Nogal, C. and Prados, L., 2013. The rise and fall of Spain (1270–1850). *The Economic History Review*, 66 (1), 1–393.

Enquête, 1867. *Enquête sur les principes et les faits généraux qui régissent la circulation monétaire et fiduciaire, observations présentées*. Impr. Impériale, Paris.

Nadal, J., 1975. *El fracaso de la revolución industrial en España, 1814–1913*. Editorial Ariel, Barcelona.

Prados, L., 1988. *De imperio a nación. Crecimiento y atraso económico en España. 1780–1930*. Alianza, Madrid.

Pro, J., 2001. La formación de la clase política liberal en España (1833–1868). *Historia Contemporánea*, (23), 445–482.

Sudrià, C., 2016. Big banks in Spain. Successes and failures on the way towards a freer market. In Lescure, M. (Ed.), *Immortal banks: Strategies, structures and performances of major banks*. Droz, Genève, pp. 139–157.

Tedde, P., 1988. *El Banco de San Carlos, 1782-1829*. Banco de España, Madrid.

Tedde, P., 1999. *El Banco de San Fernando (1829-1856)*. Alianza/Banco de España, Madrid.

Tortella, G., 1973. *Los orígenes del capitalismo en España: banca, industria y ferrocarriles en el siglo XIX*. Tecnos, Madrid.

Tortella, G. and García Ruiz, J.L., 2013. *Spanish money and banking: A history*. Palgrave Macmillan, Basingstoke.

1 Money and banking in Europe, 1700–1890

The formation of new financial systems

Carles Sudrià

The formation of an efficient financial system is a fundamental element in the process by which contemporary capitalist societies have taken shape. Neither industrialisation nor modern economic development would be conceivable without the establishment of mechanisms to mobilise resources and provide means of payment to keep up with increased trade and financing requirements.

As part of this process, the spread of fiat money plays a key role. To become effective, the extraordinary increase in trade from rising production and growing specialisation required an equivalent quantity of means of payment. Until the mid-nineteenth century, the available means of payment were limited to metallic money, basically gold and silver coins. Bills of exchange, entries in bankers' account books and other formulas facilitated remote payment and reduced the use of physical currency, but they did not replace or eliminate the need for new means of transaction. The supply of precious metals was, by definition, random. An increase in their demand and price could not be expected to spur an increase in their production. Given this state of affairs, there was a real possibility that an intense process of deflation would occur, with knock-on effects on productive activity and on the very capacity to exchange products.

This is the scenario in which it is necessary to locate the appearance of the banknote, of paper money in general and of demand deposits and current accounts. They were all instruments that could replace metallic money at large scale and become primary methods of payment. The introduction of an innovation of this scope, however, took time and effort. While paper money issued directly by the state, such as French *assignats* and Spanish *vales reales*, did have some importance at some particular periods, banknotes and current accounts were at the forefront of the new developments.

Understandably, the introduction and potential consequences of this new type of money immediately caught the attention of people concerned with economic issues, both from an analytical standpoint and from a merely practical one. The issue was also a matter of concern for the authorities, who wondered about the potential effects of the innovation and about how advisable it would be to intervene somehow in its spread. At this point, it is worthwhile looking briefly at contemporary observers' perceptions of the advantages and disadvantages of paper money and at the terms of the debate sparked by the subject.

1.1. The economics of the banknote: monopoly or plurality, a debate

Adam Smith was one of the first to call attention to the importance of banknotes and current accounts and to study their effects on the economy as a whole. In the years that Smith was at work on his famous essay, the prevailing banking system in Scotland was one in which most banks issued banknotes. Smith was a staunch supporter of the freedom to issue banknotes, though he did not deny the need to introduce some restrictions:

> The gold and silver money which circulates in any country . . . is . . . all dead stock . . . a very valuable part of the capital of the country, which produces nothing to the country. The judicious operations of banking, by substituting paper in the room of a great part of this gold and silver, enable*[s]* the country to convert a great part of this dead stock into active and productive stock; . . . *[It would be]* a sort of waggon-way through the air; *[that]* enables the country to convert, as it were, a great part of its highways into good pastures and corn fields, and thereby to increase very considerably the annual produce of its land and labour.
>
> (Smith, 1789, I, pp. 483–484)

Smith argued that over-circulation could not occur under normal circumstances because banknotes that were not needed for transactions would be returned to the banks of issue. However, he did acknowledge that the United Kingdom had witnessed episodes of over-circulation in the recent past that had spurred massive outflows of gold. In Smith's view, the reason for the anomaly lay in the glut of credit granted by the banks to merchants, which was associated with an excessive issue of banknotes. This might have been because of the banks' own rashness or a result of fraudulent practices on the part of merchants, who created and discounted bills of exchange that did not correspond to real transactions.

Smith did not propose regulatory measures to prevent episodes of an oversupply of means of payments. He did, however, give unambiguous support to prohibiting the issue of small-denomination banknotes that could be used by small merchants and individuals:

> Where the issuing of bank notes for such very small sums is allowed and commonly practiced, many mean people are both enabled and encouraged to become bankers. A person whose promissory note for five pounds, or even for twenty shillings, would be rejected by everybody, will get it to be received without scruple when it is issued for so small a sum as a sixpence. . . . It were better, perhaps, that no bank notes were issued in any part of the kingdom for a smaller sum than five pounds. Paper money would then, probably, confine itself, in every part of the kingdom, to the circulation between the different dealers.
>
> (Smith, 1789, I, pp. 486–488)

In the wake of Smith's initial assessment, however, the debate over paper money, its forms and the consequences of its spread not only did not get settled, but it went on to become one of the chief topics of discussion among social thinkers in the late eighteenth and early nineteenth centuries. The terms of the debate have already been pulled together by other authors (Arnon, 2011; Rist and Boissieu, 2002 [1951]). Of interest here are those aspects that influenced the policies adopted by states on the issuing of paper money by banks.

The most important and internationally influential discussion on the topic took place in England in the 1820s and culminated in the passage of the so-called Peel Banking Act of 1844. The terms of the debate were not unrelated to the surrounding economic and social landscape. It must be remembered that in the period from 1797 to 1819 the inconvertibility of the pound remained in effect. That is, banknotes were forced tender. This obviously affected the Bank of England, but it also affected hundreds of smaller banks that issued notes. At various stages of the period, major bouts of price inflation and the attendant depreciation of banknotes with respect to their face value were one of the triggers of the debate, which was also spurred on by the lapsing of the privileges granted to the Bank of England.

While the discussions were much more wide-ranging in scope, the focus here will be on two specific questions: first, whether the state had a responsibility to ensure the convertibility of banknotes or whether it should refrain from doing so, regarding the matter as a private transaction; and second, whether it was advisable to concentrate banknote issue in a single bank or allow several banks to issue notes. A host of people took part and many arguments were put forward. The stances, however, essentially revolved around two schools of thought known as the Currency School and the Banking School. A third strand, originating from the Free Banking School, also played a small part.

The Currency School defended the principle that price fluctuations and inflows and outflows of gold bore a direct relationship to the amount of banknotes in circulation. When the amount was 'excessive', it caused prices to go up, leading to an external accounts deficit and eventually the outflow of gold abroad. The state's introduction of a control mechanism on the issue of banknotes was, therefore, indispensable.

For the Banking School, this was a wrong approach. Under a system of fully convertible banknotes, excessive issuing was not possible. In any event, it would be temporary and have no effect because of the immediate return of unnecessary credits to the bank of issue and a corresponding reduction of banknotes in circulation. As for the inflows and outflows of gold, the Banking School attributed them to changes in international prices and took them to be circumstantial phenomena that market mechanisms would correct on their own. As a result, there was no need for any regulations and the issue of banknotes should remain in the banks' hands.

The Free Banking School concurred with the latter position, but with one important caveat: banknotes in circulation would only adjust to existing demand with the necessary speed if there was competition in the issuing of banknotes. The Bank of England's de facto monopoly was the main cause of the imbalances observed.

The legislation that was ultimately passed by the British parliament, which was called the Bank Charter Act of 1844 and known popularly as the Peel Banking Act, proved more in line with the arguments of the Currency School. The new law allowed existing banks of issue to continue, but it set total issue limits for each of them and prohibited the creation of new banks of issue. Practical and political reasons probably outweighed theoretical ones. Support for this suspicion can be found in the British parliament's passage in subsequent months of legislation with a different orientation for Scotland and Ireland, where the overwhelming hegemony enjoyed by the Bank of England in its own territory did not apply.

In spite of its undeniable importance and theoretical value, the British debate took place against a very particular backdrop that differed from other European countries. The circumstances of the financial market in the British Isles were not the same as those on the continent, nor did the authorities and the citizens themselves have the same perception of the treatment that should be given to the commercial innovation of banknotes. Accordingly, the debate on the issue of paper money took on a different character in other European countries, where it lagged behind Britain.

It is impossible to follow the debates on the topic in every country, where they reflected the specific circumstances of each one. Accordingly, it is of particular interest to look at the content of a monumental survey undertaken by the French state in 1865, followed by the publication of its findings in 1867. The survey, entitled "*Enquête sur les principes et les faits généraux qui régissent la circulation monétaire et fiduciaire*", was launched as a political response to complaints levelled at the Bank of France because of interest rate hikes at the time. The outcry against the Bank of France's monopoly grew even more intense when the institution demanded and obtained the closure of the Bank of Savoy, which held the right to issue in the Duchy of Savoy, newly annexed by France in 1860.

Politicians, businesspeople and the leading experts in France and abroad were asked to complete an extensive questionnaire. The two sections of greatest interest here focused on the utility of fiat money and the conditions that should govern its issue. One of the survey's basic reference points was the debate that had taken place in Great Britain two decades earlier. Twenty years after the enactment of the Peel Banking Law, the views of the British respondents proved particularly interesting. The three most prominent Britons were John Stuart Mill, who was then a sitting member of the British parliament; Charles Gairdner, who was general manager of the Union Bank of Scotland; and Walter Bagehot, who was editor of *The Economist*. All three had a high regard for the widespread use of fiat money in Great Britain and were even more positive about cheques drawn on current accounts, citing the same reasons of saving and convenience noted earlier by Adam Smith. They, too, took the view that abuse was impossible if the principle of convertibility of banknotes into gold at the holder's request was strictly maintained.

However, they disagreed on the question of who should issue banknotes and under what conditions. In John Stuart Mill's view, a monopoly on issue promoted circulation, freeing the public from the task of assessing the soundness of banks.

That said, he felt that any potential risk from having several banks of issue could be mitigated by demanding that the banks deposit debt securities equal in value to their issued banknotes. This was doubtless a system inspired by the United States. Ultimately, however, the dilemma between having a plurality or monopoly of issue seemed unimportant to Mill once the system's operation was assured.

Mill's position was not shared by Charles Gairdner, the general manager of a Scottish bank that issued notes. Gairdner, like others testifying before the commission, saw the freedom to issue as part of the freedom of trade in general and therefore as a right that must be respected. Beyond that, he took the view that plurality offered many advantages: facilities for the public thanks to the opening of bank branches in every district; a capital economy that resulted from the habit of depositing savings in banks; payment of interest by banks to depositors; credit facilities offered to the country's industrialists; and all of this within the framework of a system that offered complete security (no Scottish banking company had ever defaulted on its debts and the private banks had very seldom done so). Beyond these boons, Gairdner added that "there are no known drawbacks that may arise from the plurality of issue" (Enquête, 1867, V, pp. 512–513).

Walter Bagehot's position was much more nuanced. Bagehot drew a distinction between the different stages through which the process of financial modernisation had to pass. His analysis started with a description of how the system was working at the time of his testimony before the committee (February 1865):

> In England, every town has at least two banks in which every shilling of local savings is deposited. With the help of the banks, these savings are lent in the same area, if there are good opportunities to do so safely. Otherwise, they are sent to London. Thanks to this organisation, not one shilling of capital that could be saved goes to waste, and London has turned into an immense money centre without depriving other parts of the country of the resources that they could profitably invest.
>
> In all the cities of England, the bank cheque is used: every merchant, every farmer uses it regularly. The practice was introduced by the provincial banks of issue. Set up by individuals of reputation, the banks issued banknotes and, in this way, spread the knowledge of credit throughout the whole country. In each locale, there is somebody interested in replacing coinage with banknotes and this is how the substitution occurred. By becoming accustomed to credit in the form of banknotes, the population has gradually come to the use of cheques and deposits.
>
> (Enquête, 1867, I, pp. 24–26)

In Bagehot's opinion, a plurality of banknote issue was crucial to bringing off a rapid modernisation process of this sort. The issue of banknotes was the best and most straightforward way for the banks to advertise their services and the resulting earnings would make profitable branches that would otherwise not have been so. Bagehot took a negative view of the restrictions imposed on banking activity prior to 1844, but he did accept that despite the restrictions, there had been success in fully replacing coins with banknotes and in dramatically intensifying banking activity. The new restrictions imposed by the Peel Banking Act had done "no harm or very little" according to Bagehot, because they put limits on banknote issue just when it had reached its maximum. The substitution of coinage had been completed and it was now the growth in deposits and current accounts that ensured a sufficient supply of means of payment.

Under the new circumstances, a monopoly on banknote issue could have a number of advantages. In theory, it would be applicable to England and Scotland, but it proved impossible in the latter case because of the opposition of the Scots themselves ("The Scots dearly love their banknotes"). In Ireland, on the other hand, plurality continued to be advisable because the replacement of coinage had not yet been fully achieved (Enquête, 1867, I, pp. 38–39).

As opposed to the view provided by their British counterparts, the continental respondents were much more resistant to the freedom of issue and, more generally, the free operation of the banking system. Prestigious scholars like the Swiss Antoine-Elisée Cherbuliez (Zurich), the German Johann A.R. Helferich (Göttingen) and the Belgian Émile-Louis-Victor de Laveleye (Liège), in spite of their liberal ideas and general stance against state intervention, argued for the advisability of a monopoly on banknote issue and close state oversight of the activities of banks of issue. Their underlying reasons lay in the need for security in the issue of fiat currency and in the non-existence in other countries of the conditions for financial development that existed in Great Britain and that enabled the regular operation of a free issue system. Helferich summarised the advantages of a monopoly on banknote issue in five points:

1 A single central bank gives greater control to the public, which can freely debate and criticise every report from those in charge.
2 Monopoly minimises the costs of excessive plurality, which fragments the market and forces banknote users to travel to make them effective or to assume business losses.
3 Only if there is a privileged and controlled bank can the state use it as a cashier for collection and payment, which is an essential need of the public administration and promotes the widespread use of banknotes.
4 A central bank of issue can more readily obtain a large reserve of coin and bullion to streamline management in times of crisis.
5 The advantages of the free system with respect to a better use of available savings are offset by the need of small banks of issue to maintain sufficient coin and bullion reserves.

In Helferich's view, both systems were possible, but he had a preference for a single central bank of issue and was in favour of the restrictions established in the Peel Banking Act, which was, to his mind, "a major step toward the centralisation of banknote issue" in England (Enquête, 1867, V, pp. 305–312).

To these essentially economic arguments, Cherbuliez added a political argument that not only comes as a surprise from a man noted for his liberal credentials, but also seems closer in this case to French statism than to liberalism:

> State control over banks of issue is based on a principle of public order [. . .]. In every nation that has organised its circulation of money through a law, the government has the right and duty to prevent disruptions and losses that may arise from the interference of individuals in the powers that the law has granted exclusively to the nation. If the state does not permit individuals to mint coins without its consent even when they are acting in good faith, it must neither permit that fiat money be put into circulation, except under the conditions that it deems appropriate to impose.
>
> (Enquête, 1867, V, p. 786)

This position in favour of a single issuer and a strong central bank was also pervasive among the French respondents to the survey, who made up the vast majority. One of the few voices to advocate for the elimination of the Bank of France's monopoly was that of Jean-Gustave Courcelle-Seneuil, who had published a study in support of banking freedom in 1840. Only a few months after taking part in the survey, Courcelle-Seneuil sent to press a short essay whose title was unambiguous: *La Banque Libre* (Courcelle-Seneuil, 1840, 1867). Courcelle-Seneuil's arguments did not differ from the positions taken by Bagehot and Gairdner. The most significant ones were his criticism of the Bank of France's monopoly and his rigorous defence of the benefits to be gained from changing the current centralist policy.

Courcelle-Seneuil took the view that an English economist, whose name he did not reveal, was right to say that France had railways, steamships, factories and offices as in other countries, but that it did not have commercial banking. France, in his view, "was in this respect a hundred fifty years behind England and Scotland", where commerce of this sort could be found even in the smallest villages. Only with absolute banking freedom could matters improve. There was no cause to fear an excessive issue of banknotes or the lack of shareholders' equity, which would ultimately be greater in its entirety than that which the Bank of France had at the time. The only restriction on new banks of issue (between 15 and 20, he imagined) was that they must have a minimum capital of 25 or 30 million francs each (the Bank of France had 182 million francs in capital at the time). Acting in competition and free to issue banknotes, the banks would discount more paper than the Bank of France and bring their operations to areas that did not even figure in the Bank of France's plans (Enquête, 1867, III, pp. 39–42).

The position argued by Courcelle-Seneuil was strictly in the minority. It only won support from some merchants and provincial chambers of commerce that were calling for better access to credit. Most French economists, however, backed a system of monopoly on banknote issue, though in some cases their remarks did include criticisms of the lending and discount policy pursued by the Bank of

France. The latter subset featured a number of authors who wrote pamphlets and books on financial topics, such as Louis-François-Michel-Raymond Wolowski, Adolphe d'Eichthal and Clement Juglar.

In short, what can be seen from the French survey of 1865–1867 beyond the individual responses is a decisive step toward the idea of a single bank of issue rather than a plurality of issue. In broader terms, the findings asserted the right and willingness of the state to regulate banking activities in order to ensure the stable functioning of the economy as a whole. This evolution in the realm of ideas ran parallel to the introduction of reforms in many countries that reflect the same trend toward centralisation and greater state control.

1.2. The emergence of modern banking in Europe: a global view

The Riksbank, or Bank of Sweden, is typically hailed as the first bank to issue notes in Europe, which it began doing in 1661. Kindleberger attributes the Riksbank's earliness to the fact that the predominant coins in Sweden at the time were minted in copper, which made transactions of a certain size extraordinarily cumbersome. Indeed, the new banknotes soon traded at a premium to coins. When the Riksbank started issuing banknotes, it was a private bank, but the Swedish state assumed control a few years later, in 1668, making it the first central bank in the world (Kindleberger, 1984, pp. 71–74). In other countries, like the United Kingdom, the first steps toward the use of banknotes came from goldsmiths. Some of them were issuing receipts as proofs of deposits in gold or silver, and the receipts were increasingly being accepted in ordinary payments among traders and began to circulate widely.

After these initial experiences, the evolution of paper money in Europe was marked by two parallel but distinct forces. On one hand, states experienced increased financial needs, while on the other hand, the process of industrialisation gave rise to a heightened demand for means of payment and for banking services. The costs of the warfare that confronted the European powers almost without interruption from the mid-eighteenth century until 1815 forced states to seek new sources of funding that were wider than the traditional issuing of public debt and the resort to international banking houses. The key issue was that the states' growing levels of indebtedness made it gradually more difficult to place bonds, with the result that the authorities were forced to accept the bankers' increasingly unfair and one-sided conditions.

Under these circumstances, the issuing of paper money seemed an easier and less costly solution. Indeed, it meant attributing the power to discharge debts in transactions to securities issued by the state or state-authorised banks. This solved the increase in the demand for means of payment arising from the greater number of transactions that were occurring. In some cases, it was the state itself that put into circulation banknotes, which might or might not be interest-bearing. In other cases, the state granted the right to issue banknotes to one or more banks and then demanded credit from them. The two approaches converged within a few years, however, since the states that had opted for direct issuing were soon forced to create banks to manage the debt in circulation and seek to repay it.

Accordingly, a number of banking institutions, generally with private equity, came into existence primarily to provide resources to the state itself and to ensure the servicing of the public debt. The first to appear were the Bank of England (1694), the Bank of Prussia (1765), the Bank of San Carlos, in Spain (1782) and the Bank of France (1800). After the Napoleonic Wars, a second wave of 'national banks' came into being, such as the National Bank of Austria (1816), the Bank of Portugal (1846), the National Bank (Turin, 1850) and the Imperial Bank of Russia (1860). All these banks had the authority to issue banknotes, though as shall be seen, some held the right exclusively and others shared it with other entities (Collins, 1993; Conant, 1909; Kindleberger, 1984; Noël, 1888).

In parallel to the state-sponsored banks, other banking entities sprang up in every country in order to provide financial assistance to the economy's private sector, giving rise to the figure of the banker or the banking house whose main function was to discount bills, make loans to businesses and individuals and take deposits. This function was also performed by the 'national' banks, but always in a subsidiary manner, that is, only with resources that happened to be available after attending to the needs of the state.

The private banking activity carried out by individual bankers covered the financial needs of the private sector satisfactorily in most countries until the early eighteenth century. Over the course of the eighteenth century, however, it became apparent that the significant increase in production and transactions required a new type of bank that could offer new services, including new forms of credit and means of payment. To meet the demand, there was a need for entities that could systematically attract resources from the public and then distribute them among borrowers in a way that ensured the risk was spread sufficiently. This meant that the new banks needed to be larger than the traditional banking houses and have a greater capacity to assess loans, leading to increased specialisation and professionalisation.

The first country to witness banks with the new characteristics was the United Kingdom. As early as the seventeenth century, some London goldsmiths had already begun to engage in tasks associated with banking, such as taking cash deposits and making loans. Little by little, banking activity took on its own distinctive character and the same goldsmiths/bankers made the decision to split the two activities and set up banking corporations in the form of general or limited partnerships. At the beginning of the eighteenth century, it was industrial development in the North of England that led to a clamour for the modernisation of financial services. Essentially, the region's own industrialists and merchants set up banking companies to provide the needed services, giving rise to the so-called country banks.

The phenomenon was not very different in other countries. The cities and regions that experienced the impact of industrial or commercial development most intensely in those years were the ones to witness the earliest appearance of modern banking institutions. The legal forms that they adopted varied by country and their authorised operations differed too. Whether or not they were granted the right to issue banknotes must be situated in this context. The positions adopted by different governments on the subject could not have been more disparate. While Austria-Hungary and France applied the principle of a monopoly on issue after 1848, other countries like Scotland, Switzerland and many of the German states (until 1875) permitted a plurality of issue. It must be taken into account, however, that the conditions under which the issuing of paper money was authorised could vary widely and the effects could differ as well.

Figure 1.1 below shows the evolution of the issue regime in the leading countries of Europe up to 1860. It is a simplified scheme that does not take into account for example that, under monopoly systems, there were situations of currency competition that were often tolerated by the authorities, though technically illegal. The selection of countries includes the most populated ones for which there were available data. The Austro-Hungarian Empire does not appear in the table because it maintained a monopoly on issue from the moment that its first bank of issue came into operation. The graph reflects four distinct issue regimes in total:

a Monopoly: a single bank of issue, de iure or de facto.
b Plurality of issue without banknote competition (territorial monopolies).
c Plurality of issue with competing banknotes.
d Plurality of issue in residual conditions.

As the graph shows, the plurality of issue was a much more widespread phenomenon than it is usually thought to have been. Practically every country had a plurality of issue at one time or another. In 1844, when it became allowed in Spain, it was the norm in Europe with very few exceptions. Indeed, those years must be seen as the high point for the plurality of issue in Europe. The enactment of the Peel Banking Act in England in 1844, the subsequent passage of corresponding legislation for Scotland and Ireland, and the absorption of every French departmental bank by the Bank of France in 1848 all signalled a turning point in the process of banking modernisation toward greater state control over banking activities and the centralisation of banknote issue.

In any event, Figure 1.1 also shows the diversity of the paths followed by European countries in the first stage of modern financial development. To understand better what happened in Spain, it is useful to look first at the characteristics of what happened in the most significant countries.

1.3. The emergence of modern banking: national experiences

United Kingdom

Despite being ruled by the same parliament and the same government, the three countries that made up the United Kingdom had a monetary development that was as diverse as the monetary development in countries on the continent. The privileges granted to the Bank of England did not apply in Scotland, where open

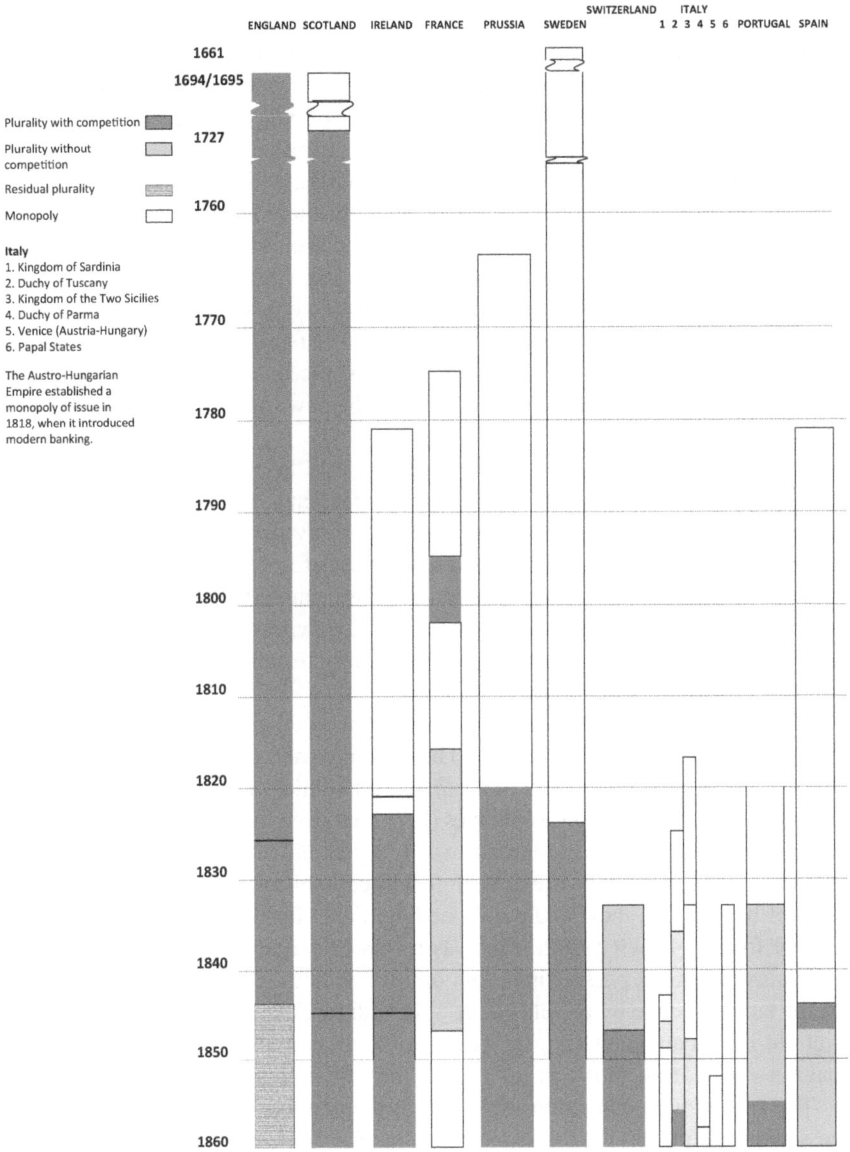

Figure 1.1 Banknote issue regimes in Europe until 1860

Source: Conant (1909) and Noël (1888)

competition prevailed among banks. Nor did it apply in Ireland, which went from a privileged system to widespread currency competition. As a result, it is worth examining each case and its circumstances in some detail, even if only cursorily.

The fact that best typifies the development of banking in Great Britain (England, Wales and Scotland) since the seventeenth century is doubtless the early introduction of modern banking mechanisms. Of course, this fact is closely related to the similarly early and ground-breaking nature of industrial development on the island. As noted above, the transformation of manufacturing activities and the associated commercial and service-related activities, which together made up the core of the Industrial Revolution, also profoundly altered the demand for financial services. The demand for short-term credit and discounting rose at the same time that the lack of payment instruments was being felt, whether in the form of banknotes, cheques or current-account transfers. It was a type of need that could not be covered by traditional banks, which were generally family enterprises with scarce capital and little capacity to attract external resources. This is what accounts for the emergence of ventures aimed at meeting the new needs from the mid-seventeenth century onwards.

Without doubt, the most emblematic venture was the establishment of the Bank of England in 1694. The circumstances of its creation are well known and it is not necessary to refer to them here. Let it suffice to say that the idea of introducing a banking entity of this sort had been discussed before, but it was the precarious situation of the Treasury that prompted the government to ask for parliamentary approval for the bank. In 1672, Charles II had suspended payments of the state's debt and his successor, William III, ran into serious trouble when seeking financial backing to face the costs of war with France.

The scheme proposed by the government involved granting a series of privileges to a new company known as "The Governor and Company of the Bank of England" in exchange for a loan of 1.2 million pounds. The new bank was given the right to administer a series of taxes (beer, maritime tonnage) as a guarantee on loan interest (8% per annum) and it was to act as the government's cashier. The shareholders also enjoyed the benefit of limited liability, which meant that in the case of bankruptcy, they would only be held liable for the amount they had paid in, not for all of their assets. This was an exclusive advantage that enabled the institution to attract passive investors of all sorts and to snatch away a good part of the business done by private bankers. In addition, the bank's charter gave it the right to issue banknotes for nine years, with a maximum circulation equal to its paid-in capital, though it was not granted the sole right to issue.

The subscription campaign for shares in the new bank was a resounding success and the company hit the ground running. Results were good. It was not long, however, before difficulties cropped up. In 1696, partly because of problems with the supply of coinage, the bank faced a run that led to the suspension of banknote convertibility for more than a year. Parliament's reaction to the situation was to fortify the bank's privileges and increase its size. Capital was increased from the original 1.2 million pounds to 2.1 million pounds, but the most striking innovation was the privilege granted by the British parliament itself not to authorise any other bank of the same characteristics as the Bank of England as long as the privilege was not revoked and to prohibit the existence of any bank with more than six shareholders, regardless of its legal status. This established the basic structure of the English banking system that would remain in force for a century, until the second interruption of convertibility in 1797.

While the system had a spirit of monopoly, it kept competition open in the lowest segment of demand for banking services and means of payment. Writing at the end of the nineteenth century, Henry D. Macleod judged the adopted formula harshly:

> It was just at this period that the original sin of the monopoly of the Bank of England began to tell with full force upon the country. Now were the seeds of future ruin, misery and desolation sown broadcast throughout the land. The prodigious development of all these industrial works demanded a great extension of the Currency to carry them out. What was required was to have banks of undoubted wealth and security to issue such a Currency. Bank of England Notes had no circulation beyond London. Its monopoly prevented any other great banks being founded, either in London or the country: and it would not establish branches in the country. England required to have a Currency, and as it could not have a good one, it had a bad one. Multitudes of miserable shopkeepers in the country, grocers, tailors, drapers, started up like mushrooms in all directions as "bankers", and issued their notes, inundating the country with their miserable rags, in many parts as low as a shilling.
>
> (Macleod, 1891, p. 550)

Aside from Macleod's disdainful tone regarding smaller bankers, it is true that practically from the very establishment of the Bank of England some private bankers started to issue their own banknotes, both in London and in the industrial shires of the North of England. At first, the banknotes were not issued in fixed denominations, but as a function of the sum requested, and they were written by hand. The first issue of partially printed banknotes by the Bank of England occurred in 1725. One of the first private banking houses to issue banknotes was Child & Co., London jewellers who, like others in the trade, had turned to banking (Richards, 1927, p. 379). As for non-London banks or country banks, the first to issue notes were the banking houses of Samuel Smith & Co. in Nottingham and Praed & Co. in Truro (Cornwall), among others. Clearly, however, the circulation of banknotes was virtually confined to London until 1750. Edmund Burke stated that there were not even a dozen banking establishments outside London prior to that year, which appears to fit with the available evidence (Pressnell, 1956, pp. 4–5).

From the century's midpoint, however, matters changed radically, and banks and bankers proliferated, especially outside London. The first reliable tally, from 1784, records 119 banks in operation in England and Wales (not counting branches), not including London. Just before the suspension of convertibility in 1797, the sources speak of up to 300 country banks established in the nation

(Pressnell, 1956, p. 11). The vast majority of these banks issued banknotes. While the amounts were modest individually, they doubtless played a key role as a whole in the supply of means of payment in industrial areas. By contrast, the evidence also points to the gradual withdrawal of London's private bankers from this activity in the latter half of the eighteenth century, with the result that the Bank of England achieved a de facto monopoly on issue in London and its environs before being officially granted a monopoly in 1826.

At first, the Bank of England kept the smallest denominations of banknotes relatively high, starting with a minimum value of £50, which was lowered to £20 around 1745 and then to £10 in 1759 in an effort to mitigate the scarcity of coinage. Without doubt, however, other banks of issue put out banknotes with much smaller values. This paved the way for the introduction of bank money in small transactions, but it also encouraged bank runs. Two successive laws in 1775 and 1777 set the lower limit first at 20 shillings and then at £5. As seen earlier, Adam Smith endorsed this restrictive policy and called for its application in Scotland too.

The outbreak of war with revolutionary France in 1793 triggered a widespread panic that forced many country banks to suspend payments. Despite the demands of bankers and merchants and the government itself, the Bank of England curtailed discounting and credit, so that suspensions and failures only spread. Finally, the British parliament approved the issue of Treasury notes to act as paper money to facilitate credit and exchanges. The result was positive. Confidence returned and a good deal of the anticipated resources did not need to be used. Four years later, however, instability struck again. According to Macleod, the reason for the new imbalance was the government's over-use of its ability to obtain credit from the Bank of England to sustain the war effort against France (Macleod, 1891, pp. 738–752). In February 1797, the bank suspended convertibility and the other banks of issue that still maintained convertibility followed suit. Banknotes were declared forced tender. The British parliament ratified the suspensions and permitted the issuing of small-denomination notes to facilitate payments.

The situation gave a fresh impetus to the creation of banks of issue outside London, because the placement of their banknotes now proved easier and less risky than before suspension. At their peak in 1815, the number of country banks in operation, according to official tallies, exceeded 700 (Pressnell, 1956, p. 11). In the same year, the end of the war on the continent ushered in a speculative process with widespread price hikes and a subsequent contraction. Many provincial banks joined the speculative bubble and were severely damaged. Nearly a hundred country banks went bankrupt and many others were forced out of business. By 1820, the number of country banks in operation had fallen to 500. The return of convertibility was halting and difficult. The process had to be postponed on several occasions and it did not come to an end until 1821.

With a return to peacetime, a less circumstantial review of the legal status of the English banking system became possible. In 1825, a new banking crisis made it easier to convince the British parliament of the need for reform. A new law that was passed in 1826 largely sought to reduce the provincial banks' weakness, which had been made clear in the crisis of the preceding decade. The chief measures were: a) to authorise the formation of banks as joint-stock companies at a distance of no less than 65 miles (105 km) from London; b) to grant the Bank of England the exclusive right to issue banknotes within 65 miles (105 km) of London; and c) to authorise the Bank of England to open branches throughout the territory of England and Wales. A new reform, which was introduced in 1833, authorised the creation of banks as joint-stock companies *within* the 65-mile limit, provided that they forfeited the privilege of banknote issue.

As an immediate result of the new regulations, many country banks that had been family enterprises were converted into joint-stock companies, enabling them to grow in size and increase their issuing capacity. From the official figures on the circulation of banknotes that are available for the years in question, the Bank of England was the issuer of approximately two-thirds of the banknotes in circulation, while the then roughly 400 country banks accounted for the remainder (Table 1.1).

The final major change in the regulation of the English banking system, which was to have a great impact on other countries, was the Peel Banking Act of 19 July 1844. As noted in the previous section, the legislation was the result of years of acrimonious debate over the need to regulate the issuing of paper money by banks. Indirectly, the debate had implications for maintaining the privileges enjoyed by the Bank of England and for the advisability of keeping a decentralised system of banknote issue. As the terms of the discussion have already been examined, the focus here will turn to the measures adopted on the issue of banknotes and on the plurality of issue.

The British government, led by Sir Robert Peel, decided to set strict regulations on banknote issue, setting aside proposals that would have left more room for the free market. In part, the decision can be explained by the bouts of inflation and of depreciation of the pound that struck in the years in which forced tender was in effect, as well as probably by the waves of bankruptcies that hit the country banks in the same period. The new law forced the Bank of England to separate its activities as a currency issuer from its activities as a commercial bank. The issue department could have up to 14 million pounds of banknotes in circulation, backed by public debt, and the remainder would have to be covered 100% by gold reserves.

Table 1.1 Yearly average of banknotes in circulation, England and Wales (£'000)

	Bank of England	*%*	*Country banks*	*%*
1833	18,476	64.9	9,991	35.1
1843	19,523	71.9	7,647	28.1
1860	21,252	76.7	6,450	23.3
1880	26,925	88.7	3,440	11.3
1900	29,366	95.9	1,243	4.1
1910	28,300	99.3	197	0.7

Source: Mitchell (1988, pp. 668–669)

The other banks of issue were given an issue limit equal to the amount of banknotes that they had in circulation at the end of the previous year. The limit would be kept fixed. Any banks that ceased issue for whatever reason would lose their issue right and three-quarters of the respective amounts would go to raise the limit granted to the Bank of England. In this manner, while a monopoly on issue was not imposed immediately, the foundations were laid for its gradual de facto establishment.

When the law took effect, there were 279 country banks of issue in England and Wales. Of these, 207 were general partnerships and 72 were joint-stock companies. In total, they had a recognised capacity to issue £8.6 million, with £5.1 million corresponding to the private banking houses and the remaining £3.5 million corresponding to the joint-stock companies.

As Table 1.1 above shows, the legislation had the expected effect of bolstering the position of the Bank of England, but the withdrawal of the country banks was extremely slow. By 1885, 143 banks of issue were still in operation, with 44 of them being joint-stock companies. In total, they enjoyed issue rights equivalent to £5.8 million, though they effectively had only £2.5 million in circulation. Of these entities, only eight were entitled to issue more than £100,000 and the largest one, Stuckey's Bristol & Somersetshire Bank, was entitled to issue £357,000. The concentration process gathered speed in the years that followed. By 1910, the plurality of banknote issue had diminished to an inconsequential phenomenon. The last independent issuer of banknotes in England and Wales was the Somerset house of Fox, Fowler & Co., that disappeared in 1921.

Scotland took a completely different path on the issuing of paper money than the one followed in England and Wales. Indeed, the Scottish system prior to 1845 is regarded as one of the few available examples of a functioning monetary system governed on strictly liberal grounds with no unnecessary regulations or privileges (L. H. White, 1984, 1992).

The first bank of issue established in Scotland was the Bank of Scotland, authorised by the Scottish parliament in 1695 a few months after the creation of the Bank of England. The Bank of Scotland was given the exclusive privilege to conduct banking activities, including the issue of banknotes, for a period of 21 years and for the entire country. Its capital was set at £100,000, though its paid-in capital was generally kept steady at 30%. The new bank had to contend with runs in 1704 and 1715 that were resolved by a procedure of paying interest on banknotes for the period in which they could not be redeemed.

In 1719, after the privilege of exclusivity had lapsed, the king authorised the creation of the Equivalent Fund, a sort of investment fund for holders of English debt. A proposal to combine the two entities was rejected by the Bank of Scotland, which was apparently making vast profits from its monopoly status. In the end, the directors of the Equivalent Fund decided to request permission to act as a bank and a charter was granted in May 1727. The restructured institution took the name of Royal Bank of Scotland and began operations with £151,000 in capital. In the years that followed, the two banks did battle, each trying to drive the other into bankruptcy.

In 1746, a new bank of issue, the British Linen Company, was granted a royal charter. The existence of these chartered banks, however, did not stop other banking houses, whether joint-stock companies or not, from issuing their own banknotes. The smaller banks typically specialised in small-denomination notes intended for retail trade and individuals. The fragility that came with issues of this sort prompted many institutions to add clauses to their banknotes to stipulate that redemption in gold could be delayed after presentation in return for interest. Adam Smith, who was very familiar with the matter, tells of how this kind of measures discouraged customers from using the banknotes, leaving many banks in dire straits. The threat forced the government to ban clauses that restricted banknote redemption and to prohibit the issue of banknotes in denominations smaller than 20 shillings (Banknotes Act [Scotland], 1765); Smith (1789, I, 417, pp. 492–493).

By pacifying competition, the new legislation paved the way for mechanisms of collaboration that soon proved effective. The most significant ones were the recognition and mutual acceptance of banknotes among all the banks and the introduction of a multilateral clearing system. The overall smooth running of the system, however, could not head off the occasional setback. The most serious calamity befell the Ayr Bank, and the origins and consequences of its misfortune highlight a number of the characteristics of a system of fully competitive plurality in operation.

The Ayr Bank opened its doors in 1769 in response to complaints over the restrictive effects of the law of 1765, and its express purpose was to offer better credit facilities to potential customers. In two years, according to Smith, the bank made loans of £800,000 at 5% interest and discounted a great many bills of exchange without regard to their provenance or the credibility of those who were discounting them. The banknotes issued by the bank to finance this credit policy were returned to the bank's branches time and again to be redeemed. As Smith explains:

> In order to support the circulation of those notes [. . .], it had been constantly in the practice of drawing bills of exchange upon London, of which the number and value were continually increasing, and, when it stopped, amounted to upwards of six hundred thousand pounds [. . .]. [Upon this amount,] it was paying, in the way of interest and commission, upwards of eight per cent, and was consequently losing more than three per cent upon more than three-fourths of all its dealings.
>
> (Smith, 1789, pp. 472–474)

The Ayr Bank collapsed in 1772, but its bankruptcy proved no impediment to the Scottish banking system, which shortly thereafter showed signs of strength and stability. As seen earlier, the Bank of England was forced in 1797 to seek authorisation from the British parliament to suspend payments in coin. When news of the suspension reached Edinburgh, a general panic broke out. A subsequent meeting convened by the authorities, however, showed full support for the banks among the capitalists and merchants and their support paved the way for a quick return to normality. Indeed, the Scottish banks kept up the suspension of payments in gold without the need for any law to permit it. Simply put, nobody complained in any way whatsoever for not being able to redeem their banknotes (Macleod, 1891, p. 601). The stability and smooth running of the Scottish banking system was officially recognised by both houses of the British parliament. In a report in 1826 commissioned by the government, the committee appointed by the House of Lords stated:

> It is also proved, by the evidence and by the documents, that the banks of Scotland, whether chartered or joint-stock companies or private establishments, have for more than a century exhibited a stability which the committee believe to be unexampled in the history of banking [sic]; that they supported themselves from 1797 to 1812 without any protection from the restriction by which the Bank of England and that of Ireland were relieved from cash payments; that there was little demand for gold during the late embarrassments in the circulation; and that, in the whole period of their establishment, there are not more than two or three instances of bankruptcy.
>
> (*Blackwood's Edinburgh Magazine*, vol. 56, 1844, num. 350, pp. 675–676)

The same committee concluded that "this circumstance, amongst others, tends to prove that uniformity, however desirable, is not indispensably necessary"; a position that helps to understand the territorial diversity of the regulations adopted in 1844–1845.

During the years of suspension and immediately afterwards, the number of Scottish banks rose dramatically, thanks to the country's development. In 1826, there were 29 banks of issue and only the three mentioned above had a specific royal charter. In total, the banks had 111 branches across the entirety of Scotland. Two decades later, the landscape pointed to some business concentration – the number of banks of issue had fallen to 19 – but there was also a simultaneous trebling of the number of branches (L. H. White, 1992, pp. 169–170). The total amount of banknotes in circulation was roughly three million pounds, but their distribution was much more balanced than it was in England. This can be seen below in Table 1.2.

This was the Scottish landscape in which the British government proposed applying the principles that had inspired the English reform of 1844, the Peel Banking Act. It was clear that the context was completely different and that the Scottish system was not beset by the ills that had justified the intervention in English banking. However, the general principle was accepted that there was a need to control the issue of banknotes by banks and, in 1845, the government introduced a specific law for Scotland that was approved.

The new legislation authorised Scottish banks to place notes in circulation to a maximum value equal to the value of their banknotes in circulation in the year prior to May 1845 plus the value of gold and silver coin in their coffers. Three-quarters of the coin had to be in gold. If banks merged, the resulting entity would

Table 1.2 Banks of issue in Scotland, 1845

Banknotes in circulation £	*No. of banks*	*Banknotes in circulation* £	*Capital* £	*No. of branches*
> 400,000	1	438,024	500,000	43
300,000–400,000	3	1,002,588	2,600,000	115
200,000–300,000	2	581,306	2,000,000	73
100,000–200,000	4	578,004	3,800,000	64
< 100,000	9	487,287	2,340,000	68
TOTAL	19	3,087,209	11,240,000	363

Source: L. H. White (1992, p. 170)

have the sum total of the issue rights granted to the merging banks. Finally, the law established that the banknotes of the Bank of England would still not be legal tender in Scotland.

As can be seen, the main difference between the Scottish law and the law passed for England and Wales was that the former contained no measures that would foster a monopoly on issue. While the overall issue limit was calculated in the same way, all the Scottish banks were still permitted to issue banknotes backed by coinage and there was no provision to transfer the amounts granted to closing or merging banks to other banks either in total or in part.

In the second half of the nineteenth century, there were no important changes in the regulatory framework of the Scottish banking system. Its evolution over the period was characterised by a gradual concentration of banks and uninterrupted expansion both within and outside Scotland. The concentration process was remarkably intense and clearly favoured the oldest and strongest banks; the eight that survived into the twentieth century were among the ten with the largest amount of banknotes in circulation in 1845. The magnitude of the expansion and concentration is reflected below in Table 1.3.

From the very outset, the banking and issue system established in Scotland has been the subject of special attention from economists, led of course by the Scotsman Adam Smith. Charles Conant, in his monumental study on banks of issue, identifies the particular and distinctive features of the Scottish banking system: freedom of issue, the use of small-denomination banknotes and cash credits. Two additional features need to be added to the list: the freedom to create new banks and the non-existence of exclusive privileges granted to any of them. This is the make-up of what has been called a free banking system similar to the one called for by the adherents of the ultra-liberal 'Austrian school'.

The benefits of the Scottish banking and issue system have been extolled alike by contemporary analysts and those who came later, and they can perhaps be boiled down to one: the system was successful in mobilising the country's available resources as much as possible and in getting these resources into the hands of investors effectively and at very low costs. It would be naïve, however, to overlook the special conditions in Scotland that made this success possible.

Table 1.3 Banks of issue in Scotland up to 1908

	No. of banks	*No. of branches*	*Banknotes in circulation £'000*	*Capital £'000*
1845	19	363	3,294	11,240
1857	17	615	4,080	11,726
1887	10	949	5,644	19,838
1908	8	1,114	7,101	27,237

Source: L. H. White (1992), Noel (1888, pp. 68–69); *Statistics for Great Britain, Germany and France, National Monetary Commission (US), 1910*

The first special condition is that Scotland was a country without a state or, in other words, the functions pertaining to the state were performed by a body (the British government) that was domiciled outside the country. This fact prevented the establishment of a privileged bank in Scotland dedicated essentially to lending to the public sector, as occurred in nearly every other European country. The equality of banking institutions before the law avoided distortions and gave full play to the mechanisms of competition. This is not to say that the Scots were not forced to bear the economic costs of their union with England. Rather, in the specific aspect of the banking structure, the absence of a 'national' bank proved undoubtedly advantageous.

The second special condition in the Scottish case is also related to England and involves the advantages that Scotland derived from its integration within the British economic area that was directed from London. Not only were there no tariffs, but transport costs were low, communication was easy and other integration factors had an effect as well. The southern Scottish shires had close ties to England's northern industrial heartland and these ties doubtless provided a crucial advantage for the Scottish economy that must not be overlooked when analysing its development.

Based on these considerations, it is possible to grasp the special interest attached to an analysis of the Irish case. At the time, Ireland was under British control, but the treatment received by the Irish bore no resemblance to the treatment of the Scottish. While Ireland could not be deemed anything other than a colony, Scotland had become, in spite of everything, an integrated part of a larger polity, the United Kingdom, on a footing of legal equality, if not economic or political equality.

The origins of banks of issue in Ireland date back to the beginning of the eighteenth century, when there are records of banknotes in circulation that had been issued by various private banking houses. While some legal provisions recognised the existence of paper money, no specific regulation was introduced. Attempts to create a banking joint-stock company with the backing of the Irish parliament that would be made in the image of the Bank of England met with failure more because of political strife than because of economic issues. In 1753, there was an episode of over-issuing that ended in an outflow of coin from the island and the subsequent bankruptcy of a large number of banks of issue. In 1760, a new crisis left only three banks of issue in operation and forced the authorities to bolster their creditworthiness with public funds. The difficulties recurred in subsequent years.

The evident instability of the banking system proved crucial in the Irish parliament's eventual approval – not without strong opposition – of the creation of the Bank of Ireland in 1782. The conditions of the new bank closely resembled those enjoyed by the Bank of England. The Bank of Ireland was to have £600,000 in capital that would be advanced to the Irish government as a loan. As a joint-stock company, the bank was to hold a monopoly. No other company with more than six partners, except the new bank itself, would be allowed to issue banknotes or bills of exchange. In 1791, an increase in capital was granted up to £1 million. The system appeared to be stable until a decree suspended payments in coin in March 1797. As noted earlier, the Bank of England had moved to suspend payments in coin in response to dire financial needs arising from the war effort against France and to uncertainty over the war's outcome. The Bank of Ireland formally contacted the island's authorities at once to obtain the same treatment, which was granted.

What is striking about the Irish case is that, once the Bank of Ireland was released from its obligation of convertibility, it undertook a most unusual policy of increased credit based on the increased circulation of money. In March 1797, the banknotes in circulation amounted to £560,000, but within a year, the figure had risen to £926,000 and in five years it stood at £2.2 million. The expansion was further magnified by the proliferation of new private banks of issue, which increased from 11 in operation in 1797 to 40 in 1804. The effect of this expansion was none other than a sharp rise in prices and the depreciation of the Irish pound. By 1804, the exchange rate between the two currencies, which ought to have been at par, stood at £118 Irish pounds per £100 English pounds. The inevitable crash came when payments in coin resumed in 1819–1820. The bank failures became widespread. From the 40 banks in operation in 1804, only 15 remained standing by the end of 1820.

Once again, a proliferation of voices called for a new reform of the system to ensure that any banks in existence would be more resilient and more stable. The problem was similar to the one observed in England and the proposal for Ireland was again very much like the one introduced in the mother country: the Bank of Ireland's monopoly as a bank of issue (in the form of a joint-stock company) was restricted to a radius of 65 miles (50 Irish miles) from Dublin (Bank of Ireland Act, 1821). It became possible, therefore, to create banks of any type outside the capital's area of influence. The new opportunity was not immediately seized on, but in 1824 a number of English capitalists founded the Provincial Bank, which was followed months later by the Hibernian, the Northern Bank and the Bank of Belfast. When these new banks were granted the required approval from the British parliament, a new period of open competition started. The main actors were the Bank of Ireland and the Provincial Bank, which launched a fierce run to open new branches. Nonetheless, the Old Bank – as the Bank of Ireland was popularly called – remained the most profitable one, delivering shareholder dividends that doubled those of its competitors.

A final wave of new banks of issue came in the 1830s. Counting only the ones that took the form of a joint-stock company, the four existing banks were joined by 13 more. Some proved very short-lived. By the early 1840s, not even half of them, seven in all, had become firmly established.

As part of the cycle that began with the Peel Banking Act, new banking legislation was enacted for Ireland that closely resembled the legislation for Scotland. For each authorised bank, there was a maximum limit on issue that was pegged to banknotes in circulation before the law took effect. Banks could further increase their issue by the amount of gold and silver coin in their coffers, with a minimum proportion of three-quarters in gold. They were prohibited, however, from issuing banknotes in denominations smaller than £1.

Banks of issue in Ireland experienced no new regulatory changes in the second half of the nineteenth century and no alteration occurred in their number. There was a sharp increase in the density of branches and in the banks' capital, but not in circulation, which remained relatively stable with only occasional fluctuations (Table 1.4). It is worth recalling that the demographic evolution of Ireland ran opposite to that of Scotland and England and Wales. Between 1841 and 1881, the population grew by 42% in Scotland and by 77% in England and Wales, while it fell by around 40% in Ireland.

There is one final consideration of a comparative nature that may be of interest. Table 1.5 sets out the figures for banknotes in circulation per inhabitant for the countries of the United Kingdom. Particularly striking is the opposite trend observed in England and Wales compared to Scotland and Ireland. In England and

Table 1.4 Banks of issue in Ireland up to 1908

	No. of banks	*No. of branches*	*Banknotes in circulation £'000*	*Capital £'000*
1845	6		6,949	4,200
1887	6	353	6,355	17,400
1908	6	785	6,882	16,800

Sources: Bodenhorn (1992); (Conant, 1909, pp. 178–185; Noël, 1888, p. 74)

Table 1.5 Annual average circulation of banknotes per inhabitant, United Kingdom

	England and Wales £	*Scotland £*	*Ireland £*
1845–1847	1.75	1.30	0.83
1858–1867	1.35	1.38	1.04
1878–1887	1.15	1.53	1.23
1898–1909	1.13	1.65	1.50

Source: *Statistics for Great Britain, Germany, and France, 1867–1909, 1910*

Wales, the banknotes in circulation per inhabitant declined, whereas there was an increase in Scotland and Ireland. By the start of the twentieth century, the circulation was clearly greater in the territories that were economically more backward.

While this state of affairs may be surprising at first glance, it reflects the higher degree of development in England of more modern means of payment, such as cheques and transfers, at the expense of banknotes and coins. Here it is worth recalling Walter Bagehot's response to the survey conducted by the French government in the 1860s:

> Peel's Act has done no harm in England, or at least very little: because it has halted provincial issuing just at the moment when it had achieved its objective: the tide had already turned. At present, the system of deposits and cheques tends to restrict provincial circulation, even among the banks with the best customers and whose credit is increasing. Peel's Law has halted the competition among the banks for circulation: it has stopped the substitution of paper by paper: it has not stopped the substitution of coin by paper because this has basically now been done.
>
> (Enquête, 1867, pp. 25–26)

France

The analysis of the plurality of issue in France must begin with a look at three events that preceded its introduction: the failed monetary experiment of John Law, the adversities of the Caisse d'Escompte and the state's issuing of *assignats*. First, Law's 'system' involved the creation of a huge bank that would take over the state's bloated debt and finance its operations through stocks and bonds and through the issue of banknotes. Licensed by the state, the bank itself or a parallel company would also take over exclusive trade with the American colonies (Upper and Lower Louisiana) as well as their settlement and exploitation. The viability of Law's system has been and continues to be a subject of controversy, but from the panic that ended the experiment in 1720, the French were certainly aware of the fragility of fiat money systems and highly suspicious of banknotes.

In 1776, the government authorised the establishment of the *Caisse d'Escompte*. While the new institution was not granted any exclusive privileges and it was created with private capital, it was closely linked to the financial needs of the state. It issued banknotes that were convertible on demand and well received at first. In 1783, the institution overcame a severe liquidity crisis that forced it to suspend payment of banknotes in coin for a few months. Four years later, the problems resurfaced, this time as a result of state pressure on the institution to obtain funds on credit. Public distrust led to increased requests for banknote redemption that once again forced the institution to restrict payments. This was the situation when revolution broke out. In the months that followed, the National Constituent Assembly ordered new loans that soon brought the entity's credit to ruin. In 1790, the institution's banknotes were decreed to be forced tender. Converted into a useless instrument, the *Caisse d'Escompte* was abolished in 1793.

The episode of the *assignats* began precisely during the first stage of the revolutionary process, when it appeared crucial to take extraordinary measures to meet the state's financial needs. After the confiscation of church property, the state issued *assignats* as a type of mortgage bond in order to realise the value of the appropriated wealth immediately. When the first issues came out in April 1790, the denominations were very large and they could not be used as money. A few months later, however, the need to assure their placement forced the government to allow *assignats* to be used in payments of all types. In the following months, new *assignats* were issued with much lower denominations and they began to lose value. In 1793, they were being exchanged at 40% of their face value. Rising prices led to the disappearance from the market of commonly used copper coins, whose nominal value was lower than the metal they contained. The need for fractional money gave rise to a proliferation of paper money issued locally by the so-called Caisses Patriotiques. By the summer of 1792, there were more than 600 recorded institutions of this sort scattered over the length and breadth of France. This peculiar episode in issue plurality was brought to an end by a decision of the National Convention in November 1792, after an acrimonious debate over the inflationary effects of these issues of banknotes and the ease with which the banknotes could be counterfeited (E. N. White, 1990).

Neither this measure nor others served to halt the ongoing depreciation of the *assignats* or stop the more well-to-do from exploiting the situation to snap up national assets at ridiculously low prices. At the beginning of 1796, *assignats* were permanently withdrawn from circulation and replaced with the new *rescriptions de l'emprunt forcé*.

The disappearance of the *assignats* and the confidence generated from the restoration of some degree of financial stability paved the way for new credit institutions to appear. This is the period in which the French had their second experience of issue plurality. In 1796, the *Caisse des comptescourants* was created, followed a year later by the *Caisse d'escomptes du commerce* and, in 1800, by both *Factorerie* and the *Comptoir commercial*. All of these establishments issued banknotes in competition with one another.

The situation changed radically when Napoleon as first consul approved the creation of the Bank of France in January 1800, shortly after his rise to power. Behind the decision was the idea of organising a hierarchical credit system with the new bank at the top and with the state participating in and, to some extent, controlling it. This intent is reflected in the size given to the new establishment. It had 30 million francs in capital, far greater than the 18 million francs of the earlier *Caisse d'escomptes* or the 2–5 million francs of the remaining Parisian banks of issue. The intention is also apparent from the state's shareholding in the institution. According to its founding charter, the Bank of France could issue banknotes, but it was not granted any privilege of exclusivity.

The new bank's first steps were bolstered by a merger agreement reached with the *Caisse des comptescourants*, which brought in resources, materials and staff with experience. The bank operated under competition until a new law awarded it the monopoly on banknote issue in Paris in April 1803. The legislation made government approval a requirement for any banks seeking to exercise the same privilege in other French departments. The argument in favour of the monopoly was simple: "a single bank is much easier to oversee than several, both for the government and for the public: whatever the economists say, it is not a case in which competition might prove useful" (Jacaud, 1999, p. 200).

The new arrangement resulted in the loss of the right to issue by all the banks that had been engaged in issuing with or without express authorisation. In addition to the four previously mentioned Parisian banking houses, there were many other banks of issue established in the French departments. The objections of the injured parties, however, fell on deaf ears. The largest competitor, the *Caisse d'escomptes du commerce*, accepted being merged into the Bank of France under the same favourable conditions offered three years earlier to the *Caisse des comptescourants*.

Although the regulations did not prohibit the Bank of France from establishing branches in the French departments, its leadership showed very little support for the idea at first. When they did finally take the plunge, the result was a sobering failure. In 1808, the bank received permission from the authorities to open branches in Lyon and Rouen, followed in 1810 by Lille. Only six years later, in 1814, the management came before the bank's board of governors to propose the advisability of closing the branches, citing serious problems of control and low profitability. After various delays, the closure of the Lyon and Rouen branches was authorised in early 1817, while the Lille branch had already been shuttered.

The Bank of France's withdrawal from the French departments encouraged the creation of new independent banks. Indeed, the Bank of France itself offered to facilitate the process in the cities where it had pulled out (Ramon, 1929, pp. 130–132). In some cases, the same directors of the former branches led the initiative to open a new establishment. The introduction of the banks came in two waves. The first wave brought three new ventures, while the second one brought six. Table 1.6 shows that the two waves came more than 15 years apart and that no new banks were created in the interim. It should be remembered that the Bourbon Restoration in France (1815–1830) was a period marked by notably sluggish economic growth.

After the July Revolution in 1830, new projects sprang up in several cities. In some of them – Lyon and Marseille – the first step was to make a request to the Bank of France to open a *comptoir* or branch. When the request was denied, the proponents decided to create a new bank. A few years later, between 1834 and 1838, fresh initiatives led to the founding of six new departmental banks (Gille, 1959, pp. 89–104). Faced with this proliferation and the evidence of a growing demand for financial services in the French departments, the Bank of France reconsidered its stance. In February 1836, the board of governors appointed a committee to study the possibility of opening branches outside Paris. In the following month, the bank sent a brief to the finance minister that gave assurances that the need for "preventive measures" against the circulation of banknotes in the departments had disappeared and that "the time had come for the Bank to establish itself in [the departments] to contribute to lower interest rates in the

Table 1.6 Departmental banks and Bank of France branches until 1848

	Departmental banks		*Branches of the Bank of France*	
	New banks	*Banks in operation*	*New branches*	*Branches in operation*
1817	Rouen	1		
1818	Nantes, Bordeaux	3		
1835	Lyon, Marseille	5		
1836	Lille	6	Reims and Saint-Étienne	2
1837	Le Havre	7	Saint-Quentin	3
1838	Orléans, Toulouse	9	Montpellier	4
1840			Grenoble and Angoulême	6
1842			Caen, Besançon, Chateauroux and Clermond-Ferrand	10
1843			Mulhouse	11
1846			Strasbourg and Le Mans	13
1847			Valenciennes	14
1848		9		14

Source: Ramon (1929)

manufacturing cities and other locales that did not have as many resources as the major centres of circulation". The authorisation for the opening of the first branches in the second wave came in May 1836 (Ramon, 1929, p. 175ff.).

From that point onward, the Bank of France's attitude toward the approval of new departmental banks became increasingly wary and the advisory reports requested by the government in response to each new application contained more caveats and demands. The debate that developed around the renewal of the Bank of France's own privilege in 1840 bolstered its position. After the renewal entered into law on 30 June of that year, opposition to the creation of new independent banks became much more forceful and successfully carried the government along with it. From 1837, as many as a dozen projects were the recipients of a negative report from the Bank of France and subsequent rejection by the government (Gille, 1959, pp. 98–99). Any parties interested in securing access to the benefits of a bank of issue opted to apply for their own *comptoir* or, more modestly, to gain acceptance of their bills of exchange in any of the existing banks. The number of departmental banks stalled at nine, while the branches of the Bank of France rose to 14 by 1848.

Table 1.7 shows the level of activity achieved by each departmental bank of issue and by the leading branches of the Bank of France. In terms of banknotes in circulation, the four most active departmental banks were Bordeaux, Lyon, Marseille and Rouen. The first three also had the greatest activity in commercial discounting, the main and practically only operation carried out by the entities. In comparison, the Bank of France's branches appear to be much less active in the introduction of their banknotes within their territories, but not in commercial

Table 1.7 Banks of issue in France in 1847. Banknotes circulation and discounts (million francs)

Departmental banks			*Bank of France*		
	Banknotes circulation	*Discounts (value)*		*Banknotes circulation*	*Discouns (value)*
			branches/comptoirs		
Bordeaux	20.9	106.2	Besançon	0.5	76.7
Rouen	12.0	79.9	Montpellier	0.9	88.3
Nantes	4.3	49.5	Saint-Étienne	1.1	84.0
Lyon	19.8	185.6	Saint-Quentin	1.0	57.1
Marseille	16.3	270.2	Others	6.0	172.7
Le Havre	4.4	67.5	**Total *comptoirs***	**9.5**	**478.8**
Lille	4.5	48.5	Bank of France, Paris	237.6	1,372.2
Toulouse	4.8	24.4	**Total Bank of France**	**247.1**	**1,851.0**
Orléans	3.0	19.8			
Total for departmental banks	**90.0**	**851.6**	**TOTAL**	**337.1**	**2,702.6**

Source: Bank of France, *Assemblée Générale des accionaires* . . . 27–6–1848. Paris

discounting. In 1847, the departmental banks of issue as a whole accounted for 26.7% of banknotes in circulation and 31.5% of the discounted value realised, two figures that are not inconsiderable.

The differences in the volume of business among the various banks were related more closely to the commercial activity in each centre than to the population. Table 1.8 below shows that the four largest banks mentioned earlier, together with the Bank of Le Havre, accounted for the greatest activity per inhabitant. It should not be forgotten that all five locations were important ports with a long-standing trading tradition.

In his analysis of the performance of the departmental banks, Bertrand Gille blamed both the regulatory restrictions and the economic relationships between the French departments and Paris for the limited development of these banks. The operational restrictions imposed by the state to authorise the banks were very narrow. The only feasible operation was the discounting of bills of exchange in their own cities or Paris. Discounting bills of exchange from other centres was generally prohibited and received authorisation only in very specific cases. The public's reluctance to use banknotes also affected the departmental banks, as did the outflows and inflows of cash in their areas of influence. For example, the banks in some southern departments experienced sharp variations in the demand for cash as a consequence of the vagaries of Spanish monetary policy and the widespread

Table 1.8 Departmental banks of issue: Relative sizes in 1847

	Banknotes in circulation per inhabitant	*Discounts. Value per inhabitant*
	francs	*francs*
Bordeaux	210.1	1,067.3
Rouen	132.6	882.9
Nantes	51.6	594.2
Lyon	137.5	1,288.9
Marseille	110.7	1,835.6
Le Havre	166.7	2,556.8
Lille	70.5	760.2
Toulouse	62.3	316.9
Orleans	76.9	507.7

use of French currency in Spain. Something similar caused the frequent monetary imbalance between the departments and Paris as a result of tax payments and investments in railways. The sluggish development of the use of current accounts and deposits prompted the banks to become too dependent on the circulation of banknotes (Gille, 1959, pp. 100–104).

In spite of everything, the departmental banks ultimately played a key role in the financial modernisation of France, especially bearing in mind the Bank of France's reluctance to extend its activities outside Paris for nearly 40 years.

The Bank of France itself had a two-faced attitude toward plurality. In various statements in 1839–1840, the bank's governor and deputy governor both acknowledged that the plurality of banks of issue had been essential to ensure an efficient distribution of credit and the introduction of fiat money and they called for greater harmony on the basis of the freedom and independence of each institution (Gille, 1959, p. 97).

This apparent acceptance of the status quo was immediately contradicted by the Bank of France's stance toward the renewal of issue privileges requested by the departmental banks. The first request came from the Bank of Bordeaux in 1846 and the Bank of France's response was to call for its transformation into a branch of the Bank of France itself. This drew indignation from the other banks of issue and from local economic forces of various kinds. Local support for the existing banks would have ensured their survival and that of the system of issue plurality for some time if the revolution of 1848 and its effects had not intervened.

The overthrow of the July Monarchy and the proclamation of the French Second Republic set off a widespread financial crisis that had devastating effects on banking in general and on the departmental banks of issue in particular (Jacaud, 1996). In Paris, several banking establishments funded through the issue of securities similar to banknotes faced a deluge of demands for redemption that forced them into liquidation, while other banking houses also suffered the effects of the crisis. The Bank of France itself was directly affected. On 25 February, in the very midst of the revolution, the bank successfully lobbied the authorities to decree a compulsory ten-day extension of maturities that enabled it to continue supplying credit to its clients for the period. However, the measure did not prevent a sharp drop in the bank's coin and bullion reserves from 140 million to 60 million francs. The situation was untenable. The bank was forced to go back to the provisional government and request relief. On 15 March, the government issued a formal decree to establish the forced tender of the Bank of France's banknotes and to suspend its obligation to redeem them in coin on demand.

Unsurprisingly, the difficulties also affected the departmental banks of issue, which had to take steps to restrict the redemption of their banknotes. On the same 15 March, they applied to the government to extend the consideration of forced tender to their banknotes and to suspend their convertibility. The government immediately directed the authorities of each department to put the measures into effect. Such extraordinary circumstances were exploited by the proponents of unified issue to impose their ideas. All indications are that the policy of France's provisional government on the matter was not disconnected from its financial needs, which forced it to turn to the Bank of France for help. The conditions agreed in the negotiation included the conversion of departmental banks of issue into branches of the Bank of France. The finance minister wanted it to appear as if the process had been agreed by the departmental banks themselves, but it did in fact entail a compulsory takeover. The authorities threatened to lift the suspension of convertibility at once if the merger was not accepted. The conditions of the purchase were relatively favourable for the shareholders of the merged departmental banks, but many of them would certainly have rejected the merger otherwise (Jacaud, 1996, pp. 208–291).

Ultimately, the plurality of banknote issue in France appears to have been a sort of anomaly in such a fiercely centralist country, and that is how it was seen by many of the political and economic decision-makers of the period. Indeed, the origins of plurality need to be located in the resistance of the Bank of France itself to extending its activities outside the capital. The institution's exacerbated centralism could be said to have spurred on the appearance of independent banks. When its leadership did at last come to appreciate the desirability of establishing a network of branches, the role of the departmental banks of issue was immediately thrown into question (Jacaud, 1997). The revolution of 1848 simply provided a pretext to impose uniformity and restore the temporarily challenged hierarchical order.

German lands

The process of forming the German Empire culminated in January 1871 with the proclamation of Wilhelm I as emperor. The timing was not happenstance. After six months of warfare, victorious Prussian troops were marching into Paris. Bismarck had achieved the impossible, the unification of the German lands under Prussian rule. The Congress of Vienna in 1815 had recognised the existence of 39 independent political entities in the German lands, including the major kingdoms of Prussia and Austria. The construction of a unified economic area had begun in

1818 with the creation of the Zollverein, a customs union that led to the removal of a large number of the existing transport barriers.

Trade integration, however, was not accompanied by a similar shift in the monetary and financial realm. The Bank of Prussia had been created by the government in 1765 exclusively with public capital. In 1847, it was converted into a joint-stock company with the participation of private capital. Nevertheless, it continued to act as the government's bank, though it had no monopoly on the issue of banknotes. It pursued an active policy of expansion, reaching 158 branches across the entirety of the kingdom by 1870. Earlier in the nineteenth century, eight additional entities had been granted authority to issue banknotes: one in 1821 and the remainder between 1848 and 1866. The hegemony of the Bank of Prussia, however, always kept their levels of banknote issue very low (see Table 1.9).

In the remaining territories that would later make up the German Empire, banks of issue emerged as well, mostly in close connection with their respective governments. The first ones sprang up in Munich (1834) and Leipzig (1839), but a huge wave followed in the mid-1850s. By 1862, there were 20 independent banks of issue in the independent German states. By the time the Imperial Bank was set up in 1875, there were 24.

As Table 1.9 shows, the size of these entities and their issue capacity varied widely. Four stood out: the Bank of Frankfurt, Bank of Munich, Bank of Leipzig and Bank of Weimar. The proximity of issuing centres to one another created competition even in states that did not allow more than one bank of issue. All of this occurred in a strongly expansionary economic environment that had a direct effect on the demand for money.

The complexity of the system of issue plurality then in effect in the German states was exacerbated by two additional factors: there were several currencies of account in the area's states and the banks were not the only parties to issue banknotes. The resulting situation was described in 1866 by Johann von Helferich, a professor at the University of Göttingen, as follows:

> We have twenty-three different types of non-bank paper money in Germany, not counting Austria, twenty-one issued by governments and the other two issued by a city council and a railway company. The minimum value of the banknotes is 1 florin (2 francs 14 cents) in the south of the country. In addition, we have thirty-one banks issuing banknotes; another one being set up and two more in the pipeline [. . .]. Four of these banks pertain to states in which the florin is the unit of currency [. . . and] one uses the franc, though it also issues in florins [. . .]. The only banknotes that are received without discount in transactions between private individuals are those of the Bank of Prussia and the Bank of Leipzig in the domain of the thaler and those of the Bank of Frankfurt in the domain of the florin. All of the others have a circulation limited to a certain distance [from the branches of the respective bank, and beyond that] their exchange supposes for the bearer a more or less considerable loss.
>
> (Enquête, 1867, V, p. 309)

Table 1.9 Banks of issue in Germany, 1862. Paid-in capital and banknotes in circulation (million francs)

Kingdom of Prussia	*Paid in capital*	*Notes in circulation*	*Zollverein countries (except Prussia)*	*Paid in capital*	*Notes in circulation*
Bank of Prussia	63.37	457.29	Bank of Leipzig	11.25	23.31
Union of Berlin	3.75	2.49	Bank of Bautzen	2.06	3.75
Bank of Stettin	7.12	3.75	Bank of Dessau	11.25	0.19
Bank of Breslau	3.75	3.75	Bank of Lübeck	1.5	2.4
Bank of Posen	3.75	3.75	Bank of Rostock	4.74	3.75
Bank of Magdeburg	3.75	3.75	Bank of Bremen	16.5	7.42
Bank of Danzig	3.75	3.75	Bank of Thuringia at Sondershausen	7.5	1.27
Bank of Cologne	3.75	3.75			
Bank of Königsberg	3.75	3.69	Bank of Gera	9.37	6.51
			Bank of Weimar	18.75	11.64
Total Prussian Banks	96.74	485.97	Bank of Gotha	5.25	6.9
			Bank of Meiningen	15.00	6.11
			Bank of Luxemburg	10.00	0.1
			Bank of Brunswick	13.12	5.00
			Bank of Hannover	20.32	5.44
			Bank of Munich	42.86	17.14
			Bank of Frankfurt	21.43	54.75
TOTAL	346.69	651.19	Bank of Darmstadt	4.57	3.89
			Bank of Hamburg	2.14	0.15
			Bank of Nassau	30.46	5.36
			Bank of Bückeburg	1.88	0.14
			Total Zollverein Banks	249.95	165.22

Source: Wirth (1896)

From 1867 onwards, a twin process of banking consolidation and increased state intervention got underway. In the same year, responsibility for the banks of issue was taken over by the North German Confederation under the de facto control of Prussia, which hugely curtailed the banks' dependence on their respective governments. In March 1870, a law established new uniform rules on monetary circulation, while three years later a new monetary system was established with the mark as the reference. Lastly, the law of 14 March 1875 restructured the entire German banking system, turning the former Bank of Prussia into the German Imperial Bank with 120 million marks in capital.

The same legislation also set the conditions under which any banks of issue whose privileges were still valid could maintain their functions. Essentially, the law stipulated that the banks in question must adhere to the same demands that the law placed on the Imperial Bank, which included severe limits on operations and on earnings distribution. The clear intent of the law was to achieve unified circulation in the near future. Indeed, 15 of the 33 banks that were entitled to issue banknotes surrendered their privilege at the very moment when the law took effect. In

1891, only seven remained in addition to the Imperial Bank itself. By 1908, only four continued to issue banknotes and all were to cease doing so in the 1920s

Italian lands

The history of banks of issue in Italy has three distinct phases that are separated by two watershed events: the creation of the National Bank of the Kingdom of Italy (Banca Nazionale nel Regno d'Italia) by merger in 1860 and the creation of the Bank of Italy (Banca d'Italia) over 30 years later in 1893. It must be taken into account, however, that the monopoly on issue was not fully introduced until 1926, when the Bank of Naples and the Bank of Sicily suspended their issuing activities (Canovai and Ferraris, 1911; Conant, 1909; De Mattia and Cardarelli, 1990; Di Nardi, 1953; La Francesca, 2004; Spinelli and Frantianni, 1991).

The first news of the issuing of securities treated as banknotes comes from Naples in 1818. Two years earlier, the Bank of the Two Sicilies had been created. It had two separate departments, one focused on state financing and the other on lending to the general public. Indeed, the bank came out of the transformation of the former Bank of Naples, a charitable financial institution created in 1796 from the merger of various pawnbrokers and similar entities. The institution's refounding was made necessary by the king's ongoing use of its funds, which he continued to do with equal or greater force after it was reconstituted as the Bank of the Two Sicilies. In 1843, an agreement was reached to hive off the branches located in Sicily and to create a new bank, which was known as the Bank of Sicily. The new bank's operation was basically the same as the operation of the former parent bank in Naples.

From the standpoint of issuing means of payment, the activities of the two southern banks were peculiar. They issued securities in the form of certificates of deposit, cash vouchers and similar instruments, but not explicitly banknotes. The documents, despite their initially high unit value, enjoyed widespread use as means of payment. During the general crisis of 1866, forced tender was introduced and the Bank of Naples received authorisation to issue money orders (quasi-banknotes) in denominations as low as 0.50 liras (Canovai and Ferraris, 1911, p. 25). In 1872–1874, both banks received formal permission to issue banknotes.

The second region to witness the appearance of banknotes in the early years of the nineteenth century was Tuscany. In 1816, Ferdinand III, the Grand Duke of Tuscany, drew capital from the ducal treasury to set up the Cassa di Sconto di Firenze. The experience was not positive and ten years later, the bank was reconstituted with an influx of private capital and the state retained only a minority shareholding. In other locations in the Grand Duchy of Tuscany, similar ventures sprang up: Livorno (1837), Siena (1841), Pisa (1846), Arezzo (1847) and Lucca (1849) (Volpi, 1997).

As their names suggest, these institutions focused primarily on commercial discounting, but they had the power to issue banknotes as well. The state had a strong presence in some of them, like the one in Florence. The establishments in Florence and Livorno, which were the two with the most business, merged in 1857 to create the National Bank of Tuscany (Banca Nazionale Toscana). In subsequent years, the process of concentration in the financial market proceeded and by the end of 1860 all of the Tuscan discounting houses mentioned above had been absorbed into the National Bank of Tuscany.

Despite the early introduction of banknotes in the Kingdom of the Two Sicilies and the Grand Duchy of Tuscany, the origins of the future Bank of Italy actually lay in the Kingdom of Piedmont-Sardinia (Conte, 1990). It was there that the Bank of Genoa was created in 1844 with the backing of Genoa's merchants, who were in need of modern credit facilities. Three years later, the Bank of Turin was created at the initiative of, and with the controlling stake of, Camillo Benso, the Count of Cavour, who was soon to be called to form part of the Sardinian government. Both new banks had a licence to issue banknotes and both went through serious hardships because of the government's constant appeals for credit. The Bank of Genoa was forced to suspend the convertibility of its banknotes in September 1848 and the Bank of Turin also faced dire straits. These circumstances account for the launch of a debate over the desirability of merging the two establishments. After lengthy negotiations, they reached agreement in 1849 to create a single bank: the National Bank of the Sardinian States (Banca Nazionale degli Stati Sardi).

Over the following ten years, the new bank experienced moderate, but significant growth. Convertibility was restored in September 1851, the circulation of its banknotes rose from 25 million liras to 40 million and the discounted values climbed from 82 million liras to 225 million. Part of the growth was the result of opening branches as required by law. Over the course of the 1850s, the bank opened eight branches, which joined the two main offices in Genoa and Turin.

In other Italian cities and regions like Rome itself, Emilia-Romagna (Bologna) and the Duchy of Parma, the spread of banknotes came later. In the case of Rome, an early banking venture that was launched in 1833 under the leadership of a French banker ended in a resounding suspension of convertibility in 1848 and the resulting implementation of forced tender for its banknotes and an expansion of issuing. To right the situation and restore public credit, the papal government spurred the creation in 1850 of the Bank of the Papal State (Banca dello Stato Pontificio), which absorbed the former institution. The circulation of banknotes rose weakly from little more than 10 million lira in 1852 to 14 million liras in 1860–1861, but it subsequently picked up to reach 30 million liras by 1870. Then, in 1870, when the Papal States were swallowed up by the Kingdom of Italy, the establishment changed its name to the Bank of Rome (Banca Romana), but it continued to enjoy the privilege of banknote issue until the creation of the Bank of Italy in 1893.

Both the Bank of the Four Legations (Banca delle Quattro Legazioni), created in Bologna in 1856, and the Bank of the Parman States (Banca degli Stati Parmensi), created in 1858, were short-lived. In 1860, each was absorbed into the National Bank of the Sardinian States as a consequence of advancing Italian unification. The expanded institution also took over the activities carried out by the National Bank of Austria in the territories that had hitherto belonged to the

Austro-Hungarian Empire, namely Lombardy and the Veneto. As a consequence of these developments, the bank came to be called the National Bank of the Kingdom of Italy.

Table 1.10 shows the state of the banks of issue in Italy at the completion of the first phase of Italian unification. The National Bank of the Sardinian States appears as the leading bank of issue, if the Bank of Naples is left aside as a special case. Also of note is the low importance of banknote circulation in the Bologna area and particularly in the regions of Italy emerging from Austrian rule. This is particularly true in Lombardy, because the imperial authorities in Venice had permitted the establishment of an independent bank of issue that continued in operation until it was absorbed by the National Bank of the Sardinian States in 1867.

Portugal

The case of Portugal is characterised by a series of legislative changes that affected the right to issue banknotes. As in Spain, the process began with a decision taken by the government in 1797 to issue paper money to cope with its financial troubles. The Portuguese problems were only compounded further by the French invasion in 1807 and the subsequent arrival of the British fleet, which initiated a seven-year period of war. The return to peace, however, did not herald any improvement in the financial situation and the depreciation of paper money reached 30% in 1821. In order to resolve the matter, the state authorised the establishment of the Bank of Lisbon, which opened its doors in 1822. The new bank was granted the exclusive right to issue banknotes, initially for 20 years and then, in 1824, for 30 years. In 1835, however, the government accepted a request from various Oporto merchants to authorise the formation of the Commercial Bank of

Table 1.10 Banks of issue in Italy circa 1860. Banknotes and metallic money in circulation (million liras)

	Banknotes in circulation (million liras)	*Coin in circulation (million liras)*	*% banknotes out of total*
National Bank of the Sardinian States	83	176	32
Bank of the Parman States	–	20	–
Bank of the Four Legations (Bologna)	3	100	3
Bank of the Papal State	44	30	59
National Bank of Tuscany	20	75	21
National Bank of Austria (Lombardy and the Veneto)	9	112	7
Mercantile Establishment of Venice	18*	100	15
Bank of Naples**	179	350	34
Bank of Sicily	30	107	22

* Figure includes state-issued banknotes.

** The Bank of Naples did not issue banknotes, but did issue certificates of deposit used as money.

Source: De Mattia and Cardarelli (1990, p. 13)

Oporto (Banco Comercial do Porto), which was also granted the right to issue banknotes. This initiated a period during which a plurality of issue was to persist in various forms for 50 years.

The crisis of 1846–1847 had a major impact on Portugal, leading to dire effects for the Bank of Lisbon. The state was deeply in debt to the bank, which had no hope of recovering its outstanding loans. It became necessary to decree the forced circulation of the bank's notes and to push through its reorganisation. The chosen formula was to merge the Bank of Lisbon with National Trust (Confiança Nacional), another financial institution that was also a state creditor. The new company was called the Bank of Portugal and it was granted the exclusive privilege to issue banknotes for another 30 years, though it also had to respect the authorisation granted to the Commercial Bank of Oporto back in 1835.

However, the provisions of the law were not observed on this occasion either. With the decree of 16 April 1850, the capital of the Bank of Portugal was reduced and its exclusive privilege to issue banknotes was restricted to the city of Lisbon. This opened the way for the creation of new banks of issue in other centres, though the opportunity was not taken up until the appearance of the Merchant Bank of Oporto (Banco de Mercantil de Porto) in 1856 and five more entities between 1861 and 1864. By the end of 1864, five banks of issue were up and running in Oporto, one in Braga and two in Lisbon, specifically the Bank of Portugal and the National Overseas Bank (Banco Nacional Ultramarino), which focused essentially on Portugal's colonies. Partial data for 1866 point to very weak circulation for the new banks (Table 1.11).

The first step toward the adoption of a monopoly on banknote issue was taken by the government when it passed a law on 29 July 1887 to award the Bank of Portugal the role of the state's cashier. The text of the law indicated that, if the Bank of Portugal accepted the new function, the government would take steps so that the seven existing banks of issue agreed to relinquish their privileges to it. Despite the government's explicit aims, however, the process does not appear

Table 1.11 Banks of issue in Portugal, 1866. Banknotes in circulation (million réis)

	Banknotes in circulation (million réis)
Bank of Portugal	1,427
Commercial Bank of Oporto	–
Merchant Bank of Oporto	142
Union Bank of Oporto	–
New Public Utility Company	168
Alliance Bank	191
Bank of Minho	40
Bank of Guimarães	–

Source: *A History of Banking in All the Leading Nations* (1896), vol. 3, pp. 310–311

to have gone far. In the end, the financial crisis of 1891 hurried the matter to a conclusion. Faced with difficulties in maintaining the convertibility of their banknotes, the smaller banks of issue came to an agreement with the Bank of Portugal in June 1891 and the government ratified the deal on 9 July. Under the arrangement, the year 1906 was set as the upper limit on the Bank of Portugal's ability to exercise its right to withdraw the banknotes of the remaining issuers from the market and replace them with its own.

1.4. A path to follow: the European way to new national financial systems

The first phase in the construction of a new financial system to meet the demands of industrialisation took on a wide variety of forms in Europe. This does not preclude the observation, however, that the processes shared many characteristics in common. Of course, the governments of later-adopting countries looked with special attention at the financial institutions that were emerging in the more advanced countries and at how the authorities supervised and eventually intervened in their operation. The most significant aspects that a careful observer might grasp from what occurred in the European financial sector up to the mid-nineteenth century can be summarised in three points:

1 The introduction of fiat money and, more generally, of modern financial habits were key elements in the process of modernisation. The way in which these processes took place and their relative pace or scope were to have a crucial influence on the extent of economic, not merely financial, development achieved by the various countries.
2 From this perspective, the plurality of banknote issue must be understood as a form of financial organisation that facilitated the introduction of instruments and practices that lie at the foundation of contemporary financial systems. Unsurprisingly, therefore, multiple issue was present in practically every country of Europe and it remained in effect until the end of the nineteenth century in most of them.
3 Despite the advantages that can be attributed to the plurality of banknote issue, it was not without costs or risks. The potential costs stemmed from the difficulties involved in handling a large volume of means of payment with varying denominations and guarantees or in effectively realising fiat money or similar instruments issued elsewhere, while the potential risks related to the fact that the ultimate guarantee of a banknote fell on the original bank of issue. This accounts for why, as the use of banknotes and current accounts spread, plurality came to appear costlier and its risks greater.

It is necessary to understand plurality, therefore, as a form of monetary organisation that was suitable to facilitate the initial growth of the modern system of fiat money, but not desirable on a permanent, widespread basis.

These reflections, drawn from the experiences of the most advanced European countries, were present in the debates and discussions that surrounded the chequered modernisation process of the Spanish financial system from the 1840s onwards. In a sense, they held up a mirror for Spain's economic decision-makers when it came time to set objectives and put government plans into action.

Sources

A History of Banking in All the Leading Nations. *Journal of Commerce and Commercial Bulletin*. New York (1896), 4 vols.

Bank of France, *Assemblée Générale des actionnaires* . . . Paris

Blackwood's Edinburgh Magazine, vol. 56, 1844.

Statistics for Great Britain, Germany and France 1867–1909. National Monetary Commission (US), Washington, 1910.

Bibliography

Arnon, A., 2011. *Monetary theory and policy from Hume and Smith to Wicksell: Money, credit, and the economy*. Cambridge University Press, Cambridge.

Bodenhorn, H., 1992. Free banking in Ireland. In Dowd, K. (Ed.), *The experience of free banking*. Routledge, New York, pp. 137–156.

Canovai, T. and Ferraris, C.F., 1911. *The banks of issue in Italy*. United States National Monetary Commission, Washington, DC.

Collins, M., 1993. *Central banking in history*. Elgar, Aldershot.

Conant, C.A., 1909. *A history of modern banks of issue*. G.P. Putnam's Sons, New York.

Conte, L., 1990. *La Banca nazionale: formazione e attivita di una banca di emissione, 1843–1861*. Edizioni scientifiche italiane, Naples.

Courcelle-Seneuil, J.G., 1867. *La Banque libre, exposé des fonctions du commerce de banque et de son application à l'agriculture, suivi de divers écrits de controverse sur la liberté des banques*. Guillaumin, Paris.

———, 1840. *Le Crédit et la banque, étude sur les réformes à introduire dans l'organisation de la Banque de France et des banques départementales, contenant un exposé de la constitution des banques américaines, écossaises, anglaises et françaises*. Pagnerre, Paris.

De Mattia, R. and Cardarelli, S., 1990. *Gli istituti di emissione in Italia: i tentativi di unificazione (1843–1892)*. Laterza, Rome.

Di Nardi, G., 1953. *Le banche di emissione in Italia nel secolo XIX*. Chieri, Tipografía Montano, Turin.

Enquête. 1867. *Enquête sur les principes et les faits généraux qui régissent la circulation monétaire et fiduciaire*. Paris: Imprimerie Impériale, 6 vols.

Dowd, K., ed., 1992. *The experience of free banking*. Routledge, New York.

Gille, B., 1959. *La banque et le crédit en France de 1815 à 1848 (vol. 14)*. Presses Universitaires de France, Paris.

Jacaud, G., 1999. A national bank or local banks? Debates on the issuing of paper money in France in the first half of the nineteenth century. In Bellet, M. and L'Harmet, C. (Eds.), *Industry, space and competition. The contribution of economists of the past*. Edward Elgar, Cheltenham, 199–218.

———, 1997. Unité ou pluralité des banques d'émission ? Les débats en France (1846–1848). *Etudes et Documents* (Comité pour l'histoire économique et financière de la France), IX, 391–413.

———, 1996. Revolution de 1848 et bouleversements monétaires. *Economies et Sociétés*, 22 (Série AF), 4–5.

Kindleberger, C.P., 1984. *A financial history of Western Europe*. Allen & Unwin, London.

La Francesca, S., 2004. *Storia del sistema bancario italiano*. Il mulino, Bologna.

Macleod, H.D., 1891. *The theory of credit*. Longmans Green and Co., London.

Mitchell, B.R., 1988. *British historical statistics*. Cambridge University Press, Cambridge.

Noël, O., 1888. *Les banques d'émission en Europe*. Berger-Levrault, Paris.

Pressnell, L.S., 1956. *Country banking in the industrial revolution*. Clarendon Press, Oxford.

Ramon, G., 1929. *Histoire de la Banque de France d'après les sources originales*. Bernard Grasset, Paris.

Richards, R.D., 1927. The evolution of paper money in England. *The Quarterly Journal of Economics*, 41, 361–404.

Rist, C. and Boissieu, C.D., 2002 [1951]. *Histoire des doctrines relatives au crédit et à la monnaie depuis John Law jusqu'à nos jours ([Reprod. en fac-sim.] réédition présentée par Christian de Boissieu, . . . ed.)*. Dalloz, Paris.

Smith, A., 1789. *An inquiry into the nature and causes of the wealth of nations*, 5th ed. A. Strahan and T. Cadell, London, 3 vols.

Spinelli, F. and Frantianni, M., 1991. *Storia monetaria d'Italia: l'evoluzione del sistema monetario e bancario*. A. Mondadori, Milan.

Volpi, A., 1997. *Banchieri e mercato finanziario in Toscana, 1801–1860*. L.S. Olschki, Florence.

White, E.N., 1990. Free banking during the French revolution. *Explorations in Economic History*, 27, 251–276.

White, L.H., 1992. Free banking in Scotland before 1844. In Dowd, K. (Ed.), *The experience of free banking*. Routledge, New York, pp. 157–186.

———, 1984. *Free banking in Britain: Theory, experience and debate, 1800–1845*. Cambridge University Press, Cambridge.

Wirth, M., 1896. The history of banking in Germany and Austria-Hungary. In *History of Banking*, vol. IV. The Journal for Commerce and Commercial Bulletin, New York, pp. 1–187.

2 Banking regulation and the emergence of provincial banks in Spain

Yolanda Blasco-Martel

This chapter and subsequent chapters analyse the development of banking in Spain between 1844 and 1874, a period that begins with the appearance of the first banks of issue and ends with the centralisation of banknote issue under the Bank of Spain (Banco de España). This was the first stage in the formation of a new financial system in Spain comparable to the systems established earlier in most countries of Western Europe. Modern banking and banknote issue attracted the interest of states that introduced very similar sorts of regulations: the requirement of certain prerequisites to be met before opening a new bank; the official approval of bank statutes and by-laws; and the establishment of a number of general operating rules by law. Banking legislation in each country typically required a percentage of capital to be held in reserve (between 10% and 50%) as well as a reserve in coin and bullion related to the amount of banknotes in the public's hands. Under some regulations like Spain's, the adequate capital to open a bank depended on circumstances and there were no set criteria. In some countries, the capital depended on the population (US), while a minimum of capital was established in others (Sweden, Belgium, Norway and Denmark). In Switzerland, for example, there was a capital requirement to cover a percentage of a bank's liabilities, which ranged from 5% to 10% at the beginning of the twentieth century (Allen et al., 1938). In most European countries, banks were regulated according to their specific legal form (joint-stock companies, general partnerships and, in the German case until the legislation of 1856, limited partnerships) (Brophy, 1992).

This section analyses the legal framework that regulated banks of issue in Spain. To this end, we have to situate the topic of regulation within a broader theoretical framework. The most recent approaches to the role of financial development in economic growth focus on the role of legal institutions as a determining factor of the differences that can be observed between the financial structures of different countries (Demirgüç-Kunt et al., 2003). Two hypotheses have been put forward. According to the first one, the countries that have better developed their financial systems (markets and intermediaries): a) had legal systems that protected property rights; b) guaranteed the enforcement of private contracts; and c) protected the interests of foreigners. By contrast, the countries that did not evolve in these respects experienced a weaker development of their financial systems. This hypothesis attaches vital importance to institutions in general (Acemoglu et al., 2004), (Lamoreaux and Rosenthal, 2005), (North, 1981), (North, 1990), (Rajan and Zingales, 2003). According to the second hypothesis, financial development can also be influenced by the existing legal framework based on its degree of enforcement and its adaptability, that is, its capacity to evolve in the face of changes in the economic environment. This hypothesis suggests that institutions do matter, but less than the specific legal framework (Beck and Demirgüç-Kunt, 2003), (La Porta et al., 1998), (Levine, 2005).

The Spanish case presents its own distinctive features. Some of these features stem from its historical trajectory, while others are related to its particular circumstances. Foremost among the first group is the closeness of the Spanish legal system to the civil law of the French tradition, typified by centralised states that make laws that have an impact on markets through political mechanisms (Merryman and Pérez-Perdomo, 2007). By the mid-nineteenth century, a body of laws was taking shape in Spain that would govern local social, political and economic life in the decades to come. The process played out in troubled, turbulent times in which various political factions did not hesitate to call on the military in order to prevail by force over their adversaries. As a consequence, political instability was one of the factors that influenced the initial stages and specific features of Spanish banking development.

Turning to Spain's particular circumstances, it is necessary to recall that the Spanish state was still being formed in the period in question and its ability to enforce new rules was tenuous. Given a situation in which any consensus is weak, regulations can become complex and end up satisfying nobody. In turn, the more complex and sophisticated the regulations are, the harder they become to understand and the less effective their application. This may explain, for instance, why unauthorised credit companies were issuing banknotes in several Spanish cities without hindrance from the competent authorities or why after the enactment of the decree of 1874 and its prohibition of further issue by provincial banks, some of these banks nonetheless continued issuing banknotes without the authorities being able to enforce the law.

In addition to the objective difficulties arising from political instability and the state's ineffectiveness in following and enforcing the law, there was an additional factor at work: the absence or narrowness of public debate on economic policy in general and financial policy in particular. Public discussion of these matters was limited and some contributions were of little value. Despite the existence of studies such as the ones by Ramón Santillán, Luís M. Pastor and Manuel Girona, there was no serious debate in Spain over the question of the freedom of issue, nor was there serious discussion of other important financial matters. The British and French debates and surveys of the period had no parallel in Spain until the twentieth century.

In the 45 years between 1829 and 1875, Spain witnessed the passage of more than 30 provisions with the status of a law or decree on the regulation of banking. The set of rules proved excessive not only because of the sheer number of provisions and the lurching back and forth that they produced, but also because of their level of detail. It was clearly a case of over-regulation, likely spurred by their chief precedent: the legislation of 1829 governing the Bank of San Fernando. The adoption of such in-depth regulations reveals the distrust of the regulator toward those who had to abide by the rules. The state defined the operations that the banks of issue could carry out, their capital requirements and the way in which share transfers had to be handled (including the procedure), how to organise their governing bodies and their administration and earnings distribution (Calbetón, 1910).

2.1. The Spanish banking system prior to 1840

Paper money was first introduced in Spain in response to the financial plight resulting from the country's defeats at the hands of Great Britain at the end of the eighteenth century. Because of the war, Spain's shipping routes to Peru and Mexico were cut off and metal from the colonies could not reach the country. In 1780, Charles III of Spain responded to the situation by authorising the issue of public debt securities (*vales reales*) at 4% interest. Between 1780 and 1783, there were three issues of *vales reales* for a total of nearly 500 million *reales*. However, they depreciated very quickly and the process managed to undermine the relationship between the monarchy and its primary groups of supporters, contributing to the fall of Spain's ancien régime (Herr, 1978). To avert disaster, a proposal was made to create a national bank, whose main objective would be to halt the continued decline in the price of *vales reales*. The result was the Bank of San Carlos, founded in 1782 under the direction of the Frenchman François Cabarrus (Santillán, 1865; Tedde, 1988). In 1783, the new bank put into circulation *cédulas*, or certificates, that were repayable to the bearer, but the parallel existence of *vales reales* (which could be also used as a means of payment and paid 4% interest) made the task more difficult. In 1795, an attempt was made to replace the *vales reales* with banknotes, but it was unsuccessful because of distrust in the institution.

After having rejected several proposals, the government finally implemented a plan to reform the old Bank of San Carlos in 1829. By agreement with its shareholders, the overall amount that the state owed to the bank (300 million *reales*) was written off by a sole payment of 40 million *reales* in cash. This money was transformed into the capital of a new entity, the Bank of San Fernando (Banco Español de San Fernando), with the same shareholders (Tedde, 1999). From the outset, the Bank of San Fernando positioned itself as the state's lender. Throughout the 1830s, the civil war triggered by the succession of Ferdinand VII greatly expanded the state's financial needs and an authentic symbiosis developed between the Public Treasury and the bank (Tedde, 1999). In some sense, the Bank of San Fernando acquiesced in becoming almost solely the state's banker, foregoing the chance to become a 'national' bank with a major presence in the financing of the private sector. This went against the spirit of the bank's own statutes. Specifically, article 5 granted the bank the right to open branch offices in any provincial capital where it was deemed advisable and to establish correspondent banks where it did not open branches. However, no branches were created until 1858 and the network of correspondent banks outside Madrid was rather limited in extent.

The royal charter of 9 July 1829 and the by-laws of 6 August 1832 encapsulated the regulations that were to govern the Bank of San Fernando. These regulations, which are of interest because they later spurred the creation of other banks in the country, were a product of their times and reflect the concerns of the day. For example, in a time of war marked by national and international turmoil, the rules provided guarantees on the wealth of foreigners in the bank's safekeeping so that such wealth would not be monitored or expropriated if the conflict involved their country of origin. The shares were registered, which is understandable when not all the capital is paid in. As a result, the shareholders were to be held liable for the outstanding capital with their assets. With the passage of time, however, the registered nature of the shares gave rise to delays and reduced the speed of transfers.

The Bank of San Fernando capital was fixed by the government according to the agreement with the Bank of San Carlos' shareholders. There was no proposal for criteria by which to evaluate its capital needs, nor did its capital relate to other requirements. As a result, the bank's issuing was not linked to capital, but rather to decisions taken by the bank's board of governors. Later banks of issue did face requirements on paid-in capital, but the criteria for capital requirements were never made explicit and they depended on each bank's governing body. Nonetheless, a committee appointed by Spain's Council of State to assess applications for the opening of new banks rejected some on the basis of insufficient capital. All indications are that the figure needed to open a bank was in the region of a million pesetas. Other countries, by contrast, did set criteria to define a bank's capital requirements. In the United States, for instance, the National Banking Act of 1864 set three prerequisites for the opening of new banks: for towns with fewer than 6,000 inhabitants, there was a minimum capital requirement of $50,000; for towns and cities with between 6,000 and 50,000 inhabitants, the minimum was $100,000; and for larger cities, the minimum was $200,000 (White, 1983, p. 16).

Article 5 of the royal charter granted the Bank of San Fernando the *facultad privativa*, or exclusive power, to issue banknotes payable on sight to the bearer. This power was to be wielded "precisely by the administration of the bank in this city and [could] not be transferred or delegated to branch offices in the provinces". The banknotes of the Bank of San Fernando were always issued in Madrid under a local monopoly, but they were allowed to circulate in the provinces and, indeed, did so. However, their circulation in the provinces fell to correspondent banks, because the Madrid bank did not open any branches until after the law of 1856.

At first, attracting liabilities through current accounts and deposits was not one of the bank's priorities. Indeed, current accounts were regarded as a banking service and a commission was charged (art. 28). This type of account could hardly serve to attract idle capital if, rather than bearing interest, it incurred fees. The Bank of San Fernando only permitted money or securities payable in Madrid to be accepted in current accounts. The funds available to a current-account holder were limited to funds paid in over the counter. The bank did not make cash advances. Indeed, there was a penalty for making withdrawals against non-existent funds. In addition, when undertaking obligations payable at the bank, it was necessary to give ten days' notice. All these elements confirm that current accounts in the period, and until the second half of the century, were regarded as a service offered by institutions to their customers in order to facilitate payments and collections. Voluntary deposits came a little closer to operations attracting liabilities. Spanish coinage was accepted for deposit, as were bills of exchange and foreign coinage in the form of gold or silver; gold and silver pastes and bars; jewels and public bonds. Voluntary deposits were free, but not interest-bearing, whereas judicial deposits incurred a custodial fee. The voluntary deposits of the period had two characteristics. First, securities were accepted as collateral for loans and, second, coins and bills of exchange were deposited so that the bank could perform the function of safekeeping in light of the uncertainties of the period. The Caja de Depósitos was founded in 1852 precisely with the aim of taking deposits as legally stipulated and paying 5% interest. In turn, the new institution's creation showed clearly the state's interest in attracting funds through deposits. As a result, the Caja de Depósitos permitted voluntary deposits in coin or notes for a fixed term, and they were interest-bearing (Sánchez-Albornoz, 1967, p. 6).

The Bank of San Fernando was chartered to carry out the operations of a commercial bank, but it was also authorised to operate with the state. Operations with the state included short-term lending, placement and negotiation of government securities and transfers of money between government agencies, among others. Its functions as a commercial bank included receiving current accounts from its customers and performing payments and collections for them, taking voluntary and judicial deposits, discounting bills of exchange and promissory notes, assessing and making loans and drafting bills of exchange.

The Bank of San Fernando discounted bills of exchange and promissory notes for a maximum period of 100 days and the operation required three bank-approved signatures, one of which had to be local. Also, one of the signatures could be substituted by shares in the bank itself, which were accepted at face value. Loans were secured with gold or silver jewels for a maximum term of six months and they could not exceed 75% of the value of the collateral. Loans could also be made for a 90-day term against government securities at their price on the stock exchange. They could not exceed 66% of the value of the collateral. Lastly, loans could be made against the bank's own shares up to 75% of the shares' value on the stock exchange.

Collateral is one of the most delicate aspects of banking operations. English law defines collateral as a "term applied to any secondary, indirect, or additional security lodged with a bank or an individual to insure the repayment of a loan. In the event of non-payment such security is available without recourse to legal proceedings" (Easton, 1926). In legal terms, the banker takes possession of collateral though it still belongs to the customer. Its effectiveness depends on its integrity and on the bank's supervision. The bank must anticipate potential changes in the value of collateral and be careful with its safekeeping. It is normal that the securities initially accepted as collateral were limited (public securities, jewels and precious metals). With the appearance of provincial banks, the accepted collateral was expanded to include merchandise, though a recurring prohibition was placed on some goods (liquids) and others were discontinued because of the risks to which they exposed the banks (cotton). Also, the creation of joint-stock companies with limited liability broadened the spectrum to include stocks and bonds as collateral for loans.

The statute of the Bank of San Fernando served as a reference point for the regulations governing banks of issue that emerged from 1844 onwards. These regulations were not the work of a committee of experts or the result of parliamentary discussions or surveys as were the regulations pushed forward in England in 1832 when the charter of the Bank of England came under review (Gregory, 1929). In the Spanish case, it was customary for the government and parliament to enact rules and regulations that were not always based on experience or expertise. As is well known, the Bank of San Fernando did not even try to meet the financial needs of the Spanish economy. Its sole occupation in the period was to finance the state. The financial requirements of the economy were actually being supplied by a set of specialised individuals and trading houses. They were currency traders, money-changers and merchants or merchant capitalists. In the absence of specific banking regulations, the banks arising in this initial period were created based on the personal experience of their promoters under the legal umbrella of the Commercial Code of 1829. According to this Code, general and limited partnerships could be created through simple registration, while joint-stock companies required approval from a commercial court, the Tribunal de Comercio (art. 293). In certain instances, royal approval was also required, for example, when some privilege was involved as it was for banks of issue (art. 294).

2.2. The first banks of issue and the restrictive laws of 1849 and 1851

In 1844, two banks of issue were created in Spain: the Bank of Isabel II in Madrid and the Bank of Barcelona.[1] The first was short-lived and its closure proved abrupt (1847), whereas the second survived much longer, but its closure in 1920 was equally precipitate, followed by a long agony for its shareholders and current-account holders.[2] Both banks opened branches: the Bank of Isabel II in Cádiz and the Bank of Barcelona in Reus, Tarragona and Palma (Majorca). However, there were also differences between the two. Foremost were differences in representation and voting in their shareholders meetings: the Bank of Isabel II opted for a system of proportionality in relation to the number of shares, while the Bank of Barcelona set a criterion of 'one shareholder, one vote' for any shareholders with five shares or more. The Bank of Isabel II was created in clear competition with the Bank of San Fernando, whereas the creation of the Bank of Barcelona came in response to the economic dynamism of its home city. While the Bank of Barcelona can be regarded as a provincial bank of issue, the Madrid bank had its own distinctive features owing to the existence of the Bank of San Fernando. For example, the paper put into circulation by the new Madrid bank was not called banknotes, but rather *cédulas al portador*, or "bearer certificates", which was a euphemism to skirt the exclusive privilege of banknote issue granted previously to the Bank of San Fernando.

Table 2.1 above clearly illustrates how the two Madrid-based banks had established the bulk of their business in government debt in 1846. However, the deposits of the Bank of Isabel II also point toward the difficulties (weak metallic reserves) that would lead to its forced merger within a few months. In that same year, an agricultural crisis precipitated by poor harvests in 1845–1847 (potatoes and grain) pushed food prices higher and the demand for manufactured goods lower throughout Europe. In Spain, the impact of the crisis was felt unevenly, including among lending institutions. In any event, the period of 1847–1848 was difficult for the new banking entities. In Madrid, the hardship forced the Bank of Isabel II into an untenable position, which prompted the government to order its amalgamation with its fierce competitor, the Bank of San Fernando, in 1847; in the Catalan case, the French political crisis of 1848 ignited a wave of fear that seriously menaced the Bank of Barcelona.

When the Bank of Isabel II went into liquidation, its Cádiz branch obtained permission to create the Bank of Cádiz in conjunction with other banks that had appeared in the period.[3] As a result, from 1847, the banks in Barcelona and Cádiz were the only ones to have the privilege to issue banknotes apart from the Bank of San Fernando. The two banks could issue banknotes equal to the total of their nominal capital, provided the banknotes were backed by holdings of gold and silver coin worth one-third of their value. The Bank of Barcelona received

Table 2.1 Main balance sheet accounts. Banks of San Fernando, Isabel II and Barcelona, 1846

December 1846 (pesetas)	*Bank of San Fernando*	*Bank of Isabel II*	*Bank of Barcelona*
Capital subscribed	20,000,000	25,000,000	5,000,000
Paid-in capital	20,000,000	17,500,000	1,868,000
Deposits	9,400,000	130,256(1)	2,007,804
Current accounts	30,100,000(2)	11,329,875(3)	2,865,048
Banknotes	20,000,000	26,668,750(4)	5,000,000
Cash and securities holdings			
Coin and bullion on hand	23,750,000(5)	1,500,000(6)	3,000,571
Bills of exchange and promissory notes in holdings	12,725,000	2,005,105(7)	12,733,734
Loans against government securities	55,925,000	22,656,293(8)	789,024

(1) The figure is estimated on the basis of earnings. (2) The figure corresponds to the line for sundry creditors. (3) This is the average between maximum and minimum current accounts during the year 1846. (4) Banknotes issued in November 1846. (5) Unspecified. (6) This item was highly unstable according to Zumalacárregui. In the preceding half-year, it had reached 20.75 million pesetas. (7) The figure only reflects bills of exchange. (8)Though there are no data available for 1846, the accounts presented by the bank in early 1847 when it merged with the Bank of San Fernando show collateralised loans totalling 22.6 million pesetas. This is the figure for February–March 1847 and must contain loans against shares too.

Source: Tedde (1999); figures for the Bank of Isabel II have been estimated based on the data provided by Zumalacárregui (1952)

permission for a second issue of banknotes up to twice its capital, provided again that one-third of the value was kept in coin in its coffers.

Interestingly, the banking regulations in Spain were not explicit and they excluded current accounts and cash deposits from the banks' reserve requirements. The founding partners did not include them either, nor did the regulator ask them to do so. However, the banks' directors were familiar with the "Palmer rule" that stated that a well-run bank was required to maintain cash in its coffers equivalent to one-third of its liabilities.[4] It is certainly odd that the painstaking regulation of the banks did not cover this aspect of deposits and current accounts. Neither the laws, nor the institutions' statutes and by-laws, nor any other rule addressed the matter. Only in the regulations of 1851 were current-account holders recognised as creditors. Perhaps the explanation lies in the fact that, while some countries had already begun to replace banknotes with bank deposits, Spain was still in the preceding phase, that is, extending the use of convertible banknotes to stand in for coinage. The substitution process stretched over the entire second half of the nineteenth century. As a result, the process of intermediation (taking savings and offering credit) had made little headway in the country. As Luís Pastor pointed out in his *Filosofía del crédito*, published in 1850:[5]

> In Spain, the number of savings banks is very small: mortgage lending is completely unheard of according to the latest advances; public funds have not been exploited because of the state of credit among us and our attitude toward it. The few banks that have existed and now exist have not paid interest on the sums that they have taken in current accounts [. . .].
>
> (Pastor 1850, p. 22)

When Pastor wrote his book, the Caja General de Depósitos did not yet exist. When it appeared in 1852, it paid interest on deposits. Beginning in the 1860s, the use of current accounts spread and when credit companies sprang up, many of them also adopted the practice of paying interest. Some banks of issue tried to follow suit. Others asked for the government's permission and were denied. Still others refused to pay interest on current accounts. The argument that took hold was that deposits should be treated as investments and therefore attract interest, whereas current accounts were a service provided by an institution to its clientele to facilitate collections and payments. In the 1840s, the Bank of Barcelona experienced first-hand the enormous cost of maintaining current accounts, when the large number of coins made procedures incredibly cumbersome (Blasco-Martel and Sudrià, 2010a). In any event, the banks had many different rationales, whereas the lawmakers remained fixated on banknote circulation.

The focus on banknote issue is borne out in the banking regulations of later years. When the position of the Bank of Isabel II became untenable, the minister Ramón Santillán signed a royal decree on 25 February 1847 to merge the bank with the Bank of San Fernando. Any monopoly on banknote issue for the resulting bank was rejected at the time: "No monopoly can result from the merger, given that issues are not industrial acts subject to competition, and with respect to discounting and other operations that do enter into the class of industrial or commercial acts, the field remains open to the free competition of bankers and individual merchants". The unified bank's capital was set at 100 million pesetas, though only half was paid in.

In 1848, the reality was that the Bank of San Fernando was struggling to place its banknotes. A royal decree on 9 September 1848 acknowledged public distrust in its banknotes and separated banknote issue from its other activities just as the Peel Banking Act had done in relation to the Bank of England. In addition, the decree restricted the bank's notes in circulation to 25 million pesetas (circulation was nearly double that amount in July 1848) and it required reserves to cover one-third of the value of the notes with coin in its coffers and the remainder with thoroughly sound securities. The banknotes were also to be accepted as cash money in the payment of rents, taxes and duties levied by the state throughout the peninsula (art. 6). As this suggests, there was a latent idea in lawmakers' minds to establish a national bank that would secure the circulation of banknotes. Ultimately, it would be a bank that had a monopoly over banknote issue throughout the national territory.

Partially paid-in capital was one of the characteristics of the earliest Spanish banks. The Bank of Barcelona and the Bank of Cádiz maintained paid-in capital at levels lower than par value. While the law of 1856 respected their right to do so, it also required of any new banks that their committed capital be fully paid in. Maintaining only partially paid-in capital had the wholehearted support of the Bank of Barcelona, with one of its directors, Manuel Girona, at the forefront (Cabana, 2002; Blasco-Martel and Sudrià, 2010a). The idea of keeping a portion of the capital in the hands of shareholders rested on a broader conception of a bank's need for equity, which was also spelled out by lawmakers, though more generically. According to this conception, the purpose of a bank's overall capital was to meet any contingency in the realisation of all financial assets accepted or owed by the bank (including banknotes). However, a bank's operating capital should be no greater than what was necessary to cover normal activity. As operating capital would be much lower than contingency capital, the difference could be retained by the shareholders with a formal commitment to bring it to the bank when needed.

As stated in a decree of the Spanish government, any excess beyond this amount "makes no sense in the organisation of a bank, which in such case would be forced, in order to obtain moderate profits, either to contravene its operations or to maintain a high premium on its discounts against the main object of these establishments which is precisely to reduce the payment of interest on capital to a minimum" (RD 30 January 1851).

Then what was the ideal capital for a bank? There is no straight answer in the Spanish legislation. As a result, each bank settled for the capital that its founder members deemed appropriate to meet the needs of the location and the bank's own interests.

Table 2.2 shows the position of the two provincial banks of issue in 1849. Their greatest similarity seems to be that their business revolved around banknotes. As

Table 2.2 Composition of assets and liabilities in the banks of Barcelona and Cádiz (1849)

ASSETS[6]	*% Bank of Cádiz*	*% Bank of Barcelona*
Coin on hand	21.86	35.83
Banknotes on hand	4.20	0.23
Holdings of redeemable bills of exchange and promissory notes	39.34	24.47
Loans against government securities	7.64	12.95
Loans against other assets	15.28	17.38
Bank properties	8.98	5.96
Others	2.69	3.18
	100.00	*100.00*

LIABILITIES	*% Bank of Cádiz*	*% Bank of Barcelona*
Paid-in capital[7]	38.09	18.79
Total banknotes issued	51.98	50.12
Deposits	0.70	8.86
Current accounts	8.51	16.83
Dividends payable	0.03	0.75
Reserve funds		1.54
Others	0.69	3.11
	100.00	*100.00*

Source: April 1849, *Archive of the Congreso de los Diputados*, file 65, no. 119; reports submitted to the Senate on the position of the different banks in existence in Spain

can be observed, the two banks had different cash policies. The explanation may lie in the crisis that had recently struck the Bank of Barcelona. The Catalan bank had also embarked on a slow, but perceptible development of current accounts.

Another important law enacted in the period (the Ley de Sociedades Anónimas) tackled the subject of joint-stock companies. On 11 December 1847, the Senate took up consideration of a draft bill for the establishment of joint-stock companies. Slightly over a month later, on 28 January 1848, the bill was signed into law by Bravo Murillo. According to Tortella (Tortella, 1968), the legislation was a reaction to the economic crisis, which was being attributed to over-speculation. In order to curb it, the new law required a royal decree or law to authorise the creation of any company with divisible share capital. This included not only joint-stock companies but also limited partnerships known as *sociedades comanditarias por acciones*. The law classified companies in two groups: a) banks of issue, transport companies and companies enjoying privileges that required approval by law; and b) any company whose purpose was of "public interest" and that required approval by royal decree. All other joint-stock companies were prohibited.

Consequently, authorisation was only granted to companies of "public interest" that had "capital proportionate to the purpose of their establishment". It is interesting to note that the concepts of "public interest" and "proportionate capital" are stated by lawmakers but not defined. The mechanism for obtaining authorisation required an application accompanied by a list of partners in the future company and by its statutes and by-laws. In any event, the shares were to be registered. Also, managers or directors had a duty to deposit a set number of shares while in office.

The law on joint-stock companies was accompanied by a regulation issued by royal decree on 17 February 1848. The royal decree regulated an array of aspects concerning the formation of such companies, the nature of their shareholders, the remuneration of their administrators, the supervision, registration and disbursement of their shares and more. The January law set a statutory two-month deadline for existing companies to ratify and comply with the law, and the regulation of 17 February reiterated the deadline. Subsequently, a royal order issued on 19 June 1848 indicated that any companies that had not complied with the rule would be dissolved, given that "the deadline had long elapsed" (it had expired nearly three months earlier). In light of the regulator's inefficiency, one might suspect that the parties involved were accustomed to not taking rules seriously and that this meant that regulations had to be repeated time and again. Irrespective of its details, the law was severely restrictive; the authorisation process for a joint-stock company was long, expensive and uncertain and authorised companies then became subject to close government oversight. While the regulations remained in effect for 20 years, modifications did mitigate some of their severity.

The banking laws of 1849 and 1851

In the years that followed, the regulator returned to the organisation of the banking system. On 19 January 1849, draft legislation was brought before the Spanish parliament to address the "reorganisation of the Bank of San Fernando". In a long explanatory memorandum, the minister, Alejandro Mon, referred exclusively to the Madrid bank and how to improve its reputation, but, as shall be seen, article 6 of the bill had other connotations. In his statement, Mon stressed the distrust in the Bank of San Fernando that existed at the time he assumed control of the ministry. He viewed this distrust as odd because "there was no known operation whatsoever that had met with misfortune". However, "there was a wariness of losses arising from some excess in lending against its shares". Even though it still held "almost" all of its capital, the capital was being employed in long-term securities that proved hard to realise. The minister further indicated that the shareholders had obtained 188% interest on their capital over 13 years and that the government would accept responsibility but that ultimately the shareholders would be held accountable and if they did not assume liability, the government would decide on the bank's continued existence or its dissolution. This was a preamble that sounds like a threat.

The reorganisation of the bank included a decrease in capital and a guarantee of issue (art. 3): "The bank must constantly keep on hand and in coin and bullion at least a third part of the value of its banknotes in circulation to ensure at all times that for all other securities it maintains an effective guarantee greater than the sum of banknotes in circulation". At the same time, the law restricted the issue of small-denomination banknotes up to 125 pesetas. In a controversial article in the first draft of the law back in January that was championed by minister Mon, the legislation stipulated that the only bank of issue and discounting would be the Bank of San Fernando.

Lastly, the law, which received approval on 4 May 1849, amended article 6, which clarified the last issue in the paragraph above as follows:

> Henceforth there shall not be more than one Bank of issue, with efforts being made to achieve agreement between the Bank of San Fernando and the banks of Cádiz and Barcelona to find the means whereby to bring about the merger of the latter two banks with the former without the least injury to their respective interests and with the approval of the government. If said merger cannot be brought about, the acquired rights of the banks of Cádiz and Barcelona shall be retained and they shall keep the power to issue banknotes for an amount equal to their effective capital paid in and existing in the bank; however, from the publication of the present law, they shall undertake to conform to the provisions of articles three, four, five, seven, twelve, fourteen and eighteen, thereby implementing the law analogously in the Statutes and By-laws of Barcelona and Cádiz.[8]

Though the law preserved the survival of the banks in Barcelona and Cádiz and their right to issue banknotes, it severely restricted their issue capacity. Until that time, it should be recalled, the two provincial banks were allowed to issue banknotes up to the amount of their nominal capital and they both had only a portion of their capital paid in. Table 2.3 shows the effects of the new issue rules on each bank. As can be seen, the adjustment forced an 85% reduction in the circulation of banknotes by the Bank of Cádiz and a 77% reduction by the Bank of Barcelona, if the latter returned as expected to a level of 25% of capital paid in.

In 1851, only two years after the reforms of Alejandro Mon, Juan Bravo Murillo pushed through a new law on the Bank of San Fernando. The process began with

Table 2.3 Capital and banknote issue for the banks of Barcelona and Cádiz at 31 December 1848 (pesetas)

	Bank of Barcelona	*Bank of Cádiz*
Nominal capital	5,000,000	25,000,000
Issued share capital	5,000,000	10,433,000
Paid-in capital	2,500,000	1,669,280
% of capital paid in	50%	16%
Banknotes issued	5,487,500	10,848,000
Banknotes in circulation	5,365,100	8,789,500
Issue limit prior to law of 5 May 1849	5,000,000	10,433,000
Issue limit set in the law of 5 May 1849	2,500,000* 1,250,000**	1,669,280

* With 50% of capital paid in.
** With 25% of capital paid in.
Source: *Gaceta de Madrid*

the submission of a report to the Spanish parliament on 30 January 1851. After a debate that went on for nearly 12 months, the new legislation was passed on 15 December of that year. Its aim was to normalise the situation of the Bank of San Fernando, which had recovered by then from the crisis that struck in 1847–1848. The minister's statement is striking. On the one hand, he acknowledged that the "exorbitance" of the capital with which the bank had been created in 1847 was due to its particular circumstances at the time. On the other hand, he indicated that it was an "embarrassment" to apply article 16 of the law of 1849 that divided the bank into two sections (issue and discounting), arguing instead for the advantages of centralisation. At the same time, he compared the Bank of San Fernando with the banks in Barcelona and Cádiz and noted that the Madrid bank was at a disadvantage because it was only allowed to issue against its effective capital, while the other two banks could issue up to their nominal capital. The minister added that the Bank of San Fernando found itself subject "by the government to an incomparably more effective intervention than the other two received". That is, he denigrated the figures put in charge of overseeing the provincial banks, indicating that they were not carrying out their role properly.

Lastly, it is useful to note that the draft legislation of January 1851 contains the first explicit mention of current-account holders as creditors by virtue of their voluntary deposits. In so doing, they were now to be regarded as such by the courts (article 6 of the draft bill of January 1851 and article 10 of the law of December 1851).

The laws of 1849 and 1851 limited the geographical extent of the banks of issue and the circulation of their banknotes. The effect was to increase their operations in current accounts. At the same time, however, the laws resulted in a significant overload for the institutions, because the management of current accounts sharply increased their work.[9] The only reference to this question in the pertinent regulations appears in the ones approved in July 1856 for the Bank of Spain. This indicates (art. 227 and 230) that the bank shall provide customers two types of cheque books: pay stub sheets, which were also called bearer stubs (*talones al portador*) and were used to pay anybody, and transfer orders (*mandatos de transferencia*), which were used only with the bank's own current-account holders.

The restrictive effects of the laws on issue not only ushered in greater use of current accounts, but they also gave rise to non-legal payment instruments that were accepted in circulation and competed against banknotes. These instruments were to play a special role in the period after 1856, when numerous credit companies circulated cheques, till receipts and other financial documents as if they were banknotes.

It is also necessary to look at another aspect that may help to understand the increasing prominence of current accounts in banking operations. With the laws of 1849–1851, current accounts flourished because the legislation had the effect of reducing the circulation of banknotes. To some extent, current accounts replaced banknotes.

Finally, after the "reorganisation" laws of 1849 and 1851, the Bank of San Fernando reorganised itself definitively with statutes approved on 18 February 1852. Interestingly, after laying out the bank's position, the report on the proceedings went on to say, "given the recognition of the Bank of San Fernando as a general bank of issue for the entire kingdom, its prompt and definitive reorganisation is therefore also a matter of the greatest public interest".

2.3. The progressive reform of 1856

In light of the foregoing, it is understandable that the progressive law of 1856, which liberalised the creation of banks of issue in Spain, was taken as an affront by the Bank of San Fernando, which was renamed the Bank of Spain (Banco de España) under the new law. Despite a discernible interest on the part of lawmakers, legislative ambiguity had repeatedly prevented the establishment of the Bank of San Fernando as a national bank with issue capacity for the entire territory.

In addition, these were years of marked growth for Europe's banks of issue. Between 1855 and 1857, a dozen banks of issue sprang up in German lands, two in the future Italy and one in Portugal. Even the rigid French system was sensitive to the eagerness for expansion: the number of branches of the Bank of France rose 30% from 35 at the beginning of 1856 to 45 by the end of 1858. This is the backdrop of keen interest in banking against which the new Spanish legislation needs to be viewed.

The law of 28 January 1856 was "the result of a compromise between Madrid bankers allied to the Bank of San Fernando who were seeking to strengthen its power [. . .] [and] a heterogeneous coalition of businessmen from the provinces and abroad tied to progressive and democratic politicians, who concurred only in their desire to restrict the monopoly position of the Bank of San Fernando and to capitalise on the promising prospects for the banking business being opened up in Spain" (Pérez de Armiñán, 1977, p. 12). In Pérez de Armiñán's view, the parliamentary discussion surrounding the law lacked technical consistency, giving rise to the famously contradictory wording of articles 3 and 4 on regulating the creation of new banks and Bank of Spain branches:[10]

> Art. 3: Within the term of one year, the Bank of Spain shall establish branches in Alicante, Bilbao, A Coruña, Málaga, Santander, Seville, Valencia, Valladolid and Zaragoza, without prejudice to the possible establishment of private banks in the aforementioned locations and others, having the same privileges granted by this law to the Bank of Spain, without the need to wait until the end of said year.
>
> Art. 4: The establishment of only one bank of issue shall be permitted in each location, whether a private bank or a branch of the Bank of Spain. After a period of three months from the publication of this law, if no authorisation has been requested to create a private Bank in one or more of the capitals listed in art. 3, the Bank of Spain shall decide whether or not to establish a branch.

Two things were unclear: 1) whether or not the Bank of Spain had a duty to open a branch in the cities listed above in the absence of a request from private applicants and 2) whether it would lose its rights if it did not so after the established three months (or one year). The rules required clarification: a royal order on 12 June 1856 made it clear that the Bank of Spain's obligation to open branches ceased "in the case that individuals or companies have requested authorisation to establish private banks within the period of 3 months" and that priority among competing applications would be given according to the date on which the applications were submitted.

Table 2.4 summarises the key concepts appearing in the law of 28 January 1856, along with some remarks that again concern the legislation's ambiguity and lack of clarity.

Table 2.4 Key concepts in the law of 1856

CONCEPT	*REGULATIONS (by article)*
Shares	1 share = 500 pesetas (art. 7). Banks were not permitted to lend against their own shares (art. 15).
Capital	100% paid in. The banks of Barcelona and Cádiz were to pay in 100% of their capital when they deemed it appropriate (art. 6 and 7).
Grant of authorisation	Authorisation granted by royal decree, agreed by the Council of Ministers, publication of statutes and by-laws in the official gazette (art. 8).
Issue	Issue = 3 x effective capital, keeping metallic reserves equivalent to 1/3 of issue (art. 9).
Denominations of banknotes issued	No banknotes with denominations lower than 25 pesetas nor greater than 1,000 pesetas shall be issued (art. 10).
Foreigners	No foreigners shall hold office in the administration of the institution (art. 12).
Operations	Discounting, issuing drafts, lending, keeping current accounts, carrying out collections, taking deposits, entering into contracts with the government and its agencies without an overdraft facility (art. 14). "They shall not be allowed to make advances to the Treasury for a sum greater than their effective capital without guarantees that are firm and easy to realise" (art. 17). (Does this wording indicate that they were permitted to lend more than their effective capital to the Treasury if they received firm guarantees?) Premium and conditions in statutes and by-laws (art. 16).
Assets	Cash and holdings in coins and readily convertible securities with terms not to exceed 90 days, ***enough*** to cover their debts because of banknotes, current accounts and deposits (art. 20). (How much is "enough"?)
Transparency	Obligation to disclose their financial position monthly (art 21).
Reserve fund	10% of effective capital, made up of net profits less 6% (art. 24).
Payment to capital/ earnings	Payment to capital shall not exceed 6% interest per annum (art. 24). After posting 10% to the reserve fund and 6% to capital, the remaining net earnings shall be divided in half between shareholders and the reserve fund (art. 24).

The law of 1856 unified the regulations, although certain exceptions remained regarding the banks in Barcelona and Cádiz. A new set of norms for the opening of banks of issue was established. For instance, banks of issue were required to be joint-stock companies with ("enough") fully paid-in capital before entering into operation. The law also set a minimum nominal value for all shares. This aspect had a downside: the banks in some provinces were left in very few hands because the share price was out of reach for many small investors. But was it more negative or positive? From the standpoint of amassing capital, it was negative. Perhaps with a lower share price, more provinces that had a less dynamic economy could have founded a bank of issue. The law also contained rules on transparency in relation to the disclosure of accounts and the making of reserve provisions. In addition, there were elements of risk reduction related to the prohibition against banks of issue making loans backed by their own shares. Loans to the Treasury were also limited and regulated. The maximum for the issue of banknotes was set at three times a bank's capital, taking for granted that the bank had to maintain gold and silver in its coffers at a value equal to one-third of its issue. Denominations of banknotes could not be lower than 125 pesetas or higher than 1,000 pesetas. Lastly, the new law installed the figure of a royal commissioner known as a *comisario regio*, a government official charged with overseeing every bank's decisions. They had to be paid by the banks themselves (around 7,500 pesetas a year).[11]

The effects of the law of 1856 were quick to appear. Between the enactment of the law and 1864, 18 banks of issue sprang up (Table 2.5).

On the same date as the law on banks of issue, whose purpose was to provide paper money and short-term credit, another law was enacted, whose goal was to encourage long-term credit and industrial promotion through so-called credit companies (*sociedades de crédito*). Credit companies had a larger share of equity

Table 2.5 Banks of issue and branches of the Bank of Spain, 1844–1864. Dates of Royal Decrees granting authorisation

	Date of Royal Decree		*Date of Royal Decree*
Bank of Barcelona	1/5/1844	Bank of Jerez	14/10/1859
Bank of Cádiz	25/12/1846	Bank of San Sebastián	13/6/1862
Bank of Málaga	27/6/1856	Bank of Reus	26/12/1862
Bank of Seville	21/11/1856	Bank of Burgos	6/11/1863
Bank of Valladolid	25/4/1857	Bank of Pamplona	6/11/1863
Bank of Zaragoza	25/4/1857	Bank of Oviedo	5/2/1864
Bank of Santander	15/5/1857	Bank of Vitoria	11/3/1864
Bank of Bilbao	18/5/1857	Bank of Palencia	11/3/1864
Bank of A Coruña	25/11/1857	Bank of Santiago	15/5/1864
Bank of Spain –		Bank Balear	5/6/1864
branches:		Bank of Tarragona	25/6/1864
Valencia	19/3/1858		
Alicante	23/5/1858		

Source: *Gaceta de Madrid*

in their liabilities than banks while their outside funds were basically made up of bonds, which were much more stable than the banks' notes and current accounts.

Another form of company was the *sociedades de giro y banca*, which focused on non-corporate discounting and short-term lending. They had been accommodated in the 1848 law on joint-stock companies and were not allowed to compete with the credit companies, because they were not authorised to issue bonds. It should be noted that while credit companies' supervision fell to the Treasury Department, that of the *sociedades de giro y banca* corresponded to the Ministry for Development. All of these companies and banks of issue had their particular tax rate in the region of 3% of net earnings (Carrasco, 1867).

2.4. The crisis of 1866 and its consequences, 1874: the end of issue plurality

In early 1866, the Spanish state faced an alarming situation arising fundamentally from its difficulties in meeting its financial commitments. The Bank of Spain, which had been acting as its principal guarantor until then, requested that the government grant permission to restrict the circulation of its banknotes.[12] However, the situation did not improve and the state's financial position came close to collapse. At that point, a programme of reforms was put forward. Draft legislation was presented for the establishment of a national bank that would absorb all then-existing banks of issue, including the Bank of Spain, and be granted predictably to a group of English investors in exchange for a very generous loan to the government.[13]

The draft bill set the new bank's capital at 300 million pesetas, which was a sum three times greater than the Bank of Spain's capital at the time. In addition, a few key conditions were laid out: the new bank's notes would circulate throughout the entirety of the national territory and the new bank would perform all the typical operations of a commercial bank while also covering the needs of the Treasury with which it was allowed to establish contracts longer than 90 days. The new bank further undertook to provide an immediate loan of 100 million pesetas for ten years at a maximum interest of 5% per annum. The new bank was also compelled to swap the shares of any Bank of Spain shareholders who wanted the new shares and, likewise, to swap those of any shareholders in the provincial banks that agreed to merge with the new national bank.[14]

The government's programme ran into stiff opposition because of its fiscal provisions (the plan included an advance on tax contributions) and because of the proposed national bank. Monetary circulation was a sensitive matter and there was very widespread fear of forced tender. Rumour had it that the new national bank would circulate currency with a face value lower than 25 pesetas, which raised general alarm. The author of one of the many pamphlets that appeared at the time, though he was in favour of the reform, cautioned the government about "the prejudice that today dominates all classes of the people against paper money", which in his opinion advised against "in such times of crisis, attempting to circulate other [banknotes] of lower value than the familiar ones" (Aguado y

Sinobas, 1866, p. 13). The same writer also wondered about the enormous capital of the new bank, which was going to permit an issue of banknotes "far greater than any other bank in Europe today", and he argued that the capital of a bank of issue should be in line with the country's population and wealth.

Be that as it may, the internal opposition to the bill was bolstered by an external event, the collapse of the London banking house Overend, Gurney & Co., which was part of the syndicate of English bankers with which the Spanish government had been negotiating authorisation to form the new bank. Government plans had to be abandoned, the minister stepped down and, as will soon be seen, a severe financial crisis broke out in several Spanish cities, decimating the country's financial system and affecting a number of banks of issue too.

Many analysts identify this situation as the beginning of the end of the moderate political system that had been hegemonic since 1856. The conservatives' ineffective management of the crisis and the progressives' growing disaffection toward the existing constitutional order ended in open confrontation that ushered in the Glorious Revolution of September 1868. The liberal radicalism of the instigators of the Glorious Revolution was reflected in a particularly exemplary fashion in the area of banking legislation.

The new regime's first order on banking was the decree of 10 December 1868, signed by Laureano Figuerola, to abolish the government commissioners in banks of issue and the inspectors of credit companies. The explanatory memorandum for the order sets out a completely new conception of banking regulation. In the minister's view, the existence of the commissioners meant "reserving to the State the impossible task of overseeing the acts and functions of the Company, placing a heavy responsibility on the State and perhaps helping to facilitate all sorts of abuses, because of the security inspired in the shareholder by the erroneous belief that such oversight can be effective in preventing [such abuses]". The minister went on to mention the consequences of the crisis of 1866, noting that "the zeal [. . .] of the Commissioners and Inspectors has been of no use in preventing the ruin of these institutions, the expense imposed on the companies being utterly fruitless [. . .]". The decree retained only the commissioners assigned to the Bank of Spain (the governor and deputy governors) and the Bank of Barcelona, "owing to the relations that these two establishments have had and continue to have with the Public Treasury".

The subsequent law, whose wording was foreshadowed in the decree itself, took nearly a year to see the light. The bill was introduced in the Spanish parliament by the minister for development, Manuel Ruiz Zorrilla, on 22 March 1869. The bill's title was telling: "Law declaring the free creation of Territorial Banks, agricultural banks, issuing and discount banks, and credit companies and other associations whose purpose is any industrial or commercial enterprise". The explanatory memorandum that accompanied the bill was the most genuine expression of the liberal doctrine inspiring the leaders of the Glorious Revolution:

> After proclaiming individual rights through the September revolution, it is logical and natural to proclaim as an immediate consequence of them the

> great principle of freedom of work [. . .]. The principle of association [. . .] is one of the highest ends toward which the peoples and races are moving under the influence of powerful social forces which are with respect to the human being what planetary attraction is to astronomical bodies [. . .]. Yet such rights are the safeguard, the only safeguard that these forces of attraction will exert their beneficent influence in all their purity [. . .] To this end, it is necessary to tear down without compunction all the regulatory impediments that today exist; it is necessary to abolish all meddling intervention; it is necessary to return to the Spanish people its freedom to form companies [. . .]. All governmental intervention in mercantile and industrial companies is unjust; it is pointless [. . .]; it is pernicious as the economic science shows it to be [. . .]

After uncontentious deliberations, the law took effect on 19 October 1869 when it was signed by José Echegaray, then minister for development. In addition to the freedom proclaimed in the bill's title, the legislation regulated other aspects of banking and company activity more broadly. For example, it established that the shares of new companies could be registered or bearer shares. Without a doubt, this was a very interesting innovation, though it would not be applied effectively until the close of the century. As for banks, they were allowed to issue banknotes up to the amount or limit set in their statutes. Under the law, the acceptance of banknotes in commercial transactions would be voluntary. That is, banknotes of banks created under the new law would not be guaranteed to discharge liabilities, nor was the recipient of a payment required to accept them. For the sake of transparency, the law mandated that each banknote convey the relationship between the bank's effective capital and its banknotes in circulation.

In its final draft, the law did not modify the status of the banks of issue, because it guaranteed their monopoly of issue in the centres where they had been established and their ability to continue under the governance of their statutes "until such time as the special conditions of their authorisation cease". This acknowledgement, however, was not obtained without debate. The committee of the lower house of the Spanish parliament removed the article, taking the view that it was not "fair to prohibit the establishment of new banks where there already existed one or more with an exclusive privilege, because not having acquired said privilege for good and fair consideration, there was no reason whatsoever of justice, and even less of fairness, to deny the benefit of this bill to places that are precisely of greatest importance [. . .]". In the plenary discussion, however, the article was restored at the behest of Manuel Cantero, then Governor of the Bank of Spain, and other members of parliament. The step was also backed by the finance minister, Constantino de Ardanaz, whose argument is worth revisiting:

> There are several Banks in Spain in close relationship with the government, which have very important negotiations pending and provide services to the State, and which the Government finds itself acknowledging here. On the basis of this reasoning and so as not to disrupt at this critical time the relationships

> that exist between the banks and the Public Treasury, which I repeat are very close, I kindly request that the Committee act accordingly [. . .].

The law was of little significance because the economic and political crisis and the existing extent of competition left little room for new banking ventures. The monarchy that emerged from the revolution collapsed when Amadeo I abdicated in February 1873 and the newly proclaimed First Spanish Republic had to deal right from the start with an armed revolt by Carlist militias. The fragile republican regime held on for only 11 months. It was dissolved by force by General Pavía in January 1874. The subsequent power vacuum was filled by a provisional government led by General Serrano, who ruled under the republican constitution without parliamentary oversight, since the Spanish parliament remained dissolved.

The provisional government, which was completely overwhelmed by Carlist advances and by the impossibility of obtaining more funds through conventional routes, issued a decree on the monopoly of issue in Spain, putting an end to three decades of plurality. Not only did the decree of 19 March 1874 represent a milestone for Spain's finances and Treasury, but it also flagrantly violated the liberal spirit that had inspired the Glorious Revolution of 1868 in the first place. It remains rather ironic that the man who bore the greatest responsibility for the decision was none other than José Echegaray, the framer and energetic champion of the ultraliberal law of 1869. All the rhetoric that had once filled pages of the *Gaceta de Madrid* appeared to have gone up in smoke. It comes as no surprise, therefore, that Echegaray dedicated the opening paragraphs of his explanatory memorandum for the decree to justifying his change of heart:

> Credit brought low by abuse, taxes depleted by the bad habits of government, disentailment neutered by the moment, it is necessary to turn to other means to consolidate the floating debt and contend with the huge costs of the war that has afflicted the greater part of our provinces for two years [. . .]. Under such critical circumstances, yielding to the demands of the present reality and to the urgent needs of the fighting [. . .].

For the minister, the problem was clearly to obtain urgent resources, not to improve the financial system. And this was resoundingly confirmed by the 500 million pesetas that the Bank of Spain undertook to lend the government when it received a monopoly on issue. After his initial rationale, much of his presentation was aimed at convincing the country that the gigantic loan was not going to put the financial system or the Bank of Spain itself in jeopardy, though the historical argument that he used must have baffled experts in the history of Spanish banking: "[. . .] there should be no fear that the Treasury would ever compromise the existence of the new Bank, just as the existence of the Bank of Spain was never compromised".

The law itself was very straightforward. It had only 18 articles. It established unified fiduciary circulation by a national bank, replacing the circulation of banknotes issued by the provincial banks. The national bank was to be the Bank of Spain and it would be reorganised with 100 million pesetas in capital. It would have the authority to issue bearer banknotes up to five times its paid-in capital and it would be required to keep reserve holdings in gold and silver bullion worth at least a quarter of its banknotes in circulation. The law required the liquidation of existing provincial banks within 30 days. They could be annexed to the Bank of Spain and, if they did so, they would contribute their capital and reserve funds and receive shares at par "as compensation for the expiration of their respective privileges". At the same time, the banknotes of these banks had to be gathered in and would cease to be legal tender three months from date of the law. Lastly, the Bank of Spain was to establish branches in the most important centres to meet the needs of trade.

Effective application of the decree was not easy. Some of the affected banks put up resistance and it proved difficult to withdraw the banknotes in circulation at the necessary speed. One of the arguments wielded by the opponents of unification was that a decree could not change provisions that had the force of law, such as the ones that had authorised the banks of issue now facing elimination. Legal appeals and protests continued, while the rule's entry into force suffered delays. After various orders urging compliance, a new decree on 20 October established prescriptively that any banks that had not complied with the provisions of the decree of 19 March "were to verify their compliance without any excuse or pretext whatsoever within three days from the date of their notification by the Governor of each province". Any banks that had gone into liquidation would not be permitted to issue more banknotes and any banknotes that were in circulation would be lawful "until 30 days from the date on which the Bank of Spain puts its own into circulation in the respective centre".

Despite the seeming firmness of the rule, the banknotes of some banks remained in circulation for months and even years. In some cities, such as Reus, this was because the Bank of Spain did not open a branch until years later. In others, such as Bilbao, it was because the public trusted the old bank of issue even though it had ceased to issue.

In any event, the last hope of the proponents of plurality vanished on 17 July 1876 when the new king, Alfonso XII, signed a law that validated as laws the legislative decrees that had been issued by the finance ministry during the months of the provisional government. The experience of issue plurality had well and truly come to an end in Spain.

This chapter has traced the development of Spanish banking regulations over the entire period in which plurality of issue persisted. The first banks to emerge (the Bank of San Carlos and the Bank of San Fernando, which later became the Bank of Spain) did so in response to the needs of the state. However, they neither had the willingness nor received the authorisation to become banks covering the national territory. The Bank of San Carlos languished until the Bank of San Fernando was raised up from its ashes. The appearance of provincial banks clearly showed the dynamism of some territories from the mid-century onwards. The regulation of these institutions was subject to the bargaining power of regional elites and the government's funding requirements. These aspects account for the variability in business and banking rules over the period and they lay the groundwork for what the future Bank of Spain would do, embarking in 1874 on a process to turn itself into a true national bank.

Notes

1 Royal resolution of 25 January 1844 for the Bank of Isabel II and royal decree of 1 May 1844 for the Bank of Barcelona.
2 For additional information on the first, see Tedde, 1999; Zumalacárregui, 1952; for more on the closure of the second, see (Blasco-Martel and Sudrià, 2016).
3 Royal order of 22 November 1847.
4 The Palmer rule appeared in 1831 in response to a query put to J. H. Palmer, governor of the Bank of England, on what principle should guide the bank in the regulation of its issue of banknotes. In his view, the principle "is to invest and retain in securities, bearing interest, a given proportion of the deposits, and the value received for the notes in circulation, the remainder being held in coin and bullion; the proportions which seem to be desirable, under existing circumstances, may be stated at about two-thirds in securities and one-third in bullion" (Gregory, 1929, p. 3). A question for further clarification was then put to Palmer: "When you say that as a general principle you think it desirable to have one-third of bullion in your coffers, against your circulation, you mean to include in that circulation not only your papers out, but all deposits, whether of Government or individuals?" And his reply was a laconic "yes". As noted later, his opinion was based on his experience. The same reply was given by George Warde Norman, a director of the Bank of England.
5 The author again takes up his reflections on the matter on page 198 and subsequent pages, expressing admiration for the US system.
6 The assets of the Bank of Barcelona in December 1849 stood at slightly more than 10 million pesetas, while the figure for the Bank of Cádiz in December 1850 was slightly more than 3 million pesetas.
7 The paid-in capital of the Bank of Cádiz (16% of its nominal capital) was 2 million pesetas and its banknotes issued stood at roughly 2.5 million pesetas. The paid-in capital of the Bank of Barcelona totalled 1,875,000 pesetas (37.5% of its nominal capital) and its banknotes issued came to 5 million pesetas.
8 Law of 4 May 1849. Article 6.
9 The circulation of depreciated coins, the management of collections and payments and all related operations sharply increased the activity of the offices and the cost.
10 For a study of the parliamentary debate sparked by the law, see (Tortella, 1973) and Blasco-Martel and Sudrià, 2010a, 2010b.
11 A warehouse clerk, whose job was one of the least skilled in the Bank of Barcelona, earned 750 pesetas in 1845 and 1,095 pesetas in 1867 (Blasco-Martel and Sudrià 2010a, p. 76).
12 "(. . .) to defend itself, [the bank obtained] authorisation from the government to limit the exchange of banknotes to what it calculated was demanded by the needs and ordinary movement in the Madrid marketplace" *Gaceta de Madrid*, 5 April 1866. The provision was not validated by the law courts, but it proved useful to avoid a formal suspension of payments by the bank.
13 See the record of parliamentary sittings (*Diario de Sesiones de las Cortes*) for the month of April 1866, particularly 24 April. For the committee's opinion, see the record covering 9 May 1866.
14 *Gaceta de Madrid*, 5 April 1866.

Sources

Gaceta de Madrid 1840–1874
Colección legislativa de España
Archive of the Congreso de los Diputados
Diario de Sesiones de las Cortes

Bibliography

Acemoglu, D., Johnson, S., and Robinson, J., 2004. *Institutions as the fundamental cause of long-run growth*. National Bureau of Economic Research, Cambridge, MA.

Aguado y Sinobas, M., 1866. *El Banco Nacional y sus consecuencias*. Imprenta El Cascabel, Madrid.

Allen, A.M., Cope, S.R., Dark, L.R.H., and Witheridge, H.J., 1938. *Commercial banking legislation and control*. Macmillan, London.

Beck, T. and Demirgüç-Kunt, A., 2003. Law and finance: Why does legal origin matter? *Journal of Comptemporary Economics*, 31, 653–675.

Blasco-Martel, Y. and Sudrià, C., 2016. *El Banco de Barcelona 1894–1920. Decadencia y quiebra*. ed. Marcial Pons, Marcial Pons, Madrid.

———, 2010a. *El Banco de Barcelona (1844–1874), historia de un banco emisor*. LID Editorial, Madrid.

———, 2010b. Regulación bancaria y pluralidad de emisión. Una perspectiva desde el Banco de Barcelona. In: Morilla Critz, J. and Tortella Casares, G. (Eds.), *Homenaje a Gabriel Tortella: Las Claves Del Desarrollo Económico y Social, Historia Empresarial* LID / Universidad de Alcalá de Henares, Servicio de Publicaciones, Madrid, 427–444.

Brophy, J.M., 1992. The political calculus of capital: Banking and the business class in Prussia, 1848–1856. *Central European History*, 25, 149–176.

Cabana, F., 2002. *Manuel Girona, semblança i antologia de textos*. Editorial Pòrtic, Barcelona.

Calbetón, F., 1910. *Antecedentes legislativos nacionales y extranjeros y proyecto de ley sobre inspección de bancos y sociedades anónimas*. Ministerio de Fomento de España, Madrid.

Carrasco, P.A., 1867. *Tratado de las contribuciones directas de España*. Establecimiento tipográfico de T. Fortanet, Madrid.

Demirgüç-Kunt, A., Laeven, L., and Levine, R., 2004. Regulations, market structure, institutions, and the cost of financial intermediation. *Journal of Money, Credit and Banking*, 36(3), 593–622.

Easton, H.T., 1926. *Money, exchange and banking...*, 3rd ed. Sir I. Pitman & Sons, London.

Gregory, T.E., 1929. *Select statutes, documents, and reports relating to British banking, 1832–1928*. Oxford University Press, London.

Herr, R., 1978. El experimento de los vales reales (1780–1808). In Otazu, A. de (Ed.), *Dinero y Crédito* (Siglos XVI Al XIX). Moneda y Crédito, Madrid, 115–124.

Lamoreaux, N.R. and Rosenthal, J.L., 2005. Legal regime and business's organizational choice: A comparison of France and the United States during the era of industrialization. *American Law and Economics Review*, 7, 28–61.

La Porta, R., Lopez-de-Silanes, F., Shleifer, A., and Vishny, R.W.W., 1998. Law and finance. *Journal of Political Economy*, 106, 1113–1155.

Levine, R., 2005. Finance and growth: Theory and evidence. In Aghion, P. and Durlauf, S.N. (Ed.), *Handbook of economic growth*. Elsevier, Amsterdam, pp. 865–934.

Merryman, J.H. and Pérez-Perdomo, R., 2007. *The civil law tradition: An introduction to the legal systems of Europe and Latin America*, 3rd ed. Stanford University Press, Stanford, CA.

North, D.C., 1990. *Institutions, institutional change and economic performance*. Cambridge University Press, Cambridge.

———, 1981. *Structure and change in economic history*. Norton, New York, London.

Pastor, L.M., 1850. *Filosofia del credito: deducida de la historia de las naciones más importantes de Europa; con un apéndice en que se aplica la teoría al estado actual de España y al arreglo de su deuda*. Impr. de D.W. Ayguals de Izco, Madrid.

Pérez de Armiñán, G., 1977. *Legislación bancaria española*, 4a ed. Banco de España, Madrid.

Rajan, R. and Zingales, L., 2003. The emergence of strong property rights: Speculation from history. *National Bureau of Economic Research*. Working Papers 9478.

Sánchez-Albornoz, N., 1967. La crisis de 1866 en Madrid: la Caja de Depósitos, las sociedades de crédito y la Bolsa. *Moneda y crédito*, 100, 3–40.

Santillán, R., 1865. *Memoria histórica sobre los Bancos Nacionales de San Carlos, Español de San Fernando, Isabel II, Nuevo Banco de San Fernando y de España*. Banco de España, Madrid.

Tedde, P., 1999. *El Banco de San Fernando*. Alianza Editorial, Madrid.

———, 1988. *El Banco de San Carlos, 1782–1892*. Banco de España, Madrid.

Tortella, G., 1973. *Los Orígenes del capitalismo en España : banca, industria y ferrocarriles en el siglo XIX*, 1st ed,. Tecnos, Madrid.

Tortella, G., 1968. El principio de responsabilidad limitada y el desarrollo industrial de España: 1829–1869. *Moneda y Crédito*, 104, 69–84.

White, E.N., 1983. *The regulation and reform of the American banking system, 1900–1929*. Princeton University Press, Princeton, NJ.

Zumalacárregui, L., 1952. *El Banco de Isabel II y la crisis de la banca de emisión española de 1847*. Gráficas Reunidas, Madrid.

3 Bourgeoisie and provincial banks

Social origins of the new banking elite

Yolanda Blasco-Martel

The social transformations of the nineteenth century, which can be characterised in Spain by the passing of the ancien régime and the rise of the liberal order, did not have the same historical antecedents as they did in other European countries like Cromwell's England or revolutionary France. Both France and England witnessed acts of regicide and the bourgeoisie's ascent to political and economic power. In Spain, a handful of liberal "revolutions" did take place over the course of the nineteenth century (in 1812, 1820–1823, 1840–1843, 1854–1856 and 1868–1874), but the changes overlapped one another. The process could best be described as intermittent and cumulative. The effects worked their way gradually into the laws and were felt unevenly at the social and territorial levels. Nor was the process linear. The transformations came one after another and some of them sometimes proved contradictory and even conflicting in a process typified by duality.[1]

If the Constitution of 1812 marked the start of the liberal process in Spain, the key dates for the social transformations come between the death of Ferdinand VII (1833) and the advent of the Bourbon Restoration (1874). From a legal standpoint, the laws arising out of the so-called Liberal or Progressive Biennium (1854–1856), which included church disentailment, railways and banking and credit companies, were core elements in the process of constructing a capitalist sector in Spain (Tortella, 1973). From a social and political standpoint, the middle decades of the nineteenth century gave shape to liberal Spain and its structure of parties, and the parties' relations with both the Crown and the armed forces were to set their mark on subsequent Spanish history. In the historiography, the middle decades of the nineteenth century have been framed as crucial to understanding the process of modernisation in Spain.[2]

By the mid-nineteenth century, what would become the Spanish economic elite was under construction. From an economic standpoint, the great fortunes were still in their infancy. Industry, trade and service-related activities like finance stood at the forefront of the period's economic dynamism. At first, these activities were done by individuals with little training. Emigration had been one way to gain access to wealth that was then, in many cases, brought home. Not everybody, however, got rich by emigrating. Many individuals who stayed home took up commerce or joined in the more dynamic sectors of agriculture, or they invested their wealth to meet the needs of the state and, given the state's constant financial difficulties, did good business alike in wartime and in peace. The reputation of these bourgeois sectors was built in the middle decades of the nineteenth century and led to their rise as the dominant group in the second half of the century.

Attempts to understand the process led to quite an extensive historiography that was not always in accord. The efforts reached a peak basically in the 1970s and 1980s and the most heavily disputed issue revolved around the existence of a "bourgeois revolution" in Spain, its characteristics and its activities. In the past 20 years, the historiographical output has revisited the old concerns on the basis of new contributions,[3] which share a common set of traits: their predilection for leading political figures, the paucity of collaboration among specialists in the social sciences who deal with these matters, an increase in biographies, the enormous weight of the local and a preference for the period of the Bourbon Restoration (Moreno, 2008).

In Spain, the origins of the "financial bourgeoisie" or "banking elite" date from the middle decades of the nineteenth century. This is the period in which banks of issue and credit companies took shape and a diverse and still undefined social sector began to emerge around them, eventually crystallising in the decades to follow. What would define this sector in the future would be its world of relationships, which began to form locally and would transcend the national as the century wore on. Undoubtedly, the sector's form and makeup reflect stereotypes put forward by sociology. The concept of the bourgeoisie is bound up with the concept of class and refers to ownership of the means of production, whereas the concept of an elite can be viewed more broadly to encompass the dominant groups or sectors in a variety of areas. The latter concept is also more closely tied to the world of relationships and practices that typify a given social sector that has or attains power. While both concepts will be addressed below, it would be more appropriate to refer to a "banking elite" because some of its members held prominent positions in major financial institutions over the entire course of the nineteenth century and have sometimes even remained in place until the present day.

The social group labelled as "bourgeoisie" has a complex origin that stretches back to Spain's ancien régime. Historians of the Middle Ages have regarded the bourgeoisie as essentially mercantile, while historians of the nineteenth century have looked for their touchstones in industrial activity. The concept of the bourgeoisie evolved and went through a host of transformations. Where should the budding financial bourgeoisie of the mid-nineteenth century be situated? Are they part of the bourgeois elite or do they fall outside it? Was their profession viewed as prestigious? Did it give them social rank? Did they make money? It must be kept in mind that considerations of their activities as moneylenders and the inescapable reference to usury meant that their profession was not regarded as one belonging rightfully to the ruling elites, although this view too was shifting over time.

It is necessary to draw on the concept of an "elite", which Tuñón de Lara defined in 1967 as a "small group of men who exercise power or have direct or indirect influence on power" (Tuñón de Lara, 1967, p. 15). This concept is marked by the occupational prestige and even the remuneration of an activity. "Special personal prestige" is the rank of a person in a particular group. The person's place in the group is independent of his or her place in other groups to which the person may belong. "These forms of prestige are then combined into a 'total social prestige', which decides a person's elite position" (Beth, 1942, p. 746). An individual's social prestige is what makes him or her a member of an elite. "The individual groups select their elites independently. But only the elite members of certain groups which in themselves enjoy a high ranking within their particular category are accorded membership in the elite of this category" (Beth, 1942, pp. 748–749). This definition is interesting precisely because some activities were still building their reputation in the mid-nineteenth century in order to climb the occupational hierarchy and become a member of the "elite". "The elite is not a 'class'; it is not even a 'group'" (Beth, 1942, p. 755). Rather, its members typically live apart, each engaged in his or her own concerns.

A more recent analysis (Rahman Khan, 2012) incorporates the contributions of Pierre Bourdieu and regards elites not only in terms of the resources under their control, but also in terms of their ability to convert those resources into other forms of capital. Throughout history, the primary resources mobilised by elites have been political, economic, cultural, social (networks) and knowledge-based (knowledge capital). These resources are created and distributed through spaces of sociability constituted by families, clubs and schools. Using these resources, elites have gained power and widened the inequality gap. According to Khan, Europe has witnessed the shift from societal control based on the power of a small group to a social organisation based on the consensus of large groups.

The international historiography has taken a variety of perspectives in its studies of bankers and banking elites. Research into the leading financial centres, like London, has been particularly plentiful. One group of heavily cited studies revolves around the incorporation of the banking bourgeoisie into the aristocracy in the late nineteenth century (Cassis, 1985), (Chapman, 1896). These studies required thorough biographical investigation to identify the partners or directors of English banks in the nineteenth century. From the analysis, one finding was that 50% of the individuals had a university education, many at Oxbridge. The evidence also identifies that their children most commonly married members of the aristocracy or landed gentry, followed by the descendants of bankers and industrialists.

In the same vein, a study by Samuel Tilman (Tilman, 2006) paints an evolving picture of Belgian bankers from the vantage of their prior training. Tilman, however, draws a clear distinction in time: they were entrepreneurs before 1850 and engineers or lawyers after 1850. Alternatively, taking a less biographical perspective, some scholars have analysed the social group in terms of a conflict or challenge, such as the legal restrictions imposed on opening joint-stock companies in Prussia and the response that was elicited from the world of banking (Brophy, 1992). More recently, a number of studies on the biographies of financiers have focused on the need to understand the evolution of the world of finance through family dynasties (Perlinge and Sjögren, 2012).

Little progress has been made in Spain since the publication of a series of studies by Nicolás Sánchez-Albornoz in the late 1960s. Sánchez-Albornoz's pioneering research laid the groundwork for subsequent Spanish historiography on banks of issue and credit companies created in the wake of the 1856 legislation. At the time, he posed a question about the period: "How, outside Madrid and Barcelona, were 328 million *reales* amassed to invest in the creation of these establishments?" (Sánchez-Albornoz, 1968, p. 51). His work gave rise to the first list of bank founders, which appeared in his footnotes. Our questions today revolve around the members of the governing bodies of the banks of issue that sprang up between 1844 and 1864. What was the top occupation among their directors? What training and education did they have? Did they belong to a local political elite? Did they engage in national politics? Were they nouveau riche or had they grown wealthy under Spain's ancien régime?

Today, nearly 50 years later, a great deal of research remains to be done. The aim of this chapter is to offer an approach to Spain's provincial banking sectors based on the individuals who sat on the governing bodies of banks of issue in the period 1844–1874. To do so, the analysis focuses first on the creation of the banks of issue and their geographical organisation. A brief review then identifies the most recognised sectors at the forefront of the different provincial banks. Lastly, the analysis looks at the nascent banking elite as a whole.

3.1. The spread of banking in Spain

In the early decades of the nineteenth century, Spain was shaken by a succession of conflicts that began with Napoleon's invasion, the war against France (1808–1814) and the loss of its Latin American empire. Then, during the so-called Liberal Triennium of 1820–1823, there was a push to restore the liberal constitution of 1812, though the initiative was defeated and Spain was plunged into an even harsher version of absolutism known as the "ominous decade". After the death of Ferdinand VII in 1833, the succession to the throne once again resulted in instability and a string of wars (the Carlist wars). By the time Ferdinand's daughter Isabella II took up her reign in 1843, there were mounting expectations that a period of political peace could be conducive to the growth of the economy. The expectations for peace, however, received a sharp jolt. While political instability marked the entirety of the nineteenth century in Spain, it was especially severe in the period from 1844 to 1874, which saw a steady stream of ministerial changes and occasional military coups.

While this political state of affairs was not the best scenario for the economy, Spain witnessed the development of a host of ventures of all sorts during the period. In some regions, industry took off and began to push at its limits. The creation of companies exploded in the industrial and service sectors. Industrial companies, insurers, banks, mining companies and still others infused a new dynamic into the Spanish economy.[4] The development, however, did not occur evenly across the entire peninsula. Spain experienced an influx of foreign capital (especially from France and Britain) that was particularly noticeable in the development of the railways and the creation of credit companies after the 1856 legislation. This is the context in which the first banks of issue began to spring up across Spain.

As indicated earlier, the first two banks outside Madrid appeared in Barcelona and Cádiz. The next ones, authorised in 1856, appeared in Málaga, Valladolid, Santander, Bilbao, Seville, A Coruña and Zaragoza. In Valencia and Alicante, branches of the Bank of Spain opened their doors. Then, between 1860 and 1863, banks opened in Jerez, San Sebastián, Burgos and Reus. While San Sebastián and Burgos were provincial capitals, Jerez and Reus were merely two important, heavily populated cities. Jerez focused on the production and export of wine and Reus combined industry with a strong agricultural impetus, but neither was a provincial capital. Last came the banks that began operations from 1864 onwards (Pamplona, Oviedo, Tarragona, Palencia, Vitoria, Balear and Santiago), which faced an additional challenge in that the economic downturn that would herald the crisis of 1866 had already begun at the time. Only one of the latecomers, the Bank of Tarragona, managed to secure a firm foothold and was able to reject merging with the Bank of Spain in 1874, whereas the rest were wound up at that time.

Table 3.1 below effectively shows the entities created as banks of issue, though the number of banks seeking authorisation was higher. Some banks were denied authorisation to issue, including Almeria in 1865, Murcia, Vigo and Logroño, to name but a few. So what guidelines did the 1856 legislation establish for the granting of authorisation to set up banks of issue in the provinces? We know that the regulator placed importance on the interest of locals in each province. Effectively, this spurred the creation of banks in places where there were unified initiatives backed by the populace as a whole. Also, certain precautions were taken so as "not to entrust the credit of specific and particular places to general associations that by the size of their businesses and their frequent need to embrace speculation greater than their effective capital may lead to a calamity [. . .], bring down others with them and put at risk the very life of interests that bear no similarity to their own and can survive independently". Such precautions were especially intended to prevent banks of issue led by sectors linked to the Péreire brothers in Paris. Fundamentally, priority went to local needs, even though the approach could not avoid some distortions and some Castilian provincial banks did reluctantly accept Basque capital.

As noted in the previous chapter, the Bank of San Fernando was renamed the Bank of Spain in the legislation of 1856. However, it was not a central bank in the mid-nineteenth century, nor even the national bank that began taking shape in 1874 (Martín-Aceña et al., 2013). It was simply a bank of issue with a special relationship to Spain's Treasury. Its links with the government made it distinct from the other banks of issue. The decision on where new banks of issue or Bank of Spain branches had to be opened was taken by the then Bank of San Fernando. And this is important because it drew the first map of Spanish banking, which depended not on local interests but on the Bank of Spain's assessment of its own business prospects. On 23 May 1855, the governor of the Bank of San Fernando committed to the Spanish finance minister to conduct the pertinent consultations on whether there would be interest in the bank's opening of branches in the provinces, at the behest of the lower house of the Spanish parliament. On 25 May, the governor informed the government that his board

Table 3.1 Provincial banks of issue. Paid-in capital and total assets, 1865

Banks of Issue	*Year founded*	*Paid-in capital, end 1865 ('000 pesetas)*	*Total assets, end 1865 ('000 pesetas)*
Bank of Barcelona	1844	5,000	29,752
Bank of Cádiz	1846	5,000	19,392
Bank of Spain	1856	50,000	181,866
Bank of Málaga	1856	2,500	11,122
Bank of Valladolid	1857	1,500	(in liquidation)
Bank of Santander	1857	1,750	6,264
Bank of Bilbao	1857	2,500	11,386
Bank of Seville	1857	4,000	8,214
Bank of A Coruña	1857	1,000	2,537
Bank of Zaragoza	1857	1,500	**
Valencia, branch of the Bank of Spain	1858	*	
Alicante, branch of the Bank of Spain	1858	*	
Bank of Jerez de la Frontera	1860	1,500	2,887
Bank of San Sebastián	1862	1,000	3,653
Bank of Burgos	1863	1,000	1,477
Bank of Reus	1863	625	1,476
Bank of Pamplona	1864	1,125	2,100
Bank of Oviedo	1864	1,000	2,065
Bank of Tarragona	1864	1,250	1,523
Bank of Palencia	1864	1,000	1,058
Bank of Vitoria	1864	1,000	1,364
Bank Balear (Palma, Majorca)	1864	1,000	3,412
Bank of Santiago	1864	750	1,317

Source: Balance sheet annexes on the banks of issue (Sudrià and Blasco-Martel, 2016) and the banks' statutes and by-laws

(*) For information on the branches, see the study by Joaquim Cuevas on the branches of the Bank of Spain in Alicante and Valencia. (**) The behaviour of the Zaragoza bank is unusual because it was split into two entities. See the study by Luis Germán. (Both studies are cited in Sudrià and Blasco-Martel, 2016.)

of governors had met in extraordinary session and taken the decision to open branches in Seville, Málaga, Alicante, Valencia, A Coruña, Santander, Bilbao, Valladolid and Zaragoza.

The Madrid bank's discretionary power had already spawned earlier instances of resentment. Back when a group of Santander residents had raised the need to revoke article 9 of the law of 1851 in order to open a bank in their city, their statement was clear: "The time of odious and harmful privileges is over and that is why the petitioners do not think it necessary to go into the reasons why the Bank of San Fernando has given no thought until today to establishing a Branch in Santander, nor into an examination of whether or not it has its own elements at present to do so [. . .]."[5] In 1856, the bank took the decision to choose centres based on whether there were locals who had an intention to open their own bank and it accepted that, if there were not, it would be the bank's responsibility to put in the capital to open branches. In this way, the guideline sought to favour local impetus in the development of banking activity. And if there was none, if no interest existed in opening banks of issue, the Madrid bank would only open branches where it might prove beneficial to its own interests.

What criteria were employed to identify the provinces of potential interest to the Bank of San Fernando? Clearly for a private entity like the Bank of San Fernando and then Bank of Spain, there would be no interest in responding solely to the actual development needs of the country. Rather, the bank made its selection in terms of the locations where business was most prosperous. One way to test the strength of this hypothesis is to look at the tax contributions from trade and industry in the respective provinces. The banking services that banks of issue intended to provide would require business that used discountable instruments (bills of exchange, promissory notes). Undoubtedly, their targets were commercial and industrial sectors. As Table 3.2 below shows, this pointed them toward centres where the figures for commercial and industrial contributions were high. Indeed, the contribution figure topped a million reales in every selected centre (with the exception of Santander). Other provinces also exceeded a million reales

Table 3.2 Tax contributions of trade and industry, 1855

Provincial capital	*Inhabitants registered in tax rolls*	*Tax-payers*	*Average taxes per registered inhabitant (reales v.)*	*Average taxes per taxpayer (reales v.)*	*Total value of taxes paid in 1855 (reales v.)*	*Created under 1856 law*
Madrid	85,621	21,723	92.17	364.20	6,806,256.50	
Barcelona	101,508	29,339	78.18	271.24	6,774,277.17	
Seville	95,767	18,579	41.13	213.15	3,165,212.18	✓
Cádiz	61,186	12,920	66.24	315.32	3,143,638.31	
Valencia	116,202	18,331	25.00	159.50	2,393,372.29	✓
Málaga	94,888	15,301	28.21	177.19	2,218,618.25	✓
Zaragoza	65,232	13,344	56.80	177.10	1,719,462.19	✓
Tarragona	47,250	10,433	35.70	159.18	1,248,167.01	
A Coruña	89,646	10,439	16.13	140.30	1,132,803.28	✓
Valladolid	39,491	11,702	34.30	115.30	1,102,613.25	✓
Alicante	66,561	11,628	21.26	124.25	1,094,431.00	✓
Santander	30,177	5,571	37.18	203.17	829,344.14	✓
Burgos	46,826	9,959	20.26	97.27	772,601.00	
Baleares	46,696	6,529	20.19	147.60	669,866.01	
Palencia	30,641	7,187	20.12	86.31	531,014.14	
Oviedo	96,743	6,145	5.31	93.33	453,368.12	

Bilbao, Pamplona, Vitoria and San Sebastián, where banks were also opened, do not appear (because they fell under the special chartered system in the Basque Country and Navarre known as the Foral Regime), while Reus and Jerez were not provincial capitals.

Source: (Trúpita Giménez, 1855, pp. 222–226, 234–235).

in 1855, namely Toledo, Girona and Córdoba. In these provinces, however, there are no reports of movements to open a bank of issue, though the Bank of Spain did open temporary branches in Toledo and Girona in 1884 and in Córdoba in 1879.

As Table 3.2 also shows the Bank of San Fernando first opened branches in places where the industrial and commercial contributions were higher. One exception is Tarragona, which had a high average contribution and was not chosen. This appears to relate to the Bank of Barcelona's preeminent claim to open a branch in the province. Indeed, the Barcelona bank had opened a branch temporarily in Tarragona as it did in Reus and Palma (Majorca). The other exception is Santander. While Santander did not figure among the provinces exceeding a million reales and the value of contributions was not very high either, the average amount per taxpayer ranked among the highest. As for the last banks to open, excluding the Bank of Tarragona, they reflected other conditions. Most probably, two arguments came into play when the Bank of San Fernando determined the provinces of interest for the establishment of banks of issue: centres where there was a known interest and willingness to open a local bank (Santander) and centres that would be of special interest to the Madrid bank if a local initiative could not move forward. However, provincial banks of issue opened in all of the locations selected by the Bank of Spain, except Alicante and Valencia, where the Madrid bank did open branches.

The table only shows provinces where banks of issue were opened. (*Reales de vellón* are a unit of money: 4 *reales de vellón* = 1 peseta.)The uneven development in the territory had been evident in the past and would continue to be so throughout the nineteenth century. Undoubtedly, Madrid benefited from being the country's capital. In 1797, there were 351 declared merchants in the urban population of Madrid (167,607 inhabitants according to Tedde de Lorca, 1983, 303). At the same time, Madrid was unique in being the province where the most credit companies were created after the legislation of 1856 (up to a total of 11). These ventures are not explained by strong local trade dynamics, but rather by being the home of the public administration and by the influx of foreign capital that played such an enormous part in the creation of many credit companies (Sánchez-Albornoz, 1966), (Tortella, 1973). As a whole, all the credit companies and banks of issue added up to nearly 400 million pesetas in effective capital (Sánchez-Albornoz, 1968, p. 50). Of the total, 63.6% was in the province of Madrid, 14.1% in Barcelona, 6% in Valladolid and 4% in Andalusia. In terms of the capital put into circulation solely by the credit companies, Madrid accounted for nearly three-quarters of the Spanish total (Sánchez-Albornoz, 1967, p. 36). Given the centrality of Madrid, it is necessary to take an overall view to grasp the development of provincial banking in Spain.

3.2. The geographical distribution of the banks of issue

The territorial organisation of Spain is the product of centuries. In 1833, only days after the death of Ferdinand VII, Javier de Burgos, minister for development, divided the country into 49 provinces after several previous attempts had been made to achieve a harmonious balance among the territories. From a historical standpoint, the kingdom of Spain is defined as a "composite state", that is, a state containing other territories within its borders that could regard themselves as units with their own identity.[6] These are the territorial units where the banks of issue would be created from the 1840s onwards. Sánchez-Albornoz (1968) groups the provincial banks of issue into five overarching areas:

a The Mediterranean coast, where six institutions were created: the banks in Barcelona, Tarragona, Reus, Palma (Majorca) and the Bank of Spain's branches in Valencia and Alicante.
b Andalusia, with four banks of issue in the cities of Cádiz, Málaga, Jerez and Seville.
c The northern coast, with a total of six entities, including two Galician banks in A Coruña and Santiago, an Asturian bank in Oviedo, a Cantabrian bank in Santander and two Basque banks in Bilbao and San Sebastián.
d The northern interior, with six banks, three in Castile: Valladolid, Palencia and Burgos; one in Araba/Álava: the Bank of Vitoria; another bank in Navarre: the Bank of Pamplona; and the last one in Aragón: the Bank of Zaragoza.
e Madrid, with one bank of issue, the Bank of Spain, which was in an intermediate stage between the national bank that it aspired to become and the provincial bank of issue that it did not succeed in being.

The territorial distribution mapped out by Sánchez-Albornoz relates to the geographical features (coastal areas and hinterlands) and historical particularities of the territories linked to the ancient kingdoms of the Iberian Peninsula. Javier de Burgos's division of the provinces was a response to the need to organise the territory on the basis of the political and administrative necessities of the centralised nation-state then under construction.

In terms of the relative capital of the banks by geographical area, Figure 3.1 above shows that the Bank of Spain, in its role as the government's banker, ranked

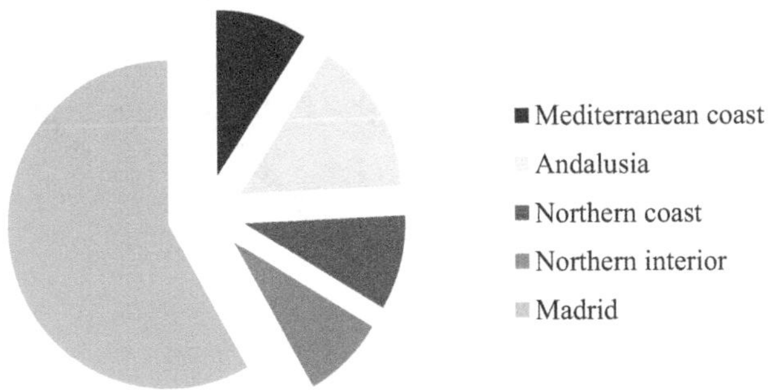

Figure 3.1 Bank capital by geographical area (1865)

Source: Table 3.1. The Mediterranean coast does not include the Bank of Spain's branches in Valencia and Alicante

higher than the provincial banks of issue. It did not rank higher, however, in terms of its effectiveness in generating business with its available capital. Figure 3.2 below shows the relationship between the banks' paid-in capital and their assets in 1865 by geographical area. It is important to note that the branches in Valencia and Alicante have been included in the Bank of Spain's figures, but would otherwise doubtless give an even greater impression of the effectiveness of the banks in coastal areas (including the Andalusian banks, whose leading institutions were located in coastal provinces). What appears clear is that all the banks, with the exception of those in the northern interior, succeeded in increasing their capital dramatically in barely a decade.

The banks on the *Mediterranean coast* arose to meet local commercial needs, but their shareholders were not homogeneous. The Bank of Barcelona brought together the capital of *Indianos* (people returning home with wealth earned in Spain's New World colonies), Catalans and people from elsewhere on the Iberian Peninsula. Because it was the first provincial banking institution and the Catalan economy was marked by dynamism in the mid-nineteenth century, the bank pulled together capital from a variety of origins. Most of its directors were merchants, but its statutes explicitly underscored the importance of industrialists to the bank, stipulating that they must be represented on the board of governors by a minimum of two members. In Barcelona, the response to the bank could not have been better. However, sectors emerged that felt excluded and, after the crisis of 1848,

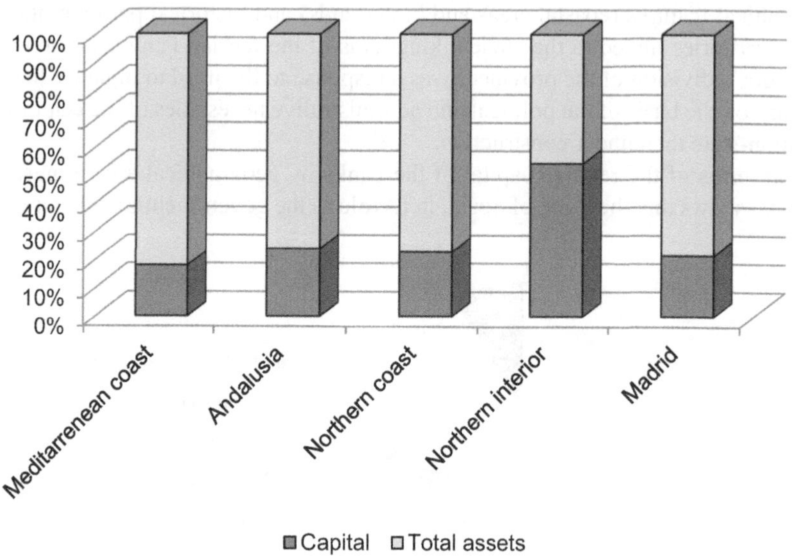

Figure 3.2 Relationship between paid-in capital and total assets by geographical area (1865)

Source: Table 3.1. The Mediterranean coast does not include the Bank of Spain's branches in Valencia and Alicante

they tried to open a new bank. The attempt failed because the central administration stepped in and stopped it. From 1856, however, the Bank of Barcelona had to face competition from credit companies that sprang up. Though the schemes of the credit companies put the strength of the Bank of Barcelona's banknotes to the test, the bank withstood the onslaught and it again became the city's flagship institution in the aftermath of the crisis of 1866. With the law of 1874, however, the bank lost its privilege to issue banknotes and it became a commercial bank that had to compete against a branch of the Bank of Spain. Ultimately, it was a battle that the Catalan bank lost.

Reus and Tarragona represent the experience of two cities caught up in a long-running competition in the nineteenth century. Banking activity in Reus appears to reflect greater dynamism, at least in the 1860s. Both banks carried on after they lost the privilege to issue banknotes in 1874, suggesting that each had gained a firm foothold in business of its home city. In Valencia, the group that formed the Bank of Spain branch was led by José Campo, who was a former mayor of the city. The group was a heterogeneous mix of merchants and of landowners who were basically agricultural in origin. Politically, they belonged to the moderate group and their businesses were engaged fundamentally in public works. At the same time, there was also a group of progressive merchants and businessmen who felt excluded and put their energies into another company, Crédito Mobiliario. In the case of Alicante, there was some unity among the local elite, which was made up of merchants and the most dynamic sector of landowners (Cuevas, 2016). In the Balearic Islands, the Bank Balear was the brainchild of a liberal group of merchants who had seen how the Bank of Barcelona had done good business on Majorca after opening a branch and they decided to take the reins.

The banks on the *northern coast* included the Galician, Asturian, Cantabrian and some of the Basque banks. The Bank of Santander grew out of the city's long tradition of merchants, merchant bankers and moneylenders. It also included manufacturing sectors (flour mills) and shipowners. The Bank of Bilbao was an accurate reflection of the city's tradition as a port and its long-standing business associations. The Bank of A Coruña arose out of joint efforts between merchants and a group of investors interested in the railway. Its representatives were closely linked to overseas trade. The Bank of Oviedo's shareholders were merchants and bankers operating in the city and the creation of the bank was promoted by the Bank of Bilbao. Some of the banks on the northern coast also held interests in the banks that would be set up in the interior. One of the most striking aspects of the group is that the Bank of Santander and the Bank of Bilbao (today's BBVA) are the only present-day survivors of the banks that began to spring up in the mid-nineteenth century across Spain.

The banks in the *northern interior* were also linked to, and sponsored by, the commercial world, but they had higher shareholdings among landowners and rentiers, who had greater levels of representation on their governing bodies. The Bank of Zaragoza grouped local merchants and property owners. The Bank of Vitoria had 32 shareholding partners and more than half identified themselves as property owners. The Bank of Valladolid is one of the best-known examples thanks to the study by Pérez García (1991). The bank's founders, who had links to the flour industry and the animal hides and textile industry, were essentially property owners and merchants, though lawyers and politicians also held shares. Many of the shareholders diversified their investments between the bank and three credit companies in a process of excessive speculation that ultimately led to the liquidation of the province's early banking experiences.

In *Andalusia*, the first entity was the Bank of Cádiz, thanks to Isabella II. Because of heavy shipping traffic with the Americas and the British Isles, local merchants were accumulating more and more paper payable in London. The various Andalusian banking ventures that emerged in the period were closely linked to commercial interests. However, the case of Jerez, located 40 km from Cádiz, is slightly different, because the founders were capitalist property owners whose core business was basically in the wine sector, including both winegrowing and winemaking. A number of the most important wine exporters in the province were among its founders. The Bank of Málaga was founded very early, having been created immediately after the legislation of 1856, and the makeup of its shareholders reflects the city's leading merchant sectors (the names of Larios, Loring, Heredia and Crooke held almost 50% of the bank's capital at the time of its founding). The Bank of Seville, like the Bank of Valladolid, is one of the most notorious banking collapses of the era. At its founding, it brought together capitalists and investors associated with trade, banking and agriculture, but the leaders of the venture were merchants and bankers who raised high expectations of easy profits among the city's investing sectors.

This entire mosaic draws on a geographical typology that should be reviewed in light of new research. It is likely necessary to add the specific time when the banks were opened and the individuals who spearheaded the process. Attention should also be paid to an analysis of the failed attempts, that is, the provinces where efforts were made to open a bank of issue in the period and either they were not granted authorisation or they did not succeed in bringing the process to fruition. To this end, there remains a need for local studies that give close attention to the development of these institutions.

3.3. The regional banking elite and banks of issue

As noted at the beginning of the chapter, it is difficult to speak of a nationwide banking elite in Spain in the mid-nineteenth century. The most prominent and complex example is Madrid, where the banking elite was made up of a set of individuals linked to the then Bank of San Fernando (from 1856, the Bank of Spain). Many of the individuals had close ties to provincial bankers. Foremost among the financiers who had carved out a place in Madrid, whether natives of the city or not, were Nazario Carriquiri, Jaime Ceriola, the house of Cerrajería and Gallo, the house of Bellón & Co. and the Marquis of Remisa.[7] The best-known financiers from the provinces who forged influential contacts at the Spanish court were Campos from Valencia, Bruil from Aragón and Jaume Girona from Catalonia. These men had established a network in the provinces and acted as a bridgehead to the capital. In this way, the provinces began to see the emergence of a local banking elite that would rise to prominence at the end of the nineteenth century and become well established in the twentieth century.

The banks of issue appeared out of the confluence of two elements: a need for means of payment to develop economic activity in the provinces more efficiently and/or the forging of relationships with influential sectors at the Spanish court. The relative importance of the elements varied by case, but both were fundamentally necessary for the creation of the first banks. Unquestionably, good relations at Court enabled the Marquis of Salamanca to open the Bank of Isabel II with greater speed (barely a few months) than was managed by the negotiators for the Bank of Barcelona, whose efforts to gain authorisation were delayed for over a year. In addition, whereas the relationships of the Bank of Spain's commissioner in A Coruña certainly helped in the opening of the local bank, the Bank of Valladolid was benefited by its proponents' links to the economic milieu in the province.[8]

In terms of regional economic specialisation, those entering the world of finance included sectors in Jerez and Tarragona who had become affluent from wine exports, though the two sectors were entirely different. The former had a key market in England that persisted throughout the century (Montañés, 2000), while the latter had a major market in the Americas that was in decline (Valls-Junyent, 2004). Some of these bourgeois sectors gravitated toward the financial sphere according to their experience and needs. When the residents of Jerez needed to negotiate bills of exchange, they developed banking activities in their trading houses. The same thing happened among Barcelona shipowners engaged in trade with the Americas and among sectors of Galician merchants engaged in trade within the Iberian Peninsula. As a result, many came together in a shared interest for banking that grew out of their business needs. Others, who had capital and were familiar with the debt market, entered banking in order to take better advantage of their networks and expertise. Some were clearly influential in national politics, while others took part in local politics. Many stood out because of their business ventures. Some were part of the political and economic elite of the country. A large number made up the financial bourgeoisie that was rising to greater prominence in Spanish economic and political life as the century wore on. Some were ennobled during the Bourbon Restoration, while others were not. The vast majority did not have university studies and their political views were disparate and changeable, with moderate liberals appearing at first, but then showing a tendency to shift toward greater conservatism over time.

Many provincial banks brought together groups of interests that had a long-standing tradition of collaborating in their businesses. The groups had some degree of stability because they had made joint investments in the past. Understandably, however, their unity was not perfect and the creation of new banking entities in the form of credit companies did, on many occasions, lead to competition with a local bank of issue. For instance, 11 credit companies sprang up in Madrid; 7 in Barcelona; 2 in Cádiz; 4 in Valencia; 3 in Valladolid; 2 each in Bilbao and Valencia; and 1 each in Seville, Zaragoza, Jerez and Pamplona. The shareholders in the new credit companies came from a variety of economic and financial sectors that were not always the same ones represented in the banks of issue.[9] At times, the banks and credit companies collaborated; at other times, they were in close competition. The capital that went into the credit companies came basically from agriculture and commerce. In some locations, capital from the *Indianos*, locals who had made good in the Americas and returned home with their wealth, was very important (Blasco-Martel and Rodrigo-Alharilla, 2015). In other places, particularly in the banks in the northern interior, agricultural capital was of enormous significance. For example, Burgos, Zaragoza, Vitoria and Palencia all stand out in terms of their directors who declared themselves to be landowners.

As notables, elites or influential sectors, the Spanish bourgeoisie (or bourgeoisies) has most often been treated from a political viewpoint. As mentioned earlier, moderate politicians embodied the hegemony of the landed gentry on the great estates, who were joined by the financial bourgeoisie, with the result that the merchants and industrialists of the north and the periphery found themselves subordinated to agricultural and financial interests (Beltrán, 2010, pp. 125–126). In general, what can be observed in the bourgeoisie that develops in the world of finance is its pragmatism. Power groups formed to apply pressure on political power. Some of these power groups took part in the parliamentary groups of their provinces or regions from which they carried out lobbying activities. As time passed, they also formed their own associations, though this would not occur until the late nineteenth and early twentieth centuries. In the mid-nineteenth century, men dedicated to finance could be found in city halls, provincial councils and boards of trade, presiding over local institutions of recognised standing, but they were fundamentally occupied with their businesses.

In any event, the characteristics of the Spanish bourgeoisie are distinctive. A country that had, for centuries, disparaged work and affected nobility would require a profound transformation both in structure and in mindset. If, drawing on the words of Aranguren, the bourgeois spirit can be defined as a "mindset peculiar to a work ethic, an industriousness, a pursuit of happiness in this world, an interest in the results of action" (Beltrán, 2010, p. 93), then where can the traces of this mindset be found in Spain? While there are certainly a host of regional differences, there appears to be a common denominator across all of them: the ease of capturing rents through a state in permanent financial crisis.

If all of the sectors that make up the financial bourgeoisie in the mid-nineteenth century have anything in common, it is their original activity in trade. In general, most of the banks on the Iberian Peninsula were founded by individuals who came from commerce. Some had made their fortune as suppliers to the government; others had brought their wealth back from the Americas (the previously mentioned *Indianos*, who were highly represented in some regions); still others had specialised in coastal domestic trade or trade overseas, and some had increased their riches thanks to the disentailment of church properties and their political contacts. The impact was not the same in every region. In particular, two cities had a denser bourgeois climate: Barcelona and Cádiz (Beltrán, 2010, p. 23). Madrid was unique in being home to the state bureaucracy. The south had close ties to trade as illustrated by the bourgeoisies in Málaga and Cádiz. In the north, the ancient trade in iron and wool underpinned a powerful mercantile sector.[10] In the middle of Spain, the case of Valladolid stands out, with its accumulation based on cereal crops. The eastern peninsula was also linked to trade, though Catalan industrial development was most prominent. The aristocracy took little part in Spain's banking ventures. Nor were the bankers, in the period covered by this study, particularly interested in burnishing their names with noble titles, which, where it did transpire, occurred later on. However, the role of lawyers was rising in importance. In nearly every bank, some men trained in the law were given a seat on the board of governors.

In the mid-nineteenth century, the educational sphere in Spain was not one of the places where the elite might meet and form connections. Spanish universities were vastly different from their English counterparts and they had little influence in the provinces, with Madrid acting as "the only factory of advanced degrees" (Carr, 1992, p. 235). Some schools specialising in commerce and other technical fields did have a certain degree of importance. Along these lines, there were notable groups of economists who, like Gabriel Rodriguez and José Echegaray, might form connections through their studies (in their case, the Madrid school of civil engineering known as the Escuela de Ingenieros de Caminos), but they were more typically politicians than entrepreneurs or businessmen. That said, it is possible to speak of a marriage policy (McDonogh, 1989) and there were shared spaces of sociability, including social clubs, cultural centres (lyceums and athenaeums), leisure associations, economic circles, professional societies, chambers of commerce and more (Calvo, 2000). Nor was this any different for the financial sector.

If one thing is clear, it is that the financial bourgeoisie joined the world of the elites converging on Madrid. Every bank needed contacts in the capital to conduct its business. Whether the banks sent their own men or they retained lawyers or representatives, the affairs of provincial banking were ultimately decided in Madrid. This convergence put a premium on the networks of influence established in the capital, showing the strength of the "weak bonds" that enabled the banks to make connections at the Spanish court, thanks to the high number of links that directors and shareholders could forge (Granovetter, 1973). In this respect, the relationships that grew out of the political connections of some members of the provincial banks' governing bodies are not to be underestimated.

As noted earlier, Sánchez-Albornoz (1968) was the first to build an overall image of the financial bourgeoisie or banking elite that developed in the mid-nineteenth century. Drawing on newly available information, the present study aims to fill in more of a picture that is still incomplete. Most of the members of the provincial banks' boards of governors in the mid-nineteenth century identified themselves as merchants. They were the ones to provide the impetus behind the banks basically because they needed means of payment for their businesses. Little is known about their individual reputations. The profession of banker is not held in esteem today, nor was it then. The link typically drawn between banking and usury omits the key role played by banking in economic development. Nor was the case different in the mid-nineteenth century. It should not be forgotten that, in the early twentieth century, a law was passed on 23 July 1908 to lay out a series of measures against usury that have remained in effect practically to the present day.

This study examines a group of 460 board members and founders of provincial banks of issue in the period 1844–1874. Some type of information (business and political activity) has been obtained for 335 of them.[11] While the information has limitations and more research of a local nature remains to be done, it can be stated categorically that the people who took the initiative to create provincial banking were merchants. In every case for which data exist, merchants represent the most important sector of provincial bank board members and founders. The data lead to a set of conclusions that are hard to confirm, given that we do not have information for every identified individual. Specifically, in relation to industrialists, the Bank of A Coruña stands out, followed to a lesser extent by the Reus and Valladolid banks. In relation to landowners, the banks in Palencia, Zaragoza and Vitoria show a relatively high percentage doing the type of activities involved in directing banks of issue. While the data remain preliminary and hard to generalise because of the lack of information on the activity of roughly 45% of all board members identified, they clearly highlight the role of merchants, who emerge as the leading players in the founding and development of Spain's provincial banks of issue.

Table 3.3 Business and political activity of bank directors (%)[12]

Bank	*No. of board members identified*	*% merchants*	*% industrialists*	*% landowners*	*% deputies/ senators*
Bank of Santander	31	93.5%	6.5%	3.2%	25.8%
Bank of Bilbao	36	44.4%	19.4%	*	16.7%
Bank of Pamplona	24	66.7%	8.3%	*	12.5%
Bank of San Sebastián	13	76.9%	*	7.7%	*
Bank of Vitoria	24	62.5%	*	20.8%	4.2%
Bank of Barcelona	43	48.8%	9.3%	*	25.6%
Bank of Zaragoza	43	30.2%	9.3%	11.6%	18.6%
Bank of Tarragona	8	*	*	*	*
Bank Balear	12	*	*	*	*
Bank of Reus	10	*	30.0%	*	10.0%
Bank of A Coruña	25	36.0%	44.0%	12.0%	20.0%
Bank of Burgos	20	15.0%	*	20.0%	35.0%
Bank of Palencia	18	27.8%	*	33.3%	22.2%
Bank of Santiago	28	50.0%	14.3%	10.7%	3.6%
Bank of Cádiz	11	*	*	*	36.4%
Bank of Seville	27	*	*	*	33.3%
Bank of Jerez de la Frontera	19	31.6%	*	*	10.5%
Bank of Málaga	8	*	*	*	50.0%
Bank of Valladolid	51	37.3%	25.5%	3.9%	9.8%
Bank of Oviedo	9	*	*	*	*
TOTAL	**460**	**38.3%**	**10.9%**	**6.5%**	**17.2%**

Source: Sudrià and Blasco-Martel 2016; Sánchez-Albornoz 1968. (* = no data available.)

The involvement of members of the provincial banks' boards of governors in national politics, while relatively limited at first, is especially significant. For example, some royal commissioners (at the banks in Barcelona, Bilbao, Cádiz and Seville) were members of the lower house of the Spanish parliament. Indeed, based on the available data, 17% of the directors in provincial banks for which data exist were sitting members in either the upper or lower house in Madrid. Most entered national politics from the middle of the 1860s onwards. As yet, there is little information on their involvement in local politics, though the evidence points to the existence of civil governors, provincial government heads and mayors among their number. It should be noted, however, that the existence of civil servants is of little importance to the provincial banks. The emergence of a group of civil servants with the creation of the liberal state (Pro, 2016) does not appear to have made itself felt through their participation in financial ventures in the provinces, though it is easier to find them on the Bank of Spain's board of governors in the period.

To conclude this recap of the development of a provincial banking elite, it is worth reflecting on the formation of the nation-state in Spain. As Juan Pro indicates, an idea emerged among moderates in the mid-nineteenth century to develop "a model of a large State identified with the material expansion of a centralised public Administration and with everything entailed in the hegemony of a Government that acted through administrative means" (Juan Pro, 2016, p. 21). This "large state" professionalised public life and brought technical experts into the public administration. In the case of the banks of issue, the idea found expression in the royal commissioners. Their role has not been studied sufficiently and it may shed light both on the penetration of the "large state" in the provinces and on its influence over provincial elites. What the chapter does confirm, however, is the role played by the world of commerce in the creation of provincial banking institutions in the mid-nineteenth century. It also addresses the way in which provincial banking elites maintained ties with the Madrid-based elite. And it leaves unanswered a host of questions for subsequent research, one of which concerns the similarities or differences, as well as the connections, between the Madrid elite linked to the Bank of Spain and the elites surrounding the provincial banks. This analysis is by no means trivial, given that, when a national bank is formed in 1874, the provincial elites are scarcely represented. This aspect would also help in understanding the subsequent development of the Spanish banking system.

Notes

1 Sánchez-Albornoz's conceptualisation of "duality" in relation to the Spanish economy in the nineteenth century can be found in (Sánchez-Albornoz, 1977), while the overlapping of modernity and tradition is examined in (Torras, 1976) and the legal discontinuity in the example of disentailment is analysed in (Tomás y Valiente, 1978).
2 The term "modernisation" is used in the compilation of Sánchez-Albornoz. Nadal identifies it as the transition from the society of Spain's ancien régime to a capitalist society (Sánchez-Albornoz, 1985, p. 89).
3 For additional information, see (Alvarez Junco, 1985), (Artola, 1973), (Jutglar, 1984), (Ortí, 1975), (Bahamonde and Cayuela, 1992), (Beltrán, 2010) y (Moreno, 2008).

4 There have been many studies on the subject. Two of the earliest to give a good account of these aspects are (Martín Aceña, 1993) and (Nadal, 1975).
5 Ibid.
6 The first studies to refer to the concept are those by (Koenigsberger, 1978) and (Elliott, 1992).
7 For the leading financiers in Madrid, consult (Mateo del Peral, 1974).
8 See the studies by (Tedde de Lorca, 1999), (Blasco-Martel and Sudrià, 2010), (Facal, 2003) and (Pérez García, 1991).
9 (Sánchez-Albornoz, 1968, p. 52) notes that, in addition to Barcelona, the only other places where capital from manufacturing might be expected were Málaga, Bilbao and Valladolid-Santander. Today, we know that even in these cities most of the capital was commercial in origin.
10 For a comprehensive study of this commerce and the development of the mercantile bourgeoisie, see (Basurto and Caro Baroja, 1983) and (Angulo, 2000).
11 The data presented here come from preliminary research for a study on the formation of a banking elite in Spain in the mid-nineteenth century. While the study is yet to be published, the work in progress was presented at the XIV Conference of the Contemporary History Association (AHC) in Alicante in 2018 by Y. Blasco and Q. Faes.
12 Information used to built this table has been taken from the banks monographs included in the full Spanish edition of this book (Sudrià and Blasco-Martel, 2016).

Sources

Archive of the Congreso de los Diputados. Madrid

Bibliography

Alvarez Junco, J., 1985. A vueltas con la Revolución Burguesa. *Zo. Abierta*, 81–106.

Angulo, A., 2000. *Del éxito en los negocios al fracaso del Consulado: la formación de la burguesía mercantil de Vitoria (1670–1840), Historia Medieval y Moderna/Universidad del País Vasco*. Universidad del País Vasco, Servicio Editorial, Bilbao.

Artola, M., 1973. *Historia de España: la burguesía revolucionaria (1808–1869), Alianza Universidad*. Alfaguara, Madrid.

Bahamonde, Á. and Cayuela, J., 1992. *Hacer las Américas : las élites coloniales españolas en el siglo XIX*. Alianza, Madrid.

Basurto, R. and Caro Baroja, J., 1983. *Comercio y burguesía mercantil de Bilbao en la segunda mitad del siglo XVIII*. Servicio Editorial Universidad del País Vasco, Bilbao.

Beltrán, M., 2010. *Burguesía y liberalismo en la España del siglo XIX: sociología de una dominación de clase*. Editorial Universidad de Granada, Granada.

Beth, M.W., 1942. The elite and the elites. *Am. J. Sociol.*, 47, 746–755.

Blasco-Martel, Y. and Rodrigo-Alharilla, M., 2015. Human capital and financial capital in the Atlantic space: From America to Catalonia, 1829–1855. *Atl. Stud.*, 12, 482–500.

Blasco-Martel, Y. and Sudrià, C., 2010. *El Banco de Barcelona (1844–1874), historia de un banco emisor*. LID Editorial, Madrid.

Brophy, J.M., 1992. The political calculus of capital: Banking and the business class in Prussia, 1848–1856. *Cent. Eur. Hist.*, 25, 149–176.

Calvo Caballero, P., 2000. La sociabilidad burguesa en Castilla y León en los siglos XIX y XX, un estado de la cuestión. *Investig. Históricas Época Mod. y Contemp*, 205–228.

Carr, R., 1992. *España 1808–1975*. Ariel, Barcelona.

Cassis, Y., 1985. Bankers in english society in the late nineteenth century. *Econ. Hist. Rev.*, 38, 210–229.
Chapman, S.D., 1896. Aristocracy and meritocracy in merchant banking. *Br. J. Sociol.*, 37, 180–193.
Cuevas, J., 2016. El Banco de España en Valencia y Alicante, 1858–1874. In Sudrià, C. and Blasco-Martel, Y. (Eds.), *La Pluralidad de Emisión En España, 1844–1874*. BBVA, Madrid, pp. 425–451.
Elliott, J.H., 1992. A Europe of composite monarchies. *Past Present*, 137, 48–71.
Facal, M.J., 2003. *El efecto de las leyes Bancarias de 1856 en Galicia: el caso del Banco de Emisión de la Coruña 1857–1875*. Facultade de Ciencias Económicas e Empresariais, Universidad de Santiago de Compostela, Santiago.
Granovetter, M., 1973. The strength of weak ties. *Am. J. Sociol.*, 68, 1360–1380.
Jutglar, A., 1984. *Historia crítica de la burguesía en Cataluña*. Anthropos Editorial.
Koenigsberger, H.G., 1978. Monarchies and parliaments in early modern Europe dominium regale or dominium politicum et regale. *Theory Soc.*, 5, 191–217.
Martín Aceña, P., 1993. *La creación de sociedades en Madrid (1830–1848)*. Un análisis del primer registro mercantil. Madrid.
Martín-Aceña, P., Martínez-Ruíz, E., Nogués-Marco, P., 2013. The bank of Spain: A national financial insitution. *J. Eur. Econ. Hist.*, 42, 11–46.
Mateo del Peral, D., 1974. Aproximación a un estudio sociológico de las autoridades económicas en España, 1868–1915. In Tortella Casares, G. (Ed.), *La Banca Española En La Restauración*. Servicio de Estudios del Banco de España, Madrid, pp. 17–106.
McDonogh, G.W., 1989. *Las Buenas familias de Barcelona : historia social de poder en la era industrial*. Omega, Barcelona.
Montañés, E., 2000. *La empresa exportadora de Jerez: historia económica de González Byass 1835–1885, Empresas centenarias*. Universidad de Cádiz, Cádiz.
Moreno, J., 2008. La historiografía sobre las élites en la España liberal. In Zurita Aldeguer, R. and Camurri, R. (Eds.), *Las Élites En Italia y En España, 1850–1922*. Universitat de València, Valencia.
Nadal, J., 1975. *El fracaso de la revolución industrial en España, 1814–1913, Ariel-Historia*. Editorial Ariel, Barcelona.
Ortí, A., 1975. Introducción. In Costa, J. (Ed.), *Oligarquía y Caciquismo, Como La Forma Actual de Gobierno En España*. Ediciones de la Revista del Trabajo, Madrid, p. 256.
Pérez García, M.P., 1991. *La bancarrota de un banco emisor: el Banco de Valladolid. Instituto de Contabilidad y Autoría de Cuentas*. Ministerio de Economia y Hacienda, Madrid.
Perlinge, A. and Sjögren, H., 2012. *Biographies of the financial world*. Gidlund, Möklinta.
Pro, J., 2016. El Estado grande de los moderados en la España del siglo XIX. *Hist. y Política Ideas, Procesos y Movimientos Soc.*, 19–48.
Rahman Khan, S., 2012. The sociology of elites. *Annu. Rev. Sociol.*, 38, 361–377.
Sánchez-Albornoz, N., 1985. *La Modernización económica de España : 1830–1930*. Alianza, Madrid.
———, 1977. *España hace un siglo*. Una economía dual. Alianza, Madrid
———, 1968. Los bancos y las sociedades de crédito en provincias: 1856–1868. *Moneda y Crédito*, 104, 39–67.
———, 1967. La crisis de 1866 en Madrid: la Caja de Depósitos, las sociedades de crédito y la Bolsa. *Moneda y crédito*, 100, 3–40.
———, 1966. De los orígenes del capital financiero: la sociedad general de crédito mobiliario español, 1856–1902. *Moneda y crédito*, 97, 29–68.

Sudrià, C. and Blasco-Martel, Y. (Eds), 2016. *La pluralidad de emisión en España, 1844–1874., Fundación BBVA*. Fundación BBVA y Ed. Biblioteca Nueva, Madrid, ES.

Tedde, P., 1999. *El Banco de San Fernando*. Alianza Editorial, Madrid.

Tilman, S., 2006. *Les grands banquiers belges, 1830–1935. Portrait collectif d'une élite, Mémoire de la classe des lettres*. Académie royale de Belgique, Bruselas.

Tomás y Valiente, F., 1978. El proceso de desamortización de la tierra en España. *Agric. y Soc.*, 7, 11–33.

Torras, J., 1976. *Liberalismo y rebeldía campesina, 1820–1823*. Ariel, Barcelona.

Tortella Casares, G., 1973. *Los Orígenes del capitalismo en España : banca, industria y ferrocarriles en el siglo XIX*, 1st ed, Serie de historia. Tecnos, Madrid.

Trúpita Giménez, J.B., 1855. *Estadística administrativa de la Dirección General de Contribuciones*. Est. Tip. de J. Antonio Ortigosa, Madrid.

Tuñón de Lara, M., 1967. *Historia y realidad del poder (el poder y las élites en el primer tercio de la España del siglo XIX)*. Cuadernos para el Diálogo, Madrid.

Valls-Junyent, F., 2004. *La Catalunya atlàntica : aiguardent i teixits a l'arrencada industrial catalana, Referències*. Eumo, Vic.

4 A profitability approach to Spanish banks' performance

Earnings and assets

Mercedes Bernal Lloréns and Juan Pedro Sánchez-Ballesta

The function of banks as distributors of the funds of citizens and private companies and, eventually, as providers of means of payment gives them a key role to play in economic development. Banks, however, are also private companies that seek to maximise profits and deliver earnings to shareholders. Though the workings of banks affect other private companies and sectors to a great extent, the fact is that their directors or owners take decisions in response to their own interests. Nonetheless, because of the importance of their function, the authorities typically impose measures of control. While the previous chapter laid out the main characteristics of the specific regulations, this chapter examines the operation of Spanish banks of issue as private businesses in the period 1858–1874, looking basically at their economic performance and their assets. The analysis will also address the regulatory measures that affected their earnings and their earnings distribution.

For the period 1858–1868, the information has been compiled from financial statements published in the *Gaceta de Madrid*. This is generally the most complete and homogeneous set of data, while supporting data have been drawn from the six-monthly reports issued by each bank. For the period 1869–1874, by contrast, the key source has been the banks' reports. By cross-checking the data from the two sources, it is apparent that they broadly concur, though they can be presented in different forms.

In terms of its structure, the chapter first lays out estimates for the banks' net income and describes the regulations pertaining to their allocation of earnings. The second section presents a calculation of the banks' return on equity (ROE) and analyses the associated factors. The third section examines their liquidity, the composition of their financial structure, and their taking of deposits as an indicator of public trust. Lastly, the fourth section concludes with the role played by financial disclosure in reducing asymmetric information and building confidence in the banks.

4.1. The banks' net income and profitability: new estimates

When analysing the banks' net income and their profitability, the first important issue concerns the calculation of the net income. Prior to the law of 1856, the statutes of each bank established how to determine its net income and reserve fund.

For instance, article 44 of the statutes of the Bank of Barcelona stipulated that a reserve fund was to be created with a quarter of its earnings, while requiring an investment of "1% in charitable works to be chosen at the shareholders meeting".

In articles 39 and 40, the first statutes of the Bank of Cádiz[1] replicated the wording of articles 43 and 44 in the statutes of the Bank of Barcelona, except for the reference to the reserve fund, which was set instead at "a fifth of the earnings". However, the new statutes of the Bank of Cádiz, which were approved by royal decree on 25 July 1847, followed the provisions established in the statutes approved on 9 July 1829 for the creation of the Bank of San Fernando. Specifically, article 69 provided for the semi-annual distribution of dividends and the payment to shareholders of 6% interest on effective capital. If profits should exceed 6%, three-quarters was to be distributed to shareholders and the rest was to go into the bank's legal reserve, which was set at 8% of paid-in capital. Should the reserve reach its limit, the profits were to be fully distributed to shareholders. If, on the contrary, profits did not reach 6% per annum, the reserve fund would be used to pay shareholders the full amount. In this manner, the reserve fund would ensure that shareholders obtained a minimum return of 6%.[2]

This system of remuneration closely resembles the one established by the law of 28 January 1856 which, as noted earlier, introduced a unified set of regulations for all banks of issue. Under the legislation, the banks were required to establish a reserve fund equivalent to 10% of their effective capital. The reserve fund was to be "formed from any net profits arising from operations, after deducting the annual interest on capital, which in no case is to exceed 6%". The calculated profits "are to be divided in half between shareholders and the reserve fund until [the latter] reaches its full amount, at which point they are to be distributed in their entirety to shareholders".

Clearly, shareholders were to be remunerated with a fixed portion, the interest on capital, which was regarded as a cost, and a variable portion, which could be half or all of the distributable earnings, depending on the sum reached by the reserve fund. In addition, by setting the requirement in relation to net earnings, the formula excluded unrealised gains. The wording of the law of 28 January 1856 was reproduced verbatim in the statutes for the banks in Valladolid, Santander and Bilbao under the heading "On earnings and their distribution" and, with slight variations, in the statutes for the banks in Málaga, Seville, Jerez, A Coruña and Zaragoza.

In the case of the reserve fund, it is important to note that the banks in Valladolid, Santander, Bilbao and Seville provided for the possibility of allocating the fund for the erection of an office building, while the banks in Málaga and Zaragoza allocated the fund to the payment of 6% interest on capital when the level of net earnings was insufficient. In addition, the Bank of Zaragoza is the only one to acknowledge explicitly that if it could not pay the 6% interest out of earnings or the reserve fund, the shortfall would not entail the recognition of a debt by the bank, but that it would pay shareholders "in accordance with the sum available".

In short, possessing shares in the banks entitled shareholders to two types of remuneration: fixed remuneration in the form of interest on capital and variable remuneration as a function of earnings.

Because the banks calculated and reported their earnings and its components in a variety of ways, it has been necessary first to standardise the collected information. The banks prepared half-yearly profit and loss accounts, so the initial step is to obtain the set of half-year results based on their reports or statements published in the *Gaceta de Madrid*. In the case of the Bank of Zaragoza, which reported on an annual basis, interpolations between consecutive annual accounts have been carried out to obtain an approximation of half-yearly data.

The second step is to calculate each half-year result as it is understood now. The result here is called half-year earnings. The approach requires the subtraction of any retained earnings from preceding periods, though the banks of issue typically did not adhere to this standard because they viewed the net income for a period as the sums available for distribution. Based on the terminology used by the banks, the method of calculation can be summarised as follows:

Definition of earnings

Half-year income
– Retained earnings from prior half-year
– Half-year costs
= Half-year earnings
+ Retained earnings from prior half-year
= Distributable earnings

Another adjustment relating to the concept of income concerns the share premium, or capital surplus, which the banks recognised as a component of half-year income and included in their results. In this case, however, the present analysis takes the view that the share premium should not be included in earnings, so it has been subtracted from income.

In the case of costs, the adjustments relate to items that the banks treated as allocations of earnings, but that are now regarded as costs. In this respect, the treatment that raises the greatest questions concerns the remuneration received by the board of governors, director, administrator, management and any unpaid trainee staff. This is because individualised information is only available for some banks, while others disclosed the data in aggregate form and it has not been possible to separate profit participation from costs. As a result, the remuneration in question has been treated as a component of costs. Something similar occurs with fixed-asset depreciation. Generally speaking, it was treated as an allocation of earnings at the time, but is considered here as a cost.[3]

Lastly, it is important to mention the introduction of a 5% tax on "any earnings that are distributed through dividends, distributions or other means among shareholders of banks and of companies of all kinds formed with Government approval". The tax was introduced in article 3 of the budgetary act of 29 June 1867 and it took effect on 1 July 1867, requiring banks to levy the tax when paying dividends and then to deposit the sum in the Treasury within 15 days. Whereas the tax on distributed net earnings was treated as a cost by the banks in Pamplona, Oviedo and Zaragoza, the other banks did not take the same approach. In this particular case, the policy followed by each bank has been left as is, without making any additional adjustment or calculation.

4.2. Analysis of return on equity (ROE)

Based on the results obtained, the ratio of earnings to shareholders' equity has been calculated to obtain an approximation of return on equity (ROE), that is, of the banks' return on owners' investments. One limitation of the approach lies in the dataset itself, given that earnings data have not always been available. Similarly, to ensure that the entry or exit of banks does not affect the average values in the dataset, interpolations have been made wherever possible when obtaining earnings and profitability.

Table 4.1 below sets out a summary of the banks' financial profitability, i.e., their return on equity (ROE).

In the aggregate, the average half-year returns for the period 1858–1874 were 4.43%, indicating that the banks of issue were profitable. A contributing factor doubtless lies in the high rates of interest being paid in Spain as a consequence of

Table 4.1 Return on equity (ROE)

	1858–1862	*1863–1868*	*1869–1874*	*1858–1874*
Bank of Barcelona	6.19%	7.85%	5.71%	6.61%
Bank of Málaga	5.28%	4.57%		4.89%
Bank of Valladolid	5.03%	5.67%		5.18%
Bank of Santander		4.24%	4.76%	4.59%
Bank of Bilbao	4.40%	6.13%	9.04%	6.65%
Bank of Zaragoza	8.29%	3.65%	–0.98%	3.38%
Bank of A Coruña	5.04%	4.67%	6.90%	5.30%
Bank of Jerez de la Frontera	3.92%	3.65%	4.81%	4.13%
Bank of San Sebastián		2.51%		2.51%
Bank of Reus				
Bank Balear		5.39%	0.01%	2.43%
Bank of Burgos		2.61%	–11.09%	–0.55%
Bank of Palencia				
Bank of Oviedo		2.40%	4.18%	3.38%
Bank of Vitoria			5.72%	5.72%
Bank of Pamplona		3.23%	3.95%	3.63%
Total	5.59%	4.45%	3.67%	4.43%

Source: Own elaboration based on the banks' reports and the *Gaceta de Madrid*

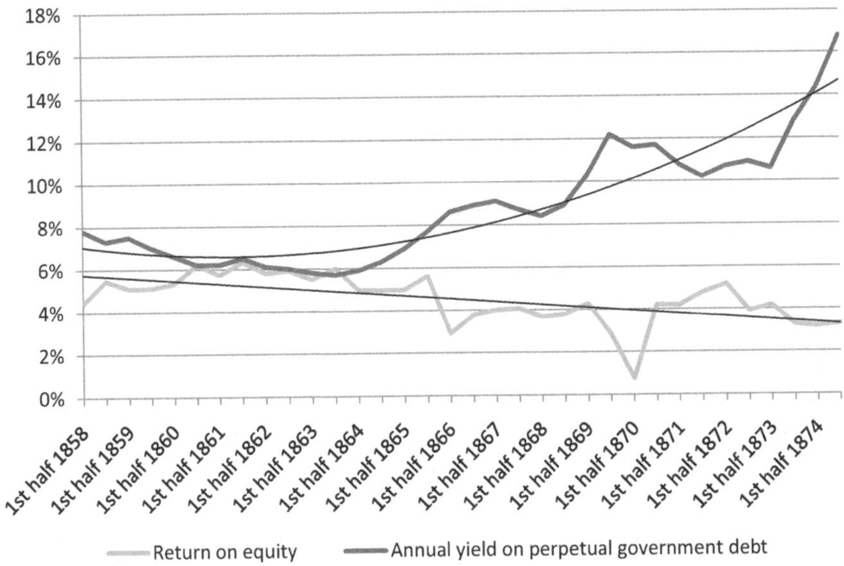

Figure 4.1 Return on equity (ROE) 1858–1874

Source: Own elaboration based on the banks' reports, the *Gaceta de Madrid* and Tafunell (2005, pp. 830, 831)

the overall situation in the country and the riskiness of operations.[4] As Figure 4.1 below shows, however, the yields from perpetual government debt were higher than the banks' returns on equity, except in the early 1860s, and the gap in profitability between the two only grew larger from then on.

Once the highest levels of profitability in the period had been reached in the early 1860s, however, the trend turned downward and there were steep drops in ROE around the crisis of 1866, which lingered in some banks until 1870. In this respect, the reports of some of the institutions, like the Bank of Málaga, highlighted the serious social upheavals of the crisis, which led to alarm in commerce, paralysis in the markets, loss of confidence and an aggravation of the financial crisis. This resulted in a credit squeeze and bank runs, with large amounts of coinage being withdrawn from the markets. Average profitability, however, remained positive even in the first half-year of 1870, which is the year with the lowest ROE in the period and a year in which banks like the ones in Zaragoza, Palma (Majorca), Burgos and Valladolid suffered losses and other banks, like the one in Pamplona, reported their lowest figures over the entire period. From that low point, there was a significant recovery in earnings during the subsequent two years triggered by the expansionary policy of the six-year period that began with the Glorious Revolution (Carreras, 1999, pp. 780, 790). Profitability topped 5% per half-year and even in 1874, when it fell, it was still higher than 3%.

Profitability and size

The main factor that accounts for the profit performance of the banks of issue is size, which has a positive and significant correlation at 1% with profitability over the whole of period, indicating that it was the larger banks that achieved greater profitability in the period.

To compare the banks' profitability by size, they have been divided into three groups: first is the Bank of Barcelona, with an effective capital on average of 6,323,000 pesetas in the period; second come the banks in Málaga and Bilbao, with an effective capital of 2,513,000 pesetas on average;[5] and third are the remaining smaller banks, with an effective capital of 1,286,000 pesetas on average. Table 4.2 below shows that the larger banks performed better than the smaller banks. While the Bank of Barcelona and the other two larger banks (Málaga and Bilbao) obtained half-year returns in the region of 6% on average, the figure was 3.6% for the smaller banks. The larger banks' upturn in profitability from after the crisis of 1866 through 1872 is also striking. Indeed, the Bank of Bilbao had the best result of the period in the first half of 1869, with an ROE greater than 16%, which the bank's own reports call very satisfactory in spite of the adverse circumstances. Similarly, the best year in the dataset for the banks in Barcelona, Oviedo and Pamplona was 1872, which was also very good for the Bank of Málaga. In 1873–1874, however, profitability among the larger banks fell sharply to 4%, perhaps because of the period of political instability set off by the abdication of Amadeo I in February 1873, compounded by the introduction of a monopoly on banknote issue in March 1874.

In addition, the size of the banks of issue was closely related to economic development in the provinces. Broadly, the more heavily populated provinces with a higher GDP were also home to the larger banks (see Table 4.3).[6]

The data further show that profitability in 1860, which is the year for which population and GDP data are available, was higher in the more heavily populated provinces. However, there is no clear correlation between GDP per capita and return on equity, because bank finance could not be used to a great extent in some provinces with high GDP.

Another question to consider is whether the banks had higher profitability in provinces where the increase in population was greater over the period 1858–1874 (as measured by the household census). As Table 4.4 above shows, there does

Table 4.2 Return on equity by bank size

	1858–1862	*1863–1868*	*1869–1874*	*1858–1874*
Bank of Barcelona	6.19%	7.85%	5.71%	6.61%
Bank of Málaga and Bank of Bilbao	4.84%	5.35%	9.04%	5.96%
Remaining banks	5.88%	3.71%	2.50%	3.59%
Total	6.19%	7.85%	5.71%	6.61%

Source: Own elaboration based on the banks' reports and the *Gaceta de Madrid*

Table 4.3 GDP, population and return on equity

Province	*GDP (million pesetas) 1860*	*Population 1860*	*GDP per capita 1860*	*Average profitability 1858–1874*
A Coruña	155.6	557,311	279.3	5.30%
Álava (Vitoria)	30.7	97,934	313.1	5.72%
Barcelona	401.3	726,267	552.5	6.61%
Biscay (Bilbao)	62.7	168,705	371.6	6.65%
Burgos	101	337,132	299.5	–0.55%
Cádiz	267.5	401,700	665.9	4.13%
Gipuzkoa (San Sebastián)	53	162,547	325.8	2.51%
Málaga	257.2	446,659	575.9	4.89%
Navarre (Pamplona)	116.8	299,654	389.8	3.63%
Oviedo	111.5	540,586	206.2	3.38%
Santander	66.8	219,966	303.8	4.59%
Valladolid	99.9	246,981	404.5	5.18%
Zaragoza	160.1	390,551	410	3.38%

* Profitability for the province of Cádiz corresponds to the Bank of Jerez de la Frontera, while profitability for the province of A Coruña to the Bank of A Coruña. The two provinces were also home to the Bank of Cádiz and the Bank of Santiago, respectively.

Source: Own elaboration based on data kindly provided by Julio Martínez Galarraga (see Rosés et al. 2010), the banks' reports and the *Gaceta de Madrid*

Table 4.4 Household census and return on equity

Province	*1857*	*1877*	*Growth*	*Average ROE*
A Coruña	5,579	9,264	66.05%	5.30%
Barcelona	46,606	75,369	61.72%	6.61%
Biscay (Bilbao)	3,988	6,927	73.70%	6.65%
Burgos	5,438	6,719	23.56%	–0.55%
Málaga	22,270	31,101	39.65%	4.88%
Oviedo	5,497	8,114	47.61%	3.38%
Navarre (Pamplona)	4,561	5,673	24.38%	3.63%
Santander	5,706	9,243	61.99%	4.59%
Valladolid	8,562	12,436	45.25%	5.18%
Zaragoza	14,410	20,545	42.57%	3.38%

Source: Own elaboration based on the INE, the banks' reports and the *Gaceta de Madrid*

appear to be some correlation between population growth in the period and the rates of return. The provincial banks of the period had a relatively small clientele; however, what the GPD and population data indicate is the society's dynamism, which doubtless had an influence on the banks' ability to achieve higher returns on equity. Next comes an examination of the conditions of representativeness in the provincial banks of issue.

Profitability and voting rights

The power relations established among shareholders are fundamental to the operation of joint-stock companies. As with today's corporations, the banks of issue set a given number of shares as a requirement to attend and vote in the shareholders' general meetings; however, the number of votes was not strictly proportional to the number of shares held. Hansmann and Pargendler (2014) explain nineteenth-century voting restrictions based on what they call consumer protection theory. Under the theory, local monopolies that provided vital services to local merchants must not be made subject to the rule of proportional voting based on the number of shares. The reason for this lay in the fact that merchants were both the customers and the major shareholders of the banking corporations, which had been created to make their own private businesses more profitable. For this reason, they had to prevent bank control from falling into the hands of investors whose sole interest was the bank's profitability or, conversely, into the hands of competitors. According to the theory, the conflict of interests occurs between investors and original shareholders on one side and customers on the other side, with the customers preferring their returns in the form of low prices, not high dividends.

Moreover, Dunlavy (2006, p. 1356) shows clearly that in the US context the dilemma between 'one person, one vote' and 'one share, one vote', a fundamental issue for the distribution of power, had already been debated in 1790. While the second option would hand the control of companies to large shareholders, the first option would give large shareholders too little power. As a result, an intermediate approach seemed preferable and rules were established to distribute power among shareholders according to a measure of proportionality. In the case of banks, the right of shareholders to the free transfer of shares was recognised, but control of a bank could not be changed simply through the sale of a large number of a person's shares, because the established rule of 'one person, one vote' ensured that control of a firm could not be lost under any circumstances (Ratner, 1970, p. 15).

In Spain, the rule of 'one shareholder, one vote' was introduced by the royal charter of 9 July 1829 that created the Bank of San Fernando and it was upheld in the royal decree of 18 February 1852. The rule also figured in the first statutes of the Bank of Barcelona (1845), though new statutes in 1859 introduced voting proportional to shares held (Blasco-Martel and Sudriá, 2010, pp. 229–230). The rule at the Bank of Cádiz was different, however, because it awarded one vote to each 40 shares with a maximum of 5 votes or 200 shares.

As for the minimum number of shares required to be eligible to vote in a shareholders' general meeting Cádiz was again an exception with 40 shares. No major differences have been observed among the remaining banks: all required a minimum of 10 shares, with the exception of the banks in Málaga, Oviedo, Palencia, Santiago and the Bank Balear, which all required 5 shares, and the Bank of Jerez, which required 8 shares. Broadly, though, the eligibility to vote required a minimum of 10 shares regardless of the number of shares issued.

For the banks in Bilbao, Santander, Valladolid, A Coruña and Jerez, the rule was 'one shareholder, one vote' regardless of the number of shares held. For the banks in Seville, Málaga and Zaragoza, the number of votes was allocated according to the number of shares, but there was a maximum limit of votes that varied between 5 votes at the Bank of Seville (with 50 shares or more), 4 votes at the Bank of Zaragoza (with 75 shares or more) and 10 votes at the Bank of Málaga (with 50 shares or more). However, all the banks created after 1862 recognised the principle of 'one shareholder, one vote', with the exception of Bank Balear, which quantified votes by the number of shares held.

Share ownership was also linked to management liability by means of a bond handed over in the form of shares. To sit on a bank's board of governors, a shareholder had to possess a given number of shares that would be deposited in the bank as a bond as long as he continued in the post in order to cover any liabilities that might be incurred by the administrators (González Huebra, 1867, p. 161). Table 4.5 shows the number of sitting members on the banks' boards of governors and the number of shares needed to occupy a seat.

Leaving aside alternate members, governors and deputy governors, the number of members sitting on the board of governors of the first-wave banks was 12, with the exception of the Bank of Zaragoza, where it was 8. By contrast, the banks created in subsequent years had 9 members, with the exception of the ones in Burgos, Santiago and Bank Balear. As for the bond required, the largest one in relation to share capital was that of the Bank of Jerez (1.067%) and the smallest one was that of the Bank of Málaga (0.3%). In the banks created later, the bond generally represented 1% of capital stock, with the exception of the Bank of Tarragona, where the figure reached 1.25%.

Table 4.5 Size of governing board and minimum capital for membership

	Number of members	*Number of shares*
Bank of Barcelona	12 members	40 shares of 500 pesetas
Bank of Cádiz	12 members and 3 trustees	50 shares of 500 pesetas
Bank of Málaga	9 members, 3 trustees and 3 alternates	30 shares of 500 pesetas
Bank of Seville	9 members and 3 trustees	20 shares of 500 pesetas
Bank of Valladolid	12 individuals and 3 alternates	25 shares of 500 pesetas
Bank of Zaragoza	8 members and 4 alternates	20 shares of 500 pesetas
Bank of Santander	12 individuals and 3 alternates	20 shares of 500 pesetas
Bank of Bilbao	12 individuals and 3 alternates	20 shares of 500 pesetas
Bank of A Coruña	12 members	20 shares of 500 pesetas
Bank of Jerez	12 members and 3 alternates	16 shares of 500 pesetas
Bank of San Sebastián	9 individuals and 3 alternates	20 shares of 500 pesetas
Bank of Reus	9 individuals and 3 alternates	20 shares of 500 pesetas
Bank of Santiago	12 individuals and 3 alternates	15 shares of 500 pesetas
Bank of Burgos	12 individuals and 3 alternates	20 shares of 500 pesetas
Bank of Vitoria	9 individuals and 3 alternates	20 shares of 500 pesetas
Bank of Palencia	9 individuals and 3 alternates	20 shares of 500 pesetas
Bank of Tarragona	9 individuals and 3 alternates	25 shares of 500 pesetas
Bank of Oviedo	9 individuals and 3 alternates	20 shares of 500 pesetas
Bank Balear	12 individuals	20 shares of 500 pesetas

Source: Own elaboration based on the banks' statutes

As for regulations on incompatibilities or conflicts of interest, all the banks generally prohibited from sitting on their governing bodies anyone who had declared bankruptcy or suspended payments until they were restored to good standing, or who had formerly been sentenced to prison or corporal punishment under the old penal code, or who was overdrawn at the bank. In addition, membership was prohibited on personal or kinship grounds. For example, every bank prohibited being a member at the same time as anyone else with whom the member shared mutual business interests or kinship.[7]

Table 4.6 shows the impact on profitability of the decision-making process in the boards of governors. As can be seen, the banks with voting rights based on the number of shares had higher returns on equity until the crisis of the 1860s, but as the country emerged from the crisis, profitability was greater in the banks abiding by 'one person, one vote'.

From the analyses above, it can be concluded that the banks of issue remained profitable at all times in spite of the severity of Spain's political, economic and social crises in the period, which resulted in business stagnation, property depreciation, social upheavals and a shortage of money and credit. Their performance did not even falter when the royal commissioners were withdrawn from all but the Bank of Spain and the Bank of Barcelona, under the decree of 10 December 1868, and with them the government's control and inspection. The removal of the royal commissioners was not only a recognition of their inability to prevent the dissolution of banks, but also a declaration of liberal principles in the oversight of banks of issue. As the preamble to the decree stated, their removal "will oblige the interested parties [. . .] to exercise effective vigilance on their own account, in place of an illusory trust in the Government". The banks faced difficult situations with the same determination and did not hesitate to modify the working conditions of employees in order to sustain earnings.

A final aspect to consider in relation to earnings is their distribution. In this respect, the banks complied with the legal requirement to allocate 10% to their reserve fund, while the remaining earnings were distributed as dividends or, as noted earlier, in the provision of credit, the creation of pension funds or the construction of future premises, with any adjustments for retained earnings being very small. Distributed dividends accounted for 90% of profits on average and the figure was quite homogeneous among the various banks. Only from 1866 onwards does the percentage decline slightly. This suggests that the banks, once

Table 4.6 Return on equity by voting rights and board

	1858–1862	*1863–1868*	*1869–1874*	*1858–1874*
Votes based on number of shares held	6.59%	5.36%	1.62%	4.47%
One person, one vote	4.77%	3.91%	4.77%	4.40%
Total	5.59%	4.45%	3.67%	4.43%

Source: Own elaboration based on the banks' reports and the *Gaceta de Madrid*

they had covered their compulsory reserve fund, did not retain earnings except for the items mentioned above. In some cases, they even distributed dividends in excess of their half-year earnings. This occurred in the first half of 1861, when the banks in Bilbao and Jerez allocated a share issue premium to their dividend distribution. Also, regardless of whether the banks were controlled by merchants or not, profitability was the factor that determined the banks' dividends. As they emerged from the crisis of the 1860s, the banks with merchants on their boards, given their higher profitability, were able to distribute more earnings than the banks without merchants on their boards.

4.3. Balance-sheet analysis of banks of issue

To perform an balance-sheet analysis of the banks, their liquidity and the composition of their financial structure have been examined. Two indicators have been used to assess their liquidity: their cash-to-assets ratio, based on holdings of coin and bullion, and their coverage of bank liabilities with the public (banknotes in circulation, current accounts and deposits), based on these holdings. Figure 4.2 below shows the behaviour of the indicators over the period. In general, their cash-to-assets ratio declines over the period, falling from 27% in the first half of 1858 to 15% in the second half of 1873, though it does rebound to its starting levels in 1874.

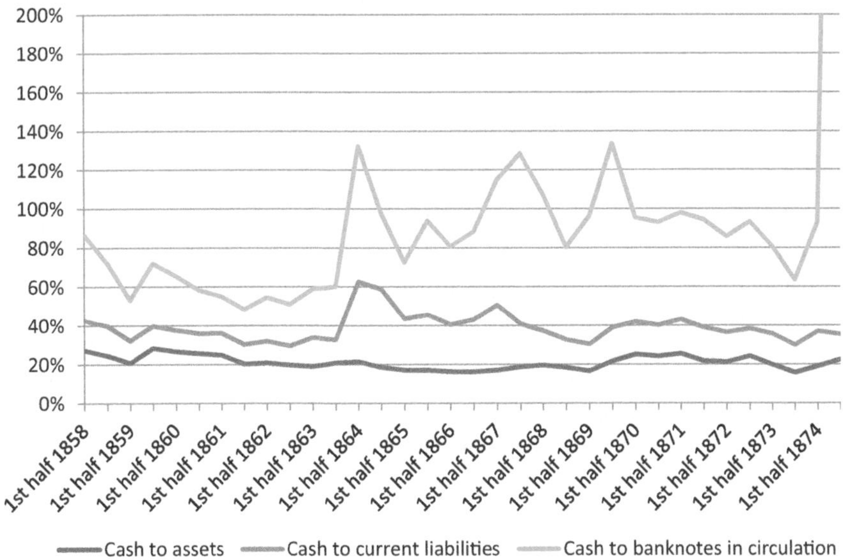

Figure 4.2 Liquidity (1858–1874)

Source: Own elaboration based on the banks' reports and the *Gaceta de Madrid*

The banks' cash position relative to liabilities follows a similar course, falling from 43% in 1858 to 30% in the second half of 1873 and rising again to 39% in 1874. This is generally consistent with the idea in the nineteenth century that a bank should keep coin and bullion equivalent to one-third of its liabilities in order to guarantee solvency. In Spain, the application of the rule hinged on the value of banknotes in circulation and the banks adhered to the rule at an aggregate level over the entire period.[8] While the cash-to-assets ratio followed a steadier trendline, however, hedged liabilities posed greater fluctuations, particularly the coverage of banknotes in circulation. This was a consequence of the sensitivity of banknotes in circulation to the level of public trust and to the banks' differing liquidity policies. For example, it is important to note the rise in the coverage of liabilities in 1864, driven by the decline of banknotes in circulation and the creation of new banks that commenced operations with a very small number of banknotes. Also, there was a decline in liquidity in the years following the crisis of 1866. Improved results after the end of the crisis, however, were associated with an improvement in liquidity in the early 1870s.Table 4.7 below lays out the liquidity indicators for each bank. As can be seen, the bank that proved most conservative in terms of liquidity and differed considerably from most of the other banks was the Bank of Barcelona, which tied up vast sums of coin and bullion to cover the large amount of liabilities that it had attracted. In 1874, available coin and bullion reached as high as 64% of assets and 82% of liabilities with the public, thanks to a loan to the government placed through the Rothschilds and backed with gold bullion (Blasco-Martel and Sudriá, 2010, pp. 341–342).

The behaviour of the other banks was more homogeneous, with the smaller ones maintaining higher liquidity, particularly in their early years of operation. The larger banks, such as Málaga and Bilbao, had sound economic management in the late 1860s and early 1870s, as observed earlier in the analysis of profitability, without needing to keep high levels of liquidity. By contrast, the Bank of Cádiz, which had an effective capital of 4,715,000 pesetas on average, showed a progressive deterioration in liquidity in the years leading up to its demise. The data also indicate that the reduced liability activity of the banks created from 1860 onwards led them to maintain a bigger cash position, though the volatility in their behaviour over the period was greater than that of their predecessors.

The financial structure has been analysed by studying the ratio of shareholders' equity to the total size of the bank and looking at the composition of liabilities across banknotes in circulation, current accounts and deposits. Figure 4.3 shows clearly that the banks operated with a high percentage of shareholders' equity during the period. For the banks as a whole, the proportion of shareholders' equity to total assets is 37% over the period, but there is a growth phase between 1860 and 1866 and the levels reach close to 50% in the crisis of 1866. The increasing ratio of shareholders' equity to borrowings was influenced by the creation of new smaller banks from 1860 with low liability activity and by the withdrawal of liabilities triggered by the public's loss of confidence during the crisis of 1866. In the second phase, there was a broad rise in borrowings in relation to shareholders' equity until 1872. As for the composition of liabilities, banknotes in circulation

Table 4.7 Liquidity of the banks of issue

	1858–1862		*1863–1868*		*1869–1874*		*1858–1874*	
	Cash/ Assets	*Cash/ Liabilities*	*Cash/ Assets*	*Cash/ Liabilities*	*Cash/ Assets*	*Cash/ Liabilities*	*Cash/ Assets*	*Cash/ Liabilities*
Bank of cádiz	27.11%	38.62%	13.44%	19.85%			19.65%	28.38%
Bank of barcelona	28.06%	38.57%	42.36%	53.81%	64.32%	80.05%	45.91%	58.59%
Bank of seville	24.18%	34.84%	15.74%	28.56%			19.76%	31.55%
Bank of málaga	28.39%	43.41%	18.65%	30.89%	17.13%	27.65%	22.17%	35.51%
Bank of valladolid	20.47%	31.14%	25.42%	37.45%			21.61%	32.60%
Bank of santander	25.27%	34.93%	16.39%	24.07%	15.36%	20.39%	18.64%	25.96%
Bank of bilbao	24.71%	36.72%	19.06%	28.14%	14.60%	22.30%	19.15%	28.60%
Bank of zaragoza	12.28%	15.54%	7.78%	11.15%	5.54%	19.89%	8.31%	15.53%
Bank of a coruña	27.74%	50.74%	16.88%	28.38%	18.37%	27.33%	20.66%	35.03%
Bank of jerez de la frontera	14.41%	24.91%	15.84%	35.98%	25.40%	43.23%	19.12%	36.61%
Bank of san sebastián			24.52%	43.74%	38.38%	57.49%	31.15%	50.32%
Bank of reus			16.63%	35.56%	13.73%	21.97%	15.74%	31.38%
Bank balear			21.00%	40.49%	10.61%	14.08%	15.28%	25.96%
Bank of burgos			13.42%	58.81%	21.95%	2.56%	15.39%	53.70%
Bank of palencia			5.94%	110%			5.94%	110%
Bank of oviedo			24.24%	69.13%	11.54%	53.59%	17.26%	60.58%
Bank of vitoria			15.45%	75.05%	6.60%	41.17%	13.41%	67.23%
Bank of pamplona			15.76%	52.37%	15.47%	42.69%	15.61%	47.30%
Bank of tarragona			16.05%	90.85%			16.05%	90.85%
Bank of santiago			14.91%	67.96%			14.91%	67.96%
Total	23.69%	35.31%	18.08%	44.06%	21.32%	37.24%	20.31%	40.08%

Source: Own elaboration based on the banks' reports and the *Gaceta de Madrid*

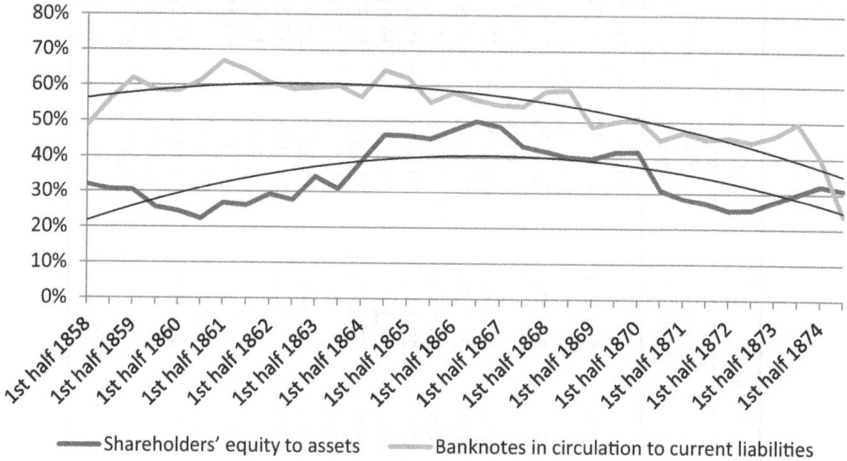

Figure 4.3 Composition of the financial structure (1858–1874)

Source: Own elaboration based on the banks' reports and the *Gaceta de Madrid*

were the chief component until the crisis of 1866, thanks to an expansionary phase in banknote issue after the legislation of 1856. During the crisis years, however, the banknotes in circulation declined and current accounts increased as a result of the distrust among banknote holders. In 1867–1868, the ratio between banknotes and current accounts stood at roughly 50%. From then on, however, the acceptance of banknotes lost ground to current accounts until 1873, at which point the decline of banknotes accelerated as a result of social and political instability triggered by the last Carlist war and the abdication of Amadeo I, as well as by the creation of a national bank.

Over the period, the banks' excessive liquidity and the high proportion of shareholders' equity in their financial structure broadly indicate prudent behaviour that reflects a value recognised by every bank as its most prized asset: the public's trust. As stated in the *Gaceta de los Caminos de Hierro* (30/03/1873), "trust is the essential need today for the safeguarding of material, political and social interests". To keep their good name and the public's trust in difficult situations, the banks of issue all employed the same sort of "prudent" policies, that is, they gradually restricted lending and discounting operations that might pose greater risks, shortened the relevant terms, curtailed the circulation of banknotes, made allowances for doubtful debts and strengthened their coin and bullion reserves so that they could satisfy bank cheques and banknotes in a timely manner. To do so, many of the banks of issue, in the absence of a lender of last resort, bore large costs to attract cash from other locales, following a maxim that appeared in the reports of the Bank of Santander: "reputation is earned, not imposed". Trust, prudence and soundness, therefore, were the three core principles of the institutions. Even under the criterion of general prudence, however, the key factor contributing to a more modernised financial structure oriented toward external resources

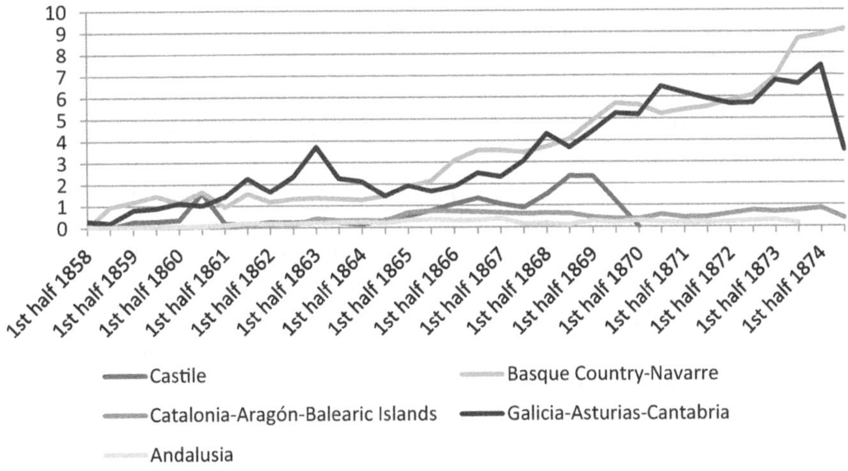

Figure 4.4 Ratio of deposits to assets by geographical area (1858–1874)

Source: Own elaboration based on the banks' reports and the *Gaceta de Madrid*

proved to be the size of the bank, just as it was in the analysis of profitability. As the data show, the larger banks had a lower percentage of shareholders' equity in their financial structure.

Confidence and securities deposits

One activity characteristic of the banks of issue was to take deposits of securities. As shown in Figure 4.4, the banks in the north (on the Bay of Biscay and in Navarre) developed this operation much more than their southern counterparts. In this respect, it is important to note that nearly all the banks recognised in their reports that one of the indicators of public confidence was the growth in voluntary deposits. The indicator may also explain the public's greater propensity to save and to trust in the banks in the north of Spain. The Bank of Bilbao noted in its report for the second half of 1862 its efforts to promote trade and to spread of the use of credit. An opposite case in the south is furnished by the Bank of Málaga, which published a report in 1865 that referred to the "abuse of credit" in the local market that was attributed to "the nature of the city's businesses". These are habits and businesses that could be explanatory of a different propensity to save and could partly explain the different behaviour of the financial institutions.

4.4. Asymmetric information, trust and disclosure

The previous section analysed the behaviour of deposits as an indicator of trust in the banks of issue. Trust, or confidence, is a key issue because the banks of issue in nineteenth-century Spain were institutions that not only competed with commercial financial entities in taking deposits, but also had to secure a clientele that would be willing to hold their banknotes. And the circulation of banknotes depended on confidence in the solvency of the bank that issued them (Tucker, 1839, p. 228). Even so, the existence of asymmetric information makes it hard to draw distinctions among the situations of different institutions and the problem can cause the run on one bank to spread (Diamond and Dybvig, 1983, p. 405; Calomaris and Khan, 1991, p. 499) and bring about the collapse of banks that were actually solvent. As a result, a fundamental pillar to safeguarding confidence in solvent institutions and ensuring the stability of the banking system as a whole is the availability of financial information on the situation of each entity (Villaumé, 1857, p. 238).

In this respect, the late eighteenth century saw the rise of the term *publicidad* as a synonym for what is now called transparency, with the basic aim being to sustain or strengthen confidence (Ciccolella, 2015, p. 216), particularly in the area of public finances. By the nineteenth century, the disclosure of information through the publication of financial statements was regarded as a public good, especially in those entities that were fundamental for the progress and stability of the economic system. In Spain, it was stated in the debate on the draft bill on banks of issue that one guarantee that would protect the interests of most people was to publish the banks' balance sheets in the official government gazette (*Gaceta de Madrid*), so that the public could know the state of each bank (*Diario de las Sesiones de las Cortes Constituyentes 1854–1856*, n° 288: 9883). As a result, rules on the publication of financial information became an additional regulatory aspect that contributed, together with regulations on activities, solvency and liquidity, to securing the stability of the financial system and maintaining the confidence of creditors in order to attract resources and ensure the circulation of banknotes.

The law on banks of issue made it compulsory to publish monthly balance sheets in the *Gaceta de Madrid*, though the government never enforced a particular reporting template (Pérez García, 1991: 87–91). As a result, the banks were free to present their balance sheets using their own templates. The oversight of financial statements fell to the royal commissioner or governor, who was a representative of the government under the law of 1856 entrusted with ensuring a bank's cash reserve ratio and carrying out other functions laid out in the bank's statutes on the auditing of its financial statements. This is a sign of the interest among the banks in reducing conflicts with their creditors and the holders of their banknotes and it points to the royal commissioner as a figure guaranteeing accountability and the credibility of the financial information provided by the banks of issue.

As a result, the banks of issue that were financially healthy had incentives to supply information to their banknote holders and depositors in order to reduce asymmetric information and prevent the spread of bank runs. At the same time, the banks' disclosure of financial information enabled their stakeholders to take decisions on whether to accept their banknotes or whether to deposit money in them. Sánchez-Ballesta and Bernal (2010) have shown that the high degree of disclosure by banks of issue can be explained by state oversight to ensure the stability of the financial system and by the banks' own desire to reduce informational asymmetries and build a reputation so as to facilitate the circulation of their banknotes. However, even with rules on the frequency of publications, banks of issue and credit companies preferred not to publish financial statements in times of crisis (Bernal, 2004), meaning that the disclosed information could be regarded as an indicator of solvency (Dupont, 2007, p. 413).

To recap, this chapter has analysed the evolution of profitability and assets in banks of issue over the period 1858–1874. Generally, the banks of issue were profitable, though the crisis of the late 1860s had a significant impact on their earnings. The primary explanatory factor of profitability was size, with the larger banks achieving higher returns on equity than the smaller ones. There was also a close relationship between their size, economic development in the provinces and urban growth.

Another aspect that has been analysed is the voting system as an indicator of the banks' governance structure. While the introduction of a system based on 'one shareholder, one vote' enabled small shareholders to participate in the management of a bank, a system of proportional voting based on the number of shares allowed large shareholders to take control. Based on an analysis of the voting system as a determinant of bank profitability, the findings show that the banks with proportional voting were more profitable than the banks with a 'one person, one vote' system until the crisis of the 1860s, but that the latter group then performed better in the wake of the crisis.

As for their asset structures, two aspects stand out: the excessive liquidity of the banks of issue and the high proportion of shareholders' equity in their financial structure. These aspects, together with the regulated publication of financial information and the banks' own disclosure policies, highlight the importance of gaining and maintaining the public's trust, which was the banks' most valuable asset.

As a final conclusion, the banks of issue clearly appear to have been created with distinct organisational and business models in cities with differing levels of economic performance, stimulated by infrastructure development and by legislation that encouraged their creation, and they helped to provide an invaluable service in the financing of the economy even in the worst of times.

Notes

1 Royal Decree of 8 January 1847.
2 The law of 14 March 1856 abolished "all taxes levied against interest on cash lending" and set legal interest rates at 6%.
3 In general, allocations of earnings have been regarded as costs. However, the allocation of earnings for the construction of a future building has been treated as reserve funds.
4 *Gaceta de los Caminos de Hierro* (19/10/1867).
5 This category would include the Bank of Seville, but no results data are available. The Bank of Cádiz falls between the second group and the Bank of Barcelona, but no results data are available in its case either.
6 The estimates of population and GDP for 1860 are taken from data kindly provided by Julio Martínez Galarraga (see Rosés et al. (2010)).
7 Broadly, relatives are individuals within the fourth degree of consanguinity or the second degree of affinity.
8 This aspect, which is known as the Palmer rule, has been studied in relation to Spanish banks of issue by Blasco-Martel (2016).

Sources

Gaceta de Madrid
Gaceta de los Caminos de Hierro
Banks' Reports (see text)

Bibliography

Bernal, M. 2004. Financial Crises and the Publication of the Financial Statements of Banks in Spain, 1844-1868. *Accounting Historians Journal*, 31(2), 1–23.

Blasco-Martel, Y., 2016. *La Palmer Rule y la Convertibilidad de los Billetes de Banco de España*. Documento de Trabajo-1614, Asociación Española de Historia Económica, Madrid.

Blasco-Martel, Y. and Sudriá, C., 2010. *El Banco de Barcelona (1844–1874)*, LID, Madrid.

Calomaris, C. and Khan, C., 1991. The role of demandable debt in structuring optimal banking arrangements. *American Economic Review*, 81 (3), 497–513.

Carreras, A., 1999. Miseria pública y prosperidad privada durante el sexenio democrático. *Doctor Jordi Nadal. La industrialización y el desarrollo económico de España / coord. por Miquel Gutiérrez i Poch*, 1, 777–794.

Ciccolella, D., 2015. False transparency: Disclosing financial data, between enlightenment and absolutism (Naples, 1870s). *Histoire et Mesure*, XXX (2), 215–256.

Diamond, D. and Dybvig, P., 1983. Bank runs, deposit insurance, and liquidity. *Journal of Political Economy*, 91, 401–419.

Dunlavy, C.A., 2006. Social conceptions of the corporation: Insights from the history of shareholder voting rights. *Washintong&Lee Law Review*, 63 (4), 1.3487–1.388.

Dupont, B., 2007. Bank runs, information and contagion in the panic of 1893. *Explorations in Economic History*, 44, 411–431.

González Huebra, P., 1867. *Curso de derecho mercantil*. Librería Sánchez, Madrid.

Hansmann, H. and Pargendler, M., 2014. The evolution of shareholder voting rights: Separation of ownership and consumption. *The Yale Law Journal*, XXXX, 100–165.

Pérez García, M.P., 1991. *La Bancarrota de un banco emisor: el Banco de Valladolid Instituto de Contabilidad y Autoría de Cuentas*. Ministerio de Economía y Hacienda, Madrid.

Ratner, D., 1970. The government of business corporations: Critical reflections on the rule of "one share one vote." *Cornell Law Review*, 56 (1), 1–56.

Rosés, J.R., Martinez-Galarraga, J., and Tirado, D.A., 2010. The upswing of regional income inequality in Spain (1860–1930). *Explorations in Economic History*, 47 (2), 244–257.

Sánchez-Ballesta, J.P., and Bernal, M., 2010. Monitoring, reputation and accountability in issuing banks in mid-nineteenth-century Spain. *Explorations in Economic History*, 47, 403–419.

Tafunell, X., 2005. Empresa y Bolsa. In Carreras, A. and Tafunell, X. (coord.), *Estadísticas históricas de España. Siglos XIX-XX*. Fundación BBVA, pp. 706–833.

Tucker, G., 1839. *The theory of money and banks investigated*, Routledge, London. (new edition: 1996).

Villaumé, M., 1857. *Nouveau Traité D'Économie Politique*, Guillaumin et Cie, Libraires, París.

5 Provincial banks of issue and the Spanish economy

Money and credit

Carles Sudrià

The years 1835–1845 in Spain saw the establishment of a representative political system which, despite its shortcomings and instability, would endure until 1923, with only one serious interruption between 1868 and 1874. It was also a time of growth for the Spanish economy, after a long period marked by both domestic and international conflicts. Far-reaching political changes were accompanied by a new set of economic rules: the regulations over most economic activities were removed; the Public Treasury was reorganised, and a new fiscal system was introduced; church and communal land were confiscated and auctioned; and legal changes allowed for the constitution of joint-stock companies. This, then, was the background to the authorisation of the new banks of issue.

This chapter analyses the evolution of banks of issue in the economic environment of the time, throughout the period that they were in existence, between 1844 and 1874. We begin by examining three of the earliest banking institutions: The Bank of Isabel II, the Bank of Barcelona and the Bank of Cádiz. Next, we assess the spread of banking practices from 1856 onwards and their effects on the economy until the crisis of 1866, which brought down many of the institutions created in the previous years. We continue with a general appraisal of the impact of banking on the Spanish economy in the mid-nineteenth century, and finish with an analysis of the effects of the crisis of 1866 on the banks of issue in Spain.

5.1. Banknotes for a select few: issuance as a restricted privilege, 1844–1856

The establishment of banks of issue in Spain was not the result of a concerted policy drafted by economic decision-makers in government or parliament, but the consequence of specific decisions taken in response to different reasons or interests. The first project that met with government support was the creation of a second bank of issue in Madrid, the Bank of Isabel II, to compete with the Bank of San Fernando.[1] The move was promoted by a small number of businessmen in the capital who needed more liquidity to expand their operations. Two of its instigators were José Salamanca from Málaga in Andalusia and Gaspar Remisa from Catalonia, both financiers with close links to the state who made their dedication to business compatible with their political responsibilities. Remisa was general director of the Treasury for many years, and a senator; Salamanca was finance minister when the merger of the Bank of Isabel II with that of San Fernando was completed.

Among the arguments put forward by the minister of the time, Juan José García Carrasco, to justify his decision to authorise a new bank of issue in Madrid, some are clearly connected with the debates that were taking place at the time in other European countries. The first was the importance of credit in the private sector to promote trade and industry ["credit institutions . . . multiplying the instruments of exchange and facilitating circulation, are the strongest lever of their prosperity"]; the second was the thinly veiled criticism of the Bank of San Fernando and its reluctance to provide credit ["the circumstances of its origin, its old practices, the misfortunes of the times have paralysed its efforts, and have removed it from large operations of discounting and exchange . . ."]; and finally, the identification of the monopoly as the underlying problem, and the need to intervene in order to bring it to an end ["knowing that it is alone, and with the power to exercise its monopoly, it sometimes prefers to earn a great deal by speculating little, than to obtain greater profits by widening the circle of its activity and its movement . . ."].[2]

The idea of creating a new bank of issue was by no means far-fetched, especially considering the lack of dynamism shown by the Bank of San Fernando in previous years.[3] The new Bank of Isabel II, however, did not live up to expectations and after a promising start it began to suffer serious problems of liquidity. The difficulties derived essentially from its involvement in the business of its main shareholder and director, José Salamanca and the practice of granting credit secured against its own shares. By the end of 1846, the bank was in crisis: at that time, the external resources repayable on demand reached the figure of 47.5 million pesetas (27.9 million in banknotes in circulation and 19.6 million in deposits and current accounts), and the paid-in capital stood at 17.7 million; these were higher than its competitor, the Bank of San Fernando, which had a short-term exposure of around 30 million pesetas, of which 20 million corresponded to banknotes in circulation, against a paid-in capital of 20 million.[4]

Given the risk that the Bank of Isabel II might go into temporary receivership (something which would undoubtedly have dragged the Bank of San Fernando along with it), the government ordered the merger of the capital's two banks of issue. Though they were independent private entities, the government argued that "the issue of banknotes payable to the bearer on demand destined to supply and serve as currency is an eminent faculty of the public authority, which it may exercise by itself or delegate . . . reserving always the right corresponding to it and the right to inspection, as a public service of the highest importance". Unlike its predecessor of 1844, this government understood that "it would be against the good principles of administration to have at the same time two different and independent establishments with the same object".[5]

The minister responsible for this decision was Ramón Santillán, a senior civil servant and conservative politician who was openly opposed to the plurality of banks of issue. Santillán served as director of the new Bank of San Fernando, the result of the merger, and of its successor the Bank of Spain, from 1849 until his death in 1863.[6]

If the experience of a second bank of issue in Madrid proved short-lived, this was not the case of the two banks of issue authorised during this period outside the capital: the banks of Barcelona and Cádiz. The Bank of Barcelona was authorised by the same government and the same finance minister who had approved the creation of the Bank of Isabel II. García Carrasco was an enthusiastic supporter of banking freedom – a position that was not shared by other political leaders who subscribed to more conservative principles. Indeed, the process that finally led to the royal approval of the Bank of Barcelona was particularly complicated. A first attempt, carried out alone by Girona Hnos. Clavé y Cia in 1842, was frustrated by the political climate of the time; in that year the Regent of Spain, General Espartero, bombarded the city of Barcelona to put down an uprising against his government.

In the second attempt to open the Bank of Barcelona, the Girona family firm, the original promoters, were accompanied by two other Barcelona-based trading houses specialising in overseas commerce, one led by Josep M. Serra and the other under the name Plandolit Hnos. The decree of authorisation was signed on the day of the fall of González Bravo's government, in which the aforementioned García Carrasco was finance minister. García Carrasco's replacement in the new markedly conservative government was Alejandro Mon, a firm opponent of the plurality of issue. Whether by the hand of the new minister or for other reasons, the fact is that the decree of authorisation was not published in the official gazette, the *Gaceta de Madrid*, until 19 August following – that is, three and a half months later.

Once official approval was obtained, a public offer of shares was convened in the city of Barcelona and it was met with such an enthusiastic reception that pro-rata measures had to be introduced to ensure that all applicants were able to access at least some shares. However, the capital remained highly concentrated: some 20 shareholders (5% of the total), who held the maximum established amount of 100 shares each, controlled just over a third of the bank's capital. The bank's statutes established the possibility of not paying in a portion of the subscribed capital, but the shareholder undertook a contractual obligation (in the presence of a notary) to provide the capital in cash if so required by the board of directors. According to Manuel Girona, one of the directors, the bank's reserves were entrusted to its own shareholders, in the conviction that these funds would be safer and more useful in their hands than in the bank's own coffers. The Bank of Barcelona opened its doors to the public on 20 August 1845, with a nominal capital of 20 million *reales*, of which 5 million were actually paid in.

The story of Cádiz is more convoluted. A brief summary would be that the city's banking experience went through two phases. During the first, between 1846 and 1847, as many as three banks of issue came to exist in Cádiz. The first, authorised in January 1846, was then stripped of the right to issue notes, although it continued to operate. A branch of the Bank of Isabel II was established in June of the same year, distributing notes from its parent company, although it had equity of its own. Finally, the conservative government officially authorised a third, independent, bank in December of the same year. This last bank and the branch of the Bank of Isabel II followed the example of Madrid and quickly entered into a merger; an agreement was reached in the summer of 1847, which was ratified by the government on 1 November of the same year. Finally, on 20 January 1848, the first bank in the saga went into liquidation, leaving just one in operation.

Though ephemeral, these competitive projects are an unequivocal sign of the dynamism of the economy of Cádiz. In fact, in the 1860s Cádiz was the province with the highest ratio of banknotes per person. This same dynamism was evident in the measures adopted in response to the legal reforms affecting the operation of the banks of issue introduced by the government in 1849 and 1851.

The information available on the operation of the three main financial entities of the period – the banks of Barcelona and Cádiz, and the Bank of San Fernando – is incomplete, as accounting documentation and some annual reports are missing. Nevertheless, we can gain a general idea of the features of the period. Figures 5.1–5.5 show the main figures on the half-yearly balance sheets of the two provincial banks until June 1856.

The first comment to be made relates to the overall structure of the balance sheet of the two pioneer banks and the proportion maintained between their own and external resources (Figure 5.1). For the period prior to the 1848 crisis, only accounting information for the Bank of Barcelona is available. These data reflect a very rapid growth in the bank's activity, which was supported by both its shareholder equity and resources from customers and the circulation of banknotes. In those first months of activity, the issue capacity established in the statutes was fully capitalised upon, but by the end of 1846 it was also considered necessary to increase the proportion of paid-in capital from 25% to 50% through two successive calls. Some shareholders reminded the board of directors that the commitment to pay in capital was limited to situations of need and that regular increases in credit demand had to be addressed by issuing new shares rather than by requiring additional paid-in capital. The board argued that it believed that the shock wave would be of short duration, and so a temporary request for more paid-in capital was the most appropriate resource to take advantage of an exceptional situation.

The situation, in fact, was one of clear expansion, as is demonstrated by the few available macroeconomic indicators. The industrial production index in Catalonia, for example, recorded an increase of more than 5% per year between 1840 and 1847, and investment in commercial companies rose from an annual average of 2.6 million pesetas in the three-year period 1839–1841 to 11.2 million between 1846 and 1848.[7] In contrast to Madrid, the international crisis of 1847 did not have a serious impact on Barcelona, although the demand for credit fell notably in the second half of the year.

Little is known about the financial activity of the first banks of Cádiz. Some references indicate that the first bank had banknotes in circulation worth almost 2 million pesetas in mid-1847, and that the bank which acted as a branch of the Bank of Isabel II managed to distribute notes worth more than 3 million pesetas, issued by its parent company in Madrid.[8] For the year 1848, the balances of the

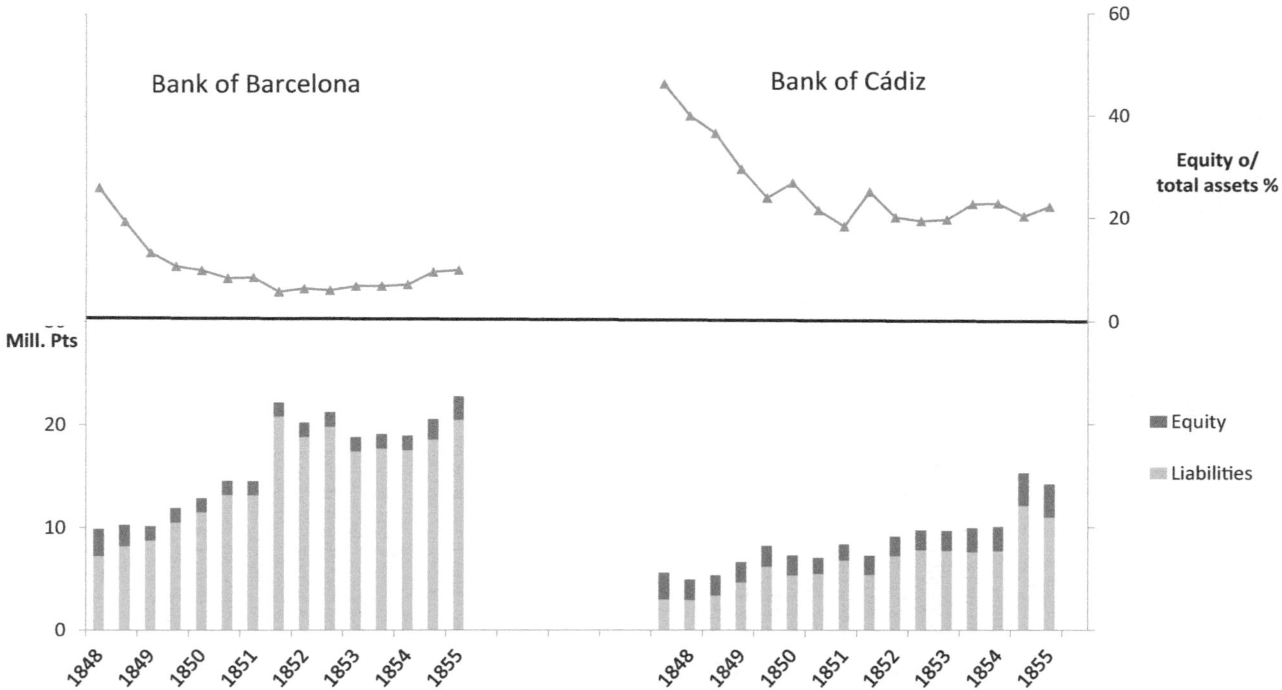

Figure 5.1 The Bank of Barcelona and the Bank of Cádiz: equity and total assets, 1846–1856 (million pesetas)

Note: Sources for banks' data from statements published in the *Gazeta de Madrid* and banks' reports. See Chapter 4.

third bank recorded 2.5 million pesetas in banknotes in circulation in the month of June, a figure that fell slightly to 2.2 million at the end of the same year.

The economic turmoil in Europe in 1847 did not have major consequences for these two provincial banking systems, but the effects of the European political crisis of 1848 were far more serious. In Barcelona there was a real panic, which was only allayed thanks to the personal contributions of members of the bank's board of directors and the positive result of the call to shareholders to pay in another fraction of the company's nominal capital.

Despite passing this test, both banks adopted a far more conservative attitude from that point onwards. The Bank of Barcelona drastically reduced the forms of credit that had been most sensitive to changes in the economic climate, such as loans secured against goods. The losses generated by the failure of some customers to pay were compounded by the losses resulting from the theft of goods that the bank had in deposit as collateral. The board decided not to publicise the real amount of the losses suffered and did not report it at the shareholders' general meeting. In the following years the losses were progressively written off in an accounting operation that ended in 1854. In any case, the bank took five half-year periods to return to the total level of assets it had recorded in December 1847. As for the Bank of Cádiz, it does not seem to have suffered such serious difficulties: in any case it only registered a decrease in the total volume of its assets in the second half of 1848.

The changes introduced by the government in the legislation regarding banks of issue in 1849 and 1851 had a much more lasting effect. We have already mentioned that the aims of this reform were to force the disappearance of the banks of Barcelona and Cádiz as independent entities, and we have noted the resistance that the banks put up against these measures. The banks managed to avoid a forced merger with the Bank of San Fernando, but they could not avoid the strict limitations imposed on the rules for note issue and reserve requirements that their statutes laid down. The new law of 4 May 1849 established the maximum limit for the issue of banknotes with regard to the effective capital of each banking company. In the case of the Bank of Barcelona, the issue limit was cut from 5 to 1.25 million pesetas, since the bank, after the crisis, had decided to return to its starting position in which it maintained 25% of its nominal capital paid in. At the time the new regulations came into force, the Bank of Barcelona had notes in circulation to the value of 4.4 million pesetas.

The case of Bank of Cádiz was slightly different. Although the statutes (amended in July 1847) already established the maximum limit of issue with regard to the amount of effective capital, the fact that the bank had redeemed a part of its issued shares meant that in practice this limit was exceeded. Specifically, as of 30 June 1849, the bank had issued notes for 2.35 million pesetas while its effective capital was 2 million. Overall, then, the new law forced the provincial banks to reduce the means of payment created by more than 50%, from the 6.75 million effectively in circulation in June 1849 to a figure of 3.25 million. Recall that the law of May 1849 limited the value of the banknotes that the Bank of San Fernando could issue to 25 million pesetas.

The effects of these decisions are shown in Figure 5.2. As can be seen, both banks strictly observed the provisions of the law and withdrew their surplus banknotes. The Bank of Barcelona completed its adjustment at the end of 1852, while the Bank of Cádiz had already done so a year earlier. A contraction of this magnitude was to have large-scale effects, both in the currency market and in the credit market.

With regard to the means of payment, the most notable effect of the restriction on the issue of banknotes seems to have been an increase in current accounts. Obviously, each of these instruments operated differently and they can only very roughly be considered substitutes. However, the relationship between the decline of one and the growth of the other seems undeniable. Figure 5.3 shows the evolution of current accounts at each of the banks, while Figure 5.4 shows the evolution of each variable jointly for each bank. Although the two phenomena are interrelated, it is clear that the fall in the issue of banknotes cannot fully explain the increase in current account balances, especially in the case of Barcelona.

For Barcelona, we have more direct proof of the connection between the two variables. As early as 1850, at the first signs of an increase in the number of current accounts (and in the amount of the operations carried out with them), the board of directors of the Bank of Barcelona studied the matter and came to the conclusion that "the circumstance of excessive multiplication of the drafts or

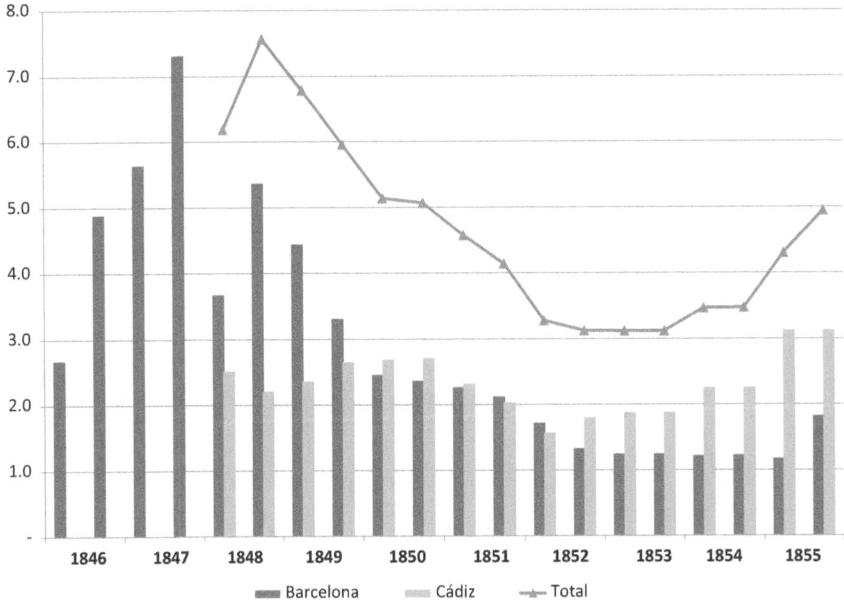

Figure 5.2 The Bank of Barcelona and the Bank of Cádiz: banknotes in circulation, 1846–1856 (million pesetas)

Note: Sources for banks' data from statements published in the *Gazeta de Madrid* and banks' reports. See Chapter 4.

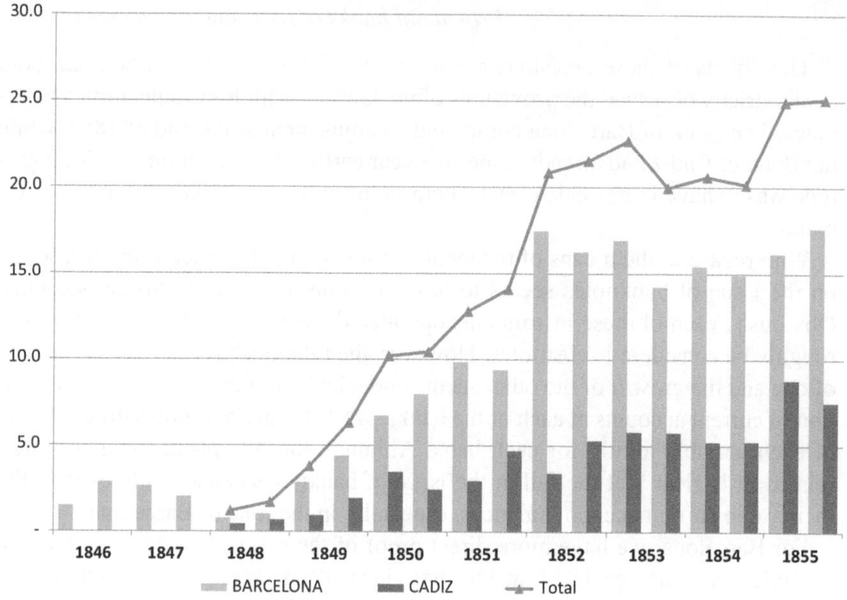

Figure 5.3 The Bank of Barcelona and the Bank of Cádiz: current accounts, 1846–1856 (million pesetas)

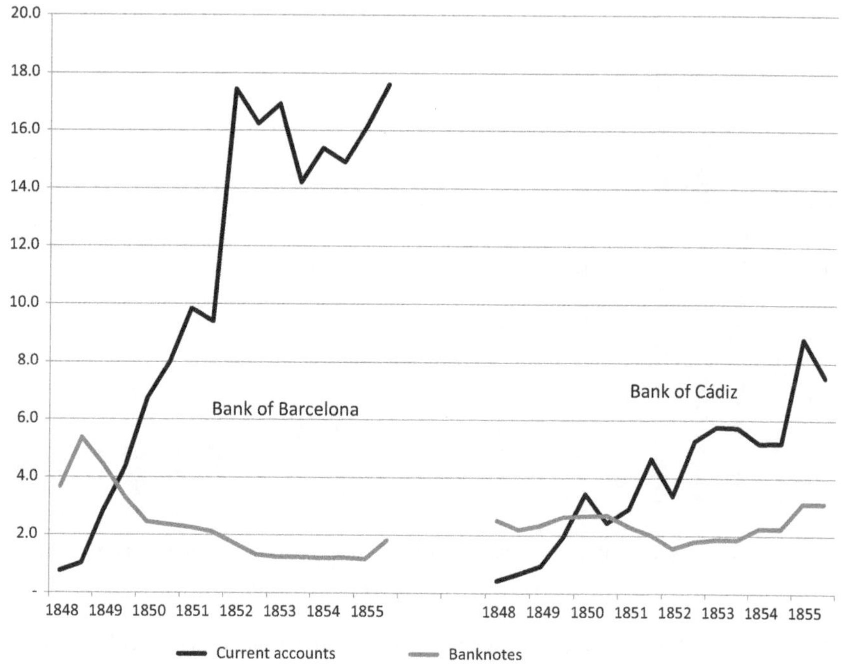

Figure 5.4 The Bank of Barcelona and the Bank of Cádiz: banknotes in circulation and current accounts, 1848–1856 (million pesetas)

Note: Sources for banks' data from statements published in the *Gazeta de Madrid* and banks' reports. See Chapter 4.

cheques by their holders [was produced] by the natural effect of the shortage of banknotes". Bankers were always apprehensive about this "inappropriate" use of current accounts, which in their opinion increased both the volume of work that the bank's employees had to do and the risks that the bank assumed. In early 1855, when the situation had become untenable and the new government appeared to be more receptive, the bank asked for authorisation for "the urgent issue of one million duros in notes from this Bank against an equal amount of cash that the Bank will set aside in its coffers in exclusive guarantee of payment of said banknotes". The aim was no longer to increase credit, but simply to provide a sufficient supply of means of payment, the shortage of which was distorting the market. The government refused the bank's request. The legal reform that would transform the Spanish financial market was already underway and the government must have thought that in this new, much less restrictive framework the problems mentioned by the bank would soon be resolved.

Obviously, there was another way to satisfy the public demand for banknotes – which was to increase the effective capital, either by increasing the paid-in capital per share or by issuing more shares. Neither option was adopted by the Bank of Barcelona until 1854. In the first case, the complaints of some shareholders regarding the decisions taken in 1847 on paying in additional capital gave the board of directors food for thought. These shareholders argued, justifiably, that the bank's philosophy implied that the portion of the capital that had not been paid in could only be called up in situations of risk to the entity, either in the case of a sudden panic or an unsuccessful operation. The board of directors eventually accepted these criticisms, especially after the persistent reduction in the bank's profits after the crisis of 1848. An increase in the number of shares – the other alternative – did not appear very attractive to shareholders either, as it might undermine the share yield if the provided resources were not profitably used. In short, all indications are that the Bank of Barcelona was more than satisfied with its privileged situation and allowed the local market of means of payment to degenerate to the point of encouraging the circulation of various kinds of paper that could be used as banknotes. As a senior finance ministry official recalled in a subsequent report,

> [. . .] before the Credit companies and Savings Banks went to cover those needs [of means of payment] with their obligations, registered cheques, and payment orders, some simple currency exchangers without the least responsibility and no other assets or possessions than some pinewood tables set up in the public squares gave in exchange for gold and silver simple IOUs that some rejected, but the majority accepted.[9]

The debate about the policies adopted by the banks and their appropriateness should not make us forget that the great majority of the bankers' decisions responded more to the movements of the markets or to the changes in the institutional variables than to strategies drawn up beforehand. In any case, the point we should try to establish is whether during this period the two existing provincial banks, in one way or another, carried out the essential function of any bank of issue – that is, to provide the society with the amount of money necessary for the proper development of commercial activities.

Figure 5.5 shows an estimate of the net money created by the two banks over this period. The calculation system used is very simple, but it has some limitations. As is well known, the definition of money is a convention that tends to vary depending on the analytical objective pursued. The very high degree of disaggregation available today of the various monetary instruments according to their degree of liquidity and other characteristics makes it possible to carry out extremely refined analyses, but a precise knowledge of the functioning of each monetary instrument is beyond the reach of historians. Thus, for example, it is difficult to determine the degree of liquidity of the current accounts, or whether the cash deposits were in fact payable on demand or if they required prior notice, as indicated by the bank's rules. We do not even know the level of acceptance of the notes issued by the banks.[10] Our estimate of the 'money created' by the banks of issue is based on adding up the banknotes in circulation and the current accounts and subtracting the coin and bullion in their coffers.

Figure 5.5 shows an irregular evolution, albeit with an unmistakable upward trend. Note, however, that the trajectory of each of the banks considered differs substantially both in terms of the rate of overall growth and, particularly, in the

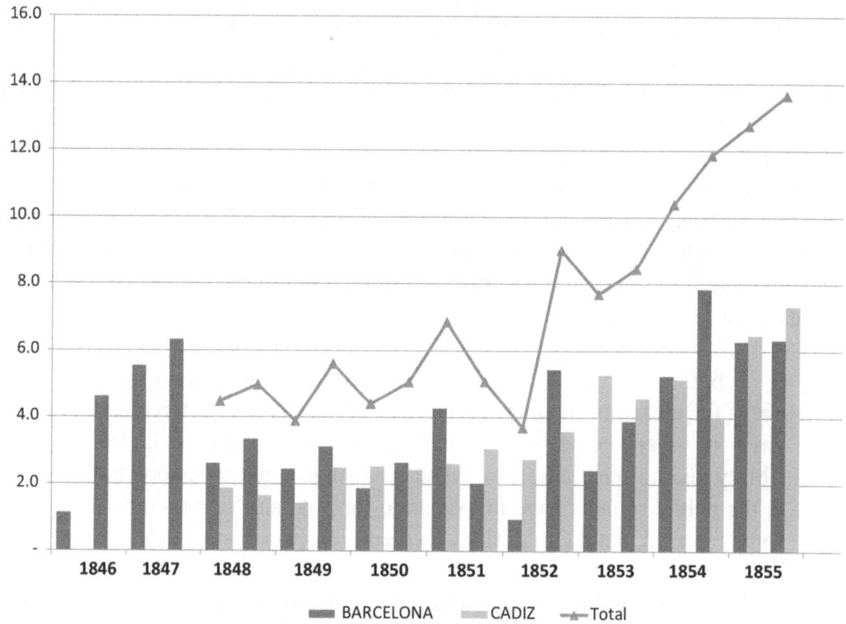

Figure 5.5 The Bank of Barcelona and the Bank of Cádiz: money created, 1846–1856 (million pesetas)

Note: Sources for banks' data from statements published in the *Gazeta de Madrid* and banks' reports. See Chapter 4.

half-yearly variability. Despite its greater size, the Bank of Barcelona presents extreme instability in terms of the net supply of money. The situation of near collapse in 1848 was prolonged by the forced adaptation to the new banking regulations and had become far more intense by 1852. Nor did the subsequent recovery remain steady: the peak of late 1854 (almost 8 million pesetas) preceded another fall (of 30%!) in the following half-year periods, even though these were moments of extreme financial stress at the local level.

In comparison, the evolution of the Bank of Cádiz followed the progress of the markets much more closely. We should note that both entities were providing their respective markets with very similar amounts of money, despite the differences in population and income. Indeed, if we take as a reference the close of June 1854, we see that while the levels of monetary circulation were clearly higher in Cádiz, Barcelona was well ahead in terms of current accounts. The joint result in net terms (the money created) was also higher in the province of Cádiz, both in relation to the population and to the level of income (Table 5.1).

Although at first these figures may appear surprising, they reflect this first phase of the introduction of modern financial instruments. The use of bank money at the time was strictly limited to the commercial sphere and, in fact, both the authorities and the credit institutions themselves took measures to prevent its proliferation outside professional groups. For this reason, they imposed relatively high minimum amounts for banknotes and limited the opening of current accounts to people who could demonstrate a commercial or professional activity. Under these conditions, the greater commercial concentration of Cádiz prevailed over the much more diversified structure of the province of Barcelona.

Much the same could be said about the other fundamental function of banking, the granting of credit. Figure 5.6 shows the evolution of the two entities' portfolios

Table 5.1 Means of payment offered by provincial banks of issue (30 June 1854)

		Barcelona	*Cádiz*
Banknotes in circulation			
• Total	Million ptas	1.2	2.3
• Per inhabitant	Pesetas	1.7	5.6
• Per 1,000 pts of GDP	Pesetas	3.0	8.4
Current accounts			
• Total	Million ptas	15.4	5.2
• Per inhabitant	Pesetas	21.2	13.0
• Per 1,000 pts of GDP	Pesetas	38.4	19.5
Money created			
• Total	Million ptas	5.2	5.1
• Per inhabitant	Pesetas	7.2	12.8
• Per 1,000 pts of GDP	Pesetas	13.1	19.2

Source: Provincial population and GDP for 1860

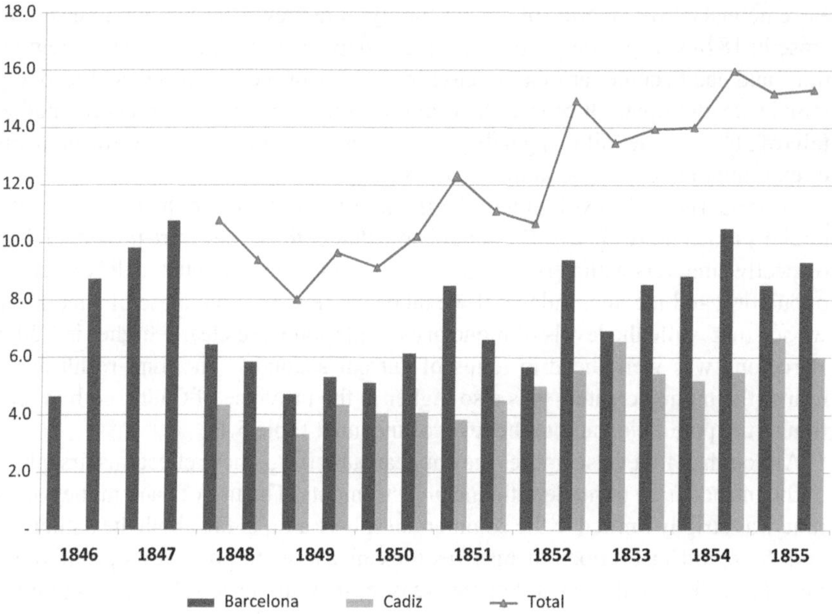

Figure 5.6 The Bank of Barcelona and the Bank of Cádiz: discounts and loans (million pesetas)

Note: Sources for banks' data from statements published in the *Gazeta de Madrid* and banks' reports. See Chapter 4.

and their total. After the crisis of 1848, which affected Barcelona but not Cádiz, the trend is clearly upward, even though the Bank of Barcelona shows the same erratic performance already mentioned in the creation of money. We have details about credit policy for the Bank of Barcelona, but not for the Bank of Cádiz.

Table 5.2 shows the changes in the credit granted by the Bank of Barcelona. The discounting of bills and promissory notes represented around 50% of the total in the 1850s, the rest being loans against goods or securities. The discounts constituted what in the internal jargon of the bank were termed credit 'on signatures' and were granted, in principle, on the sole guarantee of the supposed solvency of the person making the discount. For these purposes, the bank 'qualified' its customers by granting them a maximum discount limit. These rating lists, which were constantly updated, contained around 500 individuals and companies over this period.

Besides discount, the Bank of Barcelona offered also loans in the form of promissory notes backed by securities or goods (raw or manufactured cotton, colonial foodstuffs, etc.). These guaranties had to be placed in the bank or under the bank's supervision.

As can be seen in Table 5.2, before the crisis of 1848, the bank lent considerable amounts on raw and manufactured goods, mainly raw cotton or fabrics. The crisis

Table 5.2 Credit granted by the Bank of Barcelona (1847–1854)

	1847		*1851*		*1854*	
	Million Ptas	*%*	*Million Ptas*	*%*	*Million Ptas*	*%*
Discounts of bills and promissory notes	14.8	30.1	22.5	50.4	23.2	45.2
Loans against:						
raw materials (cotton)	9.7	19.7	3.6	8.1	3.1	6.0
colonial goods	1.4	2.8	0.2	0.5	0.9	1,8
manufactured goods	4.5	9.2	–	–		
debt securities	10.1	20.6	11.8	26.6	10.8	21.0
shares	8.6	17.5	6.4	14.3	13.3	25.9
Total	49.2	100.0	44.6	100.0	51.3	100.0

Source: Blasco-Martel and Sudrià (2010, pp. 129–130, 190)

came to show that in an economy so dependent on the cotton industry it was easy for a general contraction of economic activity to coincide with a fall in the prices of raw materials and intermediate or finished products in that industry. For the bank this could mean (in addition to the increased risk of default of many of its clients) a fall in the market value of the goods securing the loans, and the storage and preservation of these products represented a considerable cost and risk. As a result, transactions of this kind were limited, and only recovered (and then only partially) when a company was set up in Barcelona dedicated to the storage of merchandise and the issue of warrants of deposit, which the bank could discount under the usual conditions.

In these years, it should also be noted that the bank extended the acceptance of the shares of joint-stock companies listed on the Barcelona Stock Exchange as a guarantee. This move was crucial to the development of companies of this kind, a phenomenon closely linked to the development of modern capitalism itself. The bank internally agreed on a maximum limit of shares that it was willing to accept as collateral for each company, in order to avoid an excessive concentration of risk.

These first steps in modern provincial banking, though modest in terms of the number of entities and their size, meant that two of the most prominent commercial centres in the country now had formal credit institutions which, apparently at least, were managed in a professional way and with a thorough knowledge of banking techniques.[11] To close this first section, it may be of interest to compare this still incipient activity of the provincial banks with the activity of Spain's first bank, the Bank of San Fernando.

The data displayed in Figure 5.7 summarise the differences in the activities of the Bank of San Fernando and the two provincial banks created in the mid-1840s. The close relationship of San Fernando with the state and with public businesses certainly made a difference. The enormous distance between the circulation of banknotes accredited by the Bank of San Fernando and those issued by the other

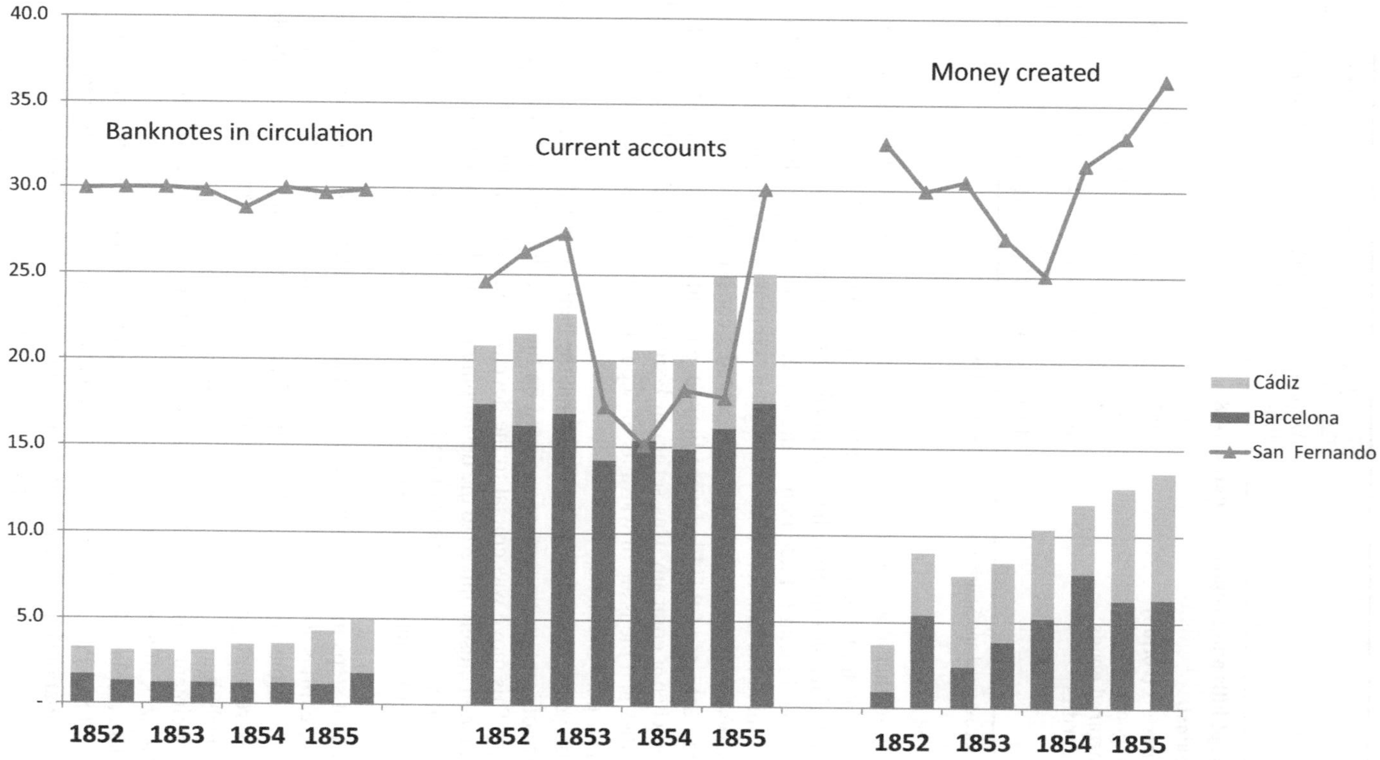

Figure 5.7 Banknotes in circulation, current accounts and money created by the banks of issue (million pesetas)

Note: Sources for banks' data from statements published in the *Gazeta de Madrid* and banks' reports. See Chapter 4.

two banks is striking: naturally, this was a direct reflection of the capital that each entity had accumulated. Recall that the reform approved by law on 15 December 1851 fixed the maximum total value of banknotes that could be issued with regard to a bank's paid-in capital: thus, the maximum issue was 30 million pesetas for the Bank of San Fernando, and 3.1 million for the two provincial banks of issue combined.

It is safe to suppose that banknotes were used differently in Madrid than they were in the commercial centres. The mere fact that banknotes could be used to make payments to the state gave them a use value that they would certainly not have had if their acceptance depended on the willingness of the contracting parties. We must remember, however, that for Barcelona at least there is evidence that the circulation of banknotes offered by the local bank in those years did not cover the demand for means of payment in the local market. So, the differences in the use of banknotes were due to public business, but also to a clear reluctance on the part of the most important bank of issue after San Fernando to supply these notes to the trading community in which it held a monopoly.

With regard to current accounts, the recorded amounts differ less, and in certain years the provincial banks collected more current account deposits than the Bank of San Fernando. In a way this finding corroborates the point we have just mentioned: it was their use in transactions with the government that made banknotes particularly useful in Madrid. The behaviour of its current accounts, which could only be used between individuals, was quite similar to that recorded in the other two cities. Nor should we forget that a part of those current accounts in the provincial markets substituted for banknotes, which were in short supply.

Finally, as regards the evolution of the net money created, clear differences can be seen between Madrid on the one hand and Cádiz and Barcelona on the other. While in the two provincial cities a steady upward trend is observed, in the capital the contraction of 1854 was particularly intense. The scarce number of years for which we can make the comparison makes it impossible to determine whether this is a temporary phenomenon or a pattern of behaviour. We must bear in mind the significant role of the state as a demander of funds, and the crowding-out effect that this role might have had on the economy of the country as a whole.[12] We will return to this subject in our analysis of the boom in issue plurality that began in 1856.

5.2. The plurality of issue expands: the banking system of 1856

The law of 1851 enabled the government to authorise new banks of issue in the provinces which had none at the time. However, the successive finance ministers of the so-called moderate party maintained the restrictive policy initiated in 1845 and turned down applications submitted by various groups of businessmen from Málaga, Jerez and Santander. The Bank of San Fernando, keen to expand, pressed for a legislative change that would allow it to extend its field of operation.[13]

This explains why, when the progressives came to power in July 1854, the subject of banks of issue was particularly controversial. A succession of proposals for the reform of the legal framework of the banking system were put forward. The Banking Act of 1856 established a system of juxtaposed monopolies, in which each bank had the exclusive power of issue in the territory assigned to it. Thus, on paper at least, there was no possible competition between the banknotes. As we will see later, competition did indeed arise – not between the banknotes issued by the authorised banks, but between the banknotes of certain banks and the monetary instruments issued by other financial intermediaries such as credit companies, exchange houses and private banking houses.

The law included an initial list of nine cities where a local bank with the power to issue banknotes should be created – or, failing that, a branch of the Bank of Spain. These cities were A Coruña, Alicante, Bilbao, Málaga, Santander, Seville, Valencia, Valladolid and Zaragoza. The first entity to seize the opportunity was the *Crédito Mobiliario Español*, a firm created under the Credit Companies Act, which had been approved on the same day as the Banks of Issue Act. The *Crédito Mobiliario Español* was set up and controlled by the Pereire brothers, the owners of the famous *Crédit Mobilier* in Paris. The company itself explained the events in the report presented to its shareholders on 30 May 1857:

> We requested authorisation from the government to found banks in several points indicated in the same law, namely: Seville, Valencia, Santander, Valladolid, Bilbao, Alicante, La Coruña and Zaragoza. The project was well received by the government, but not in the provinces, where, either spontaneously or encouraged, an opposition so strong was manifested that, however unjustified we believed it to be . . . we decided to abandon our plan.[14]

With the failure of this nationwide operation, local interests came into play. Between June 1856 and November 1857, seven of the nine banks listed in the law received authorisation from the government and obtained the funds necessary to start business. In 1858, the Bank of Spain was authorised to open branches in the cities of Valencia (in March) and Alicante (in May), which did not have independent banks at the time. There were no new approvals of banks of issue until October 1859, when the Bank of Jerez received permission to open. Another time span of almost three years followed until June 1862, when the last phase began, involving ten entities: the banks of San Sebastián, Reus, Burgos, Pamplona, Oviedo, Vitoria, Palencia, Santiago, Bank Balear (Majorca) and Tarragona, the last bank approved, in June 1864.

We know that the government chose these nine cities on the advice of the Bank of San Fernando; but we do not know why some subsequent requests were accepted (up to ten) and others rejected.[15] In this second phase, it seems that the government limited itself to checking compliance with the requirements established by law and to approving the corresponding statutes and regulations. In any event, the fact is that the process of the spread of banknotes and modern banking reflected the performance of the indicators of economic activity only partially. Table 5.3 shows the top 20 provinces according to various tax criteria and GDP. The indicators used are the following: a) the sum of each province's share of the

Table 5.3 The top 20 Spanish provinces in 1860

	*Territorial plus industrial and commercial contribution tax**	*Industrial and commercial contribution tax**	*Estimated GDP*
1	**Madrid**	**Madrid**	**Barcelona**
2	**Barcelona**	**Barcelona**	**Madrid**
3	**Seville**	**Cádiz**	*Granada*
4	**Valencia**	**Seville**	**Cádiz**
5	**Cádiz**	**Valencia**	**Valencia**
6	**Zaragoza**	**Zaragoza**	**Málaga**
7	**Málaga**	**Málaga**	**Seville**
8	*Córdoba*	**Valladolid**	**Zaragoza**
9	*Toledo*	**Tarragona**	**A Coruña**
10	*Badajoz*	**Alicante**	*Murcia*
11	*Granada*	*Toledo*	**Alicante**
12	**A Coruña**	*Granada*	*Jaén*
13	*Jaen*	**A Coruña**	*Almeria*
14	**Alicante**	**Santander**	*Córdoba*
15	**Tarragona**	*Córdoba*	*Badajoz*
16	*Murcia*	*Murcia*	**Navarre**
17	**Valladolid**	*Badajoz*	**Tarragona**
18	*Ciudad-Real*	**Burgos**	**Oviedo**
19	*Cáceres*	**Balearic Isl.**	*Toledo*
20	*Leon*	*Girona*	**Balearic Isl.**

* The provinces with their own tax systems (Navarre, Gipuzkoa, Araba/Álava and Biscay) are not included.

Province	**With banks of issue created before 1856**
Province	**With banks of issue or Bank of Spain branches created between 1856 and 1858**
Province	**With banks of issue created after 1858**

Sources: *Anuario Estadístico de España* and GDP data kindly provided by Julio Martínez Galarraga (see Rosés et al. 2010)

land contribution and the industrial and commercial contribution taxes; b) each province's share of the industrial and commercial contribution tax only; and c) an estimate of each province's GDP. As can be seen, the indicator that reflects most closely the selection made is the share of industrial and commercial contribution only: this is as to be expected, given the close relationship in those years between trade and finance.

It is more difficult to explain the absence (both in this initial group and in the group of banks that were subsequently authorised) of cities such as Granada, Toledo, Murcia, Córdoba and Badajoz, which made higher contributions as tax-payers and had a higher level of income than others that did have a bank of issue, such as Palencia, Burgos, Oviedo or even Santander, which is present in only one of the three lists considered. The indications are that, in the first list, maritime trade was considered a key factor: of the 12 cities that had a bank of issue in 1858, once the first provisions of the law were fulfilled, only 3 (Madrid, Zaragoza and Valladolid) did not have direct access to the sea.

The economic heterogeneity of the cities in which banks of issue were established also had an undoubted influence on the level of activity that they attained in the immediately following years. Table 5.4 shows the total assets of each bank at the end of 1864, the peak year of the system's expansion, and its relationship with the number of inhabitants and with the income level of the respective province. Taken together, the figures suggest the existence of two groups of banks, divided according to the amount of their assets. The group with fewer assets comprised nine entities: the banks of A Coruña, Pamplona, Burgos, Oviedo, Palencia, Santiago, Reus, Tarragona and Bank Balear. All of them, except for A Coruña, had been created after 1862 and, therefore, had been in operation for less than two years at the end of 1864.

As for the remaining 11, the clear hegemony of the Bank of Barcelona in absolute terms is significantly reduced when we relate the assets of the banks to the population or to the income level of each province. In both cases, the Bank of Bilbao emerges as the entity with the greatest relative importance followed by the two Cádiz banks, in banking assets per capita, and by the Bank of Santander in assets per unit of GDP. Interestingly, all these cities presented a strong commercial specialisation in those years, ahead of others such as Málaga or Barcelona itself, where industrial activity was significant. If the calculation is done in regional terms, using the limits of the current autonomous communities, the result is not very different. Now Andalusia is the region with the most banks (4) and the most banking assets, surpassing Catalonia; however, the positions of predominance in relative terms are held by the Basque Country and Cantabria, a considerable distance ahead of a second regional group comprising Catalonia, Andalusia and Aragon. The relative levels are lower in the remaining regions, even those such as Castile-León and Galicia, which had several banks in their territories (Table 5.5).

Naturally enough, the role played by the provincial banks of issue in each region and in Spain as a whole was also conditioned by the existence of other financial entities competing with them either directly or indirectly. As already mentioned, the law that allowed the proliferation of banks of issue was approved on the same

Table 5.4 Total assets of provincial banks of issue, 1864

Banks	*Total assets*	*Total assets per inhabitant*		*Total assets per 1,000 ptas of GDP*	
	Thousands of pts	*Province*	*pesetas*	*Province*	*pesetas*
Barcelona	24,341	Biscay	59	Biscay	159
Cádiz	19,472	Cádiz	56	Santander	102
Seville	13,654	Barcelona	34	Cádiz	84
Zaragoza	12,480	Zaragoza	32	Zaragoza	78
Málaga	11,907	Santander	31	Gipuzkoa	63
Bilbao	9,962	Seville	29	Barcelona	61
Santander	6,786	Málaga	27	Valladolid	54
Valladolid	5,402	Valladolid	22	Seville	54
San Sebastián	3,317	Gipuzkoa	20	Málaga	46
A Coruña	3,193	Araba/Álava	14	Araba/Álava	45
Jerez	2,932	Tarragona	10	A Coruña	29
Pamplona	1,986	A Coruña	8	Tarragona	28
Balear	1,964	Balearic Isl.	7	Balearic Isl.	19
Reus	1,727	Navarre	7	Navarre	17
Burgos	1,604	Palencia	6	Burgos	16
Oviedo	1,509	Burgos	5	Palencia	15
Tarragona	1,458	Oviedo	3	Oviedo	14
Vitoria	1,395				
Santiago	1,317	Total	22	Total	52
Palencia	1,114				
Total	127,520				

Sources: GDP data kindly provided by Julio Martínez Galarraga (see Rosés et al. 2010)

Table 5.5 Total assets of banks of issue according to region, 1864

	Total assets	*Per inhabitant*		*Per 1,000 pts of GDP*	
	'000 pesetas	*Region*	*pesetas*	*Region*	*pesetas*
Andalusia	47,964	Basque Country	34	Santander	102
Catalonia	27,526	Cantabria	31	Basque Country	100
Basque Country	14,675	Catalonia	16	Catalonia	39
Aragon	12,480	Andalusia	16	Aragon	37
Castile-León	8,121	Aragon	14	Andalusia	32
Cantabria	6,786	Balearic Isl.	7	Balearic Isl.	19
Galicia	4,509	Navarre	7	Navarre	17
Navarre	1,986	Castile-León	4	Galicia	14
Balearic Isl.	1,964	Asturias	3	Oviedo	14
Asturias	1,509	Galicia	3	Castile-León	12
Regions*	127,520		11		31
Bank of Spain	209,540				
Total Spain	337,060		22		58

*Regions with independent banks of issue

Sources: *Anuario Estadístico de España* and GDP data kindly provided by Julio Martínez Galarraga (see Rosés et al. 2010)

day as the Credit Companies Act, which paved the way for the creation of a large number of credit companies throughout Spain. Table 5.6 shows the capital paid in by each type of bank in each location in 1864.

The first point to highlight is the importance of the change in the legislative framework of the financial system introduced in 1856. Of the 58 banking corporations in operation in 1864, only 5 had existed before this change, and only 4 of the 27 cities which now had a banking establishment had had one before 1856. The second point to note is the higher rate of paid-in capital in the credit companies than in the banks of issue. However, it should be borne in mind that in general the banks of issue presented a much higher degree of leverage than the credit companies. For example, in the same years, shareholder equity represented around 22% of the total in both the Bank of Spain and the Bank of Barcelona, compared with a figure of 85% in the Crédito Mobiliario Español and 35% in the Barcelona credit companies.[16]

The main business interest of most of these credit companies was the railway. In some cases, they were promoters of railway lines, in others they acted as contractors and, in almost all cases, as financial agents. This explains in part why towns characteristically associated with the railway like Valladolid, Santander and Bilbao had several credit companies. With regard to Catalonia, it should

Table 5.6 Joint-stock banking companies: paid-in capital, 1864

	Banks of issue	*Credit companies**		*TOTAL*
	Paid-in capital		*Paid-in capital*	*Paid-in capital*
	Million Pts	*N°.*	*Million Pts*	*Million Pts*
Barcelona	5.00	6	36.25	41.25
Valladolid	1.50	3	22.20	23.70
Santander	1.75	2	8.40	10.15
Bilbao	2.50	2	6.75	9.25
Valencia**		4	8.00	8.00
Cádiz	5.00	2	2.35	7.35
Seville	4.00	1	1.25	5.25
Jerez de la Frontera	1.50	1	1.00	2.50
Pamplona	1.10	1	0.60	1.70
Banks of issue in towns without credit companies (13)	13.60			13.60
Credit companies in towns without banks of issue (4)		4	4.00	4.00
Total Spain (bar Madrid)	35.95	26	90.80	126.75
Madrid	40.70	11	192.90	233.60
Total Spain	**76.65**	**37**	**283.70**	**360.35**

* Including banks covered by the general legislation on joint-stock companies
** The branches of the Bank of Spain had no assigned capital
Source: Tortella (1973, pp. 108–109)

be recalled that practically all the railway lines were financed internally, which helps to explain the existence of four credit companies and two discount houses in Barcelona. Some credit companies engaged in other businesses, ranging from the construction of canals and property development to the exploitation of timber.[17] However, neither the railways nor most other businesses attained the levels of profits expected, and from 1863 onwards the credit companies faced serious financial difficulties; as we will see below, they were deeply affected by the crisis that reached its peak in mid-1866.

As for the relations between the banks of issue and the credit companies, a distinction should be made between the interactions that occurred via the financial market and those of an institutional nature. In the financial context, credit companies started to issue quasi-banknotes, that is, financial assets that were used as currency, a practice that flouted the differentiation that the legislator had sought to impose in 1856. Indeed, article 4 of the Banks of Issue Act established that "in each locality, only one issuing establishment may be created, either a private bank or a branch of the Bank of Spain". However, the Credit Companies Act authorised credit firms to issue bearer and short-term bonds of not less than one month. It was easy for this type of short-term bond to circulate like banknotes; indeed, some members of parliament drew attention to this, but their warnings were ignored.[18] As a result, in several cities the bank of issue and local credit companies competed to issue banknotes. The best-known case is Barcelona, where, in the months prior to the crisis of 1866, quasi-banknotes were issued by no less than half a dozen banking entities, some of them private in nature. Their presence angered the Bank of Barcelona, which now had difficulties in placing its own banknotes on the market.[19]

While some banks and credit companies clashed over the right to issue, others established mechanisms of cooperation. The agreements signed between the Bank of Barcelona and *Crédito Mercantil* and later *El Comercio* are well-known examples: the two credit companies agreed to place Bank of Barcelona banknotes on the market, which the bank gave them under guarantee. In fact, the bank assigned part of its own credit capacity to *Crédito Mercantil* and *El Comercio* on the understanding that these firms could offer customers much more favourable and flexible conditions than the Bank itself.[20] Other forms of cooperation were much more dangerous and irregular: for example, transactions with companies in which some or all of the directors of the bank of issue had interests. The most common mechanism consisted of transferring part or all of the credit company's portfolio to the bank, which might include highly depreciated bonds that were accepted at their face value or, at any event, above their market price. The bank's ability to issue banknotes managed to postpone the crisis, but there was always a serious risk that the bank itself would eventually be dragged down by it.

Despite the management problems they experienced and the irregularities that some committed, the credit companies played a decisive role in the financial modernisation that took place in Spain in the third quarter of the nineteenth century. Their main contribution was undoubtedly their role in the mobilisation of previously hoarded savings through the placement of bonds, stocks and other modern financial assets. The extraordinary availability of resources that resulted was used essentially in the construction of the railway network. Some authors have recently suggested that the role of domestic capital in financing the investment boom of those years was greater than had previously been believed.[21]

5.3. Dimensions of the new banks: capital, money and credit

After establishing the scale and the characteristics of the banking expansion promoted by the 1856 reform, we should now try to assess its economic impact. To do so, in this section we analyse the joint evolution of the most significant items on the banks' balance sheets during the period 1856–1868, and compare them with those corresponding to the Bank of Spain and other indicators.

Figure 5.8 shows the evolution of the equity of the banks of issue during this period. As can be seen, and apart from the initial years, there were two main periods in which their equity rose considerably – between 1860 and 1861 and throughout 1864. On both occasions the increase was due to the entry of new banks. In fact, between 1857 and 1866 no provincial bank of issue increased its capital. The Bank of Spain did so in 1864: in two phases it raised its capital from 30 to 50 million pesetas in response to the difficulties it faced in trying to maintain the convertibility of its banknotes, and the harsh criticisms it received for failing to do so.[22] In any case, it is clear that the provincial banks doubled the resources of the banking system – a significant development, especially since it took place in cities which had previously lacked any entities of a certain size able to supply credit.

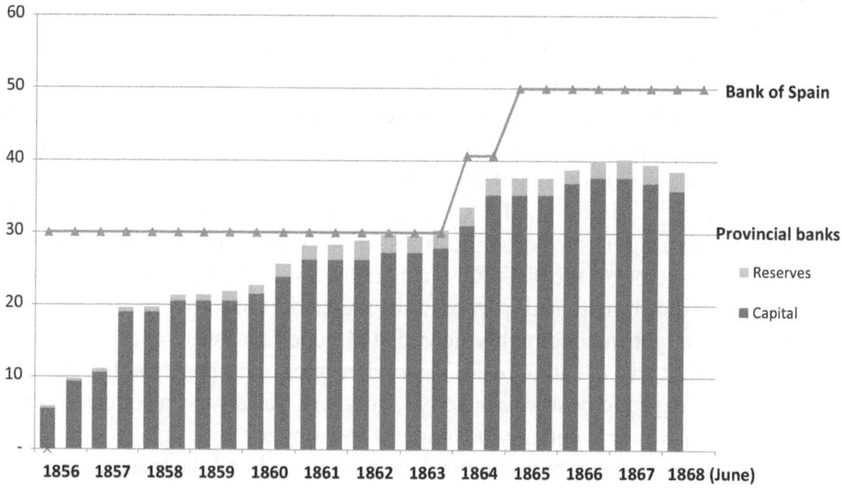

Figure 5.8 Banks of issue: equity, 1856–1868 (million pesetas)

Note: Sources for banks' data from statements published in the *Gazeta de Madrid* and banks' reports. See Chapter 4.

The variability is far greater in relation to the external resources obtained by the banks of issue. Figure 5.9 shows their evolution between 1856 and 1868. The huge difference between the Bank of Spain on the one hand and the provincial banks of issue on the other is immediately evident. After the initial phase of implementation, and after the crisis of 1857–1858, the provincial banks had raised close to 80 million pesetas, a level they maintained, with slight fluctuations, until the end of 1868. The Bank of Spain, however, experienced strong variations in the amount of resources it obtained, with highs close to 120 million and lows of 80 and 60 million. Such disparate behaviour shows that the forces that impacted on the financial market in Madrid were different from those affecting the markets of other Spanish cities.

The reasons for this difference can be analysed better if we distinguish between the main instruments that these entities could use to attract resources: the issue of banknotes, and the maintenance of current accounts. Figure 5.10 shows the evolution of these figures for the Bank of Spain and the banks of issue. This closer perspective also shows that the differences affected both the Bank of Spain and the banks of issue, so they cannot be attributed to the particular features of either. Indeed, we see that both the banknotes in circulation and the current accounts oscillated much more markedly in the Bank of Spain than in the provincial banks. The balance sheets of the Bank of Spain reported sharp falls in banknotes in circulation and in current accounts between 1859 and 1861 (30%), in banknotes between 1864 and 1866 (35%) and in current accounts between 1863 and 1864

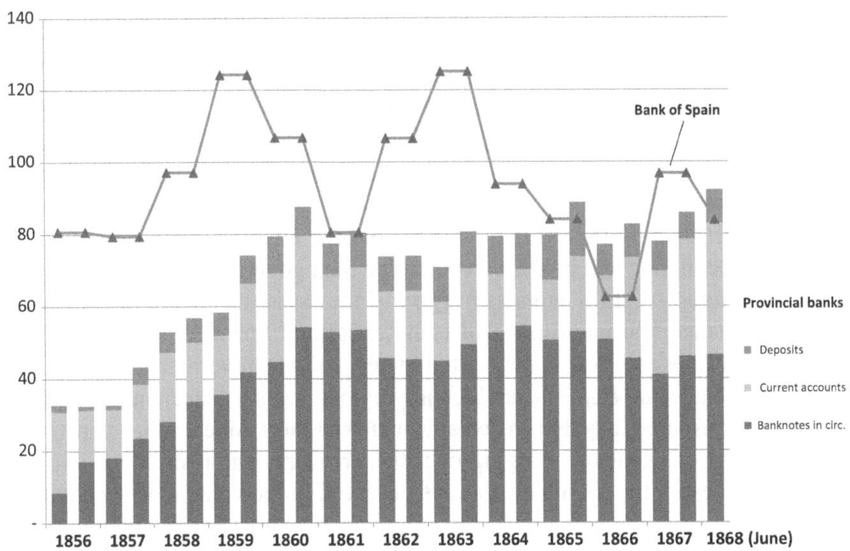

Figure 5.9 Banks of issue: liabilities, 1856–1868 (million pesetas)

Note: Sources for banks' data from statements published in the *Gazeta de Madrid* and banks' reports. See Chapter 4.

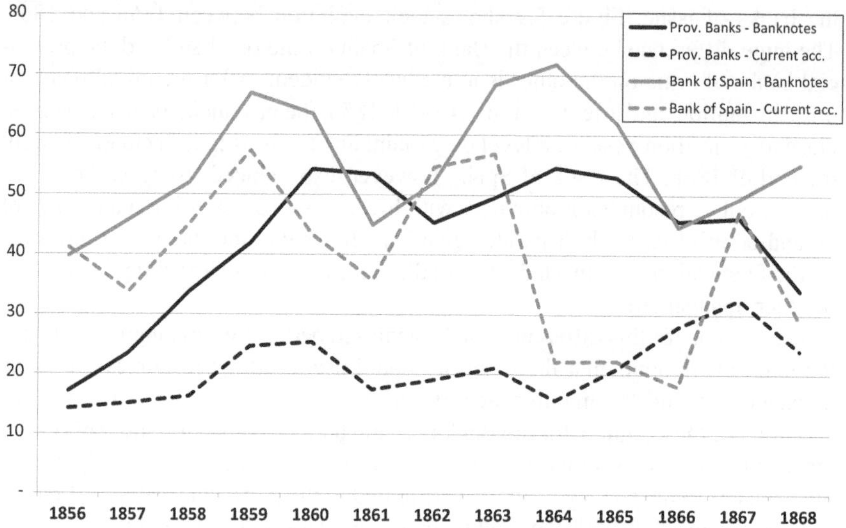

Figure 5.10 Banks of issue: banknotes in circulation and current accounts (million pesetas)

Note: Sources for banks' data from statements published in the *Gazeta de Madrid* and banks' reports. See Chapter 4.

(more than 50%), but no falls of this intensity were recorded by the provincial banks.

These were years of severe difficulties for the Bank of Spain, and these difficulties were responsible for the sharp fluctuations that we see in their accounts. The bank faced serious problems in meeting its obligations in mid-1861. In April of that year, under pressure from the growing demand for cash, the board of directors decided to make all its payments in banknotes and maintain a single counter open for the conversion of banknotes into coins. The measure alarmed holders of banknotes who rushed to convert their money, and the ensuing "queue" became the subject of economic and political debate. The then governor of the bank, Ramón Santillán, noted several factors as triggers of the crisis: the deficit in the current account balance; the interruption of commercial and financial flows with Cuba as a result of the civil war in the United States; and the government's decision to clean up the *Caja de Depósitos*, which in previous years had accumulated a large quantity of resources payable on demand or at very short notice, which constituted a real sword of Damocles hanging over the Treasury. The restrictions imposed could not prevent the sharp contractions observed in the volume of banknotes in circulation and in the current accounts between the end of 1859 and the end of 1861.[23]

After a few months of calm, liquidity tensions appeared again in early 1863. On this occasion, Santillán blamed the fall in foreign exchange rates, which led to a flow of cash abroad, especially to France. But he also censured some provincial banks for "the large sums that were extracted from the Bank, mainly for the banks of Seville and Cádiz which were in the greatest difficulties, and for the bank in Bilbao, which had continued to feed on our cash ever since the works of the railway from that city to Miranda and Tudela began."[24] The exchange of banknotes once again suffered restrictions, and they once again were traded at below par in the informal market. In June 1864 a new attempt to remove the limitations on the conversion of banknotes into cash ended in resounding failure, as the Bank of Spain itself acknowledged.[25] Again, the circulation of banknotes contracted, and many clients reduced the balances of their current accounts. The problem persisted until after the crisis of 1866.

The reasons given by Santillán and by the bank itself to justify its liquidity problems seem plausible, but they are not borne out by other indicators. Firstly, this was clearly a period of expansion. To quote Luis María Pastor, an expert in the subject, "the country is calm, industry and commerce are moving steadily forward, agriculture is thriving, public works are advancing, the Bank is prosperous. . . . And yet, banknotes cannot be exchanged . . . an obligation so peremptory, so sacred, cannot be fulfilled". And he concludes, "the cause of the conflict . . . in which the Bank finds itself does not come from external causes; it is necessary to look for it in the very heart of the situation."[26]

A second indication along the same lines is the fact that the other banks of issue did not suffer similar problems in these years. In fact, one might have expected the effects of an imbalance in the foreign balance of payments to appear earlier in the cities in the provinces than in Madrid. And, indeed, we have proof of constant departures of silver from the port of Barcelona to be re-minted in Marseille, or to pay for the purchase of products abroad. However, this does not seem to have affected the Bank of Barcelona, which had been more concerned in the immediately preceding years by competition from the new credit institutions established in the city.

Another of the factors that Santillán blamed for the problems of the Bank of Spain was the performance of the *Caja de Depósitos*, but this problem was not restricted to the Madrid market. The *Caja* operated in all the provinces, and in some of them it represented a significant drain on resources. Therefore, the difficulties of the Bank of Spain were of its own making, and were due specifically to its strong specialisation in the provision of credit to the public sector: its famous "queue" was the direct result of the imbalance in the state's accounts and the public's growing feeling that the situation was untenable. It was natural to assume that the decisions that the government would have to make to rectify the situation could seriously affect the state's debt to the bank and, therefore, its solvency and liquidity. Holding more banknotes than necessary was a risk to be avoided, even if it meant waiting forever in the queue (or paying someone else to do so).

The situation of the external resources of the banks of issue is mirrored by the evolution of the money created (Figure 5.11). A simple glance indicates the existence of three sub-periods: one of general expansion and establishment of the provincial banks, until 1860; a second period of prosperity between that year and 1866, and the third, until 1868, marked by the consequences of the crisis.

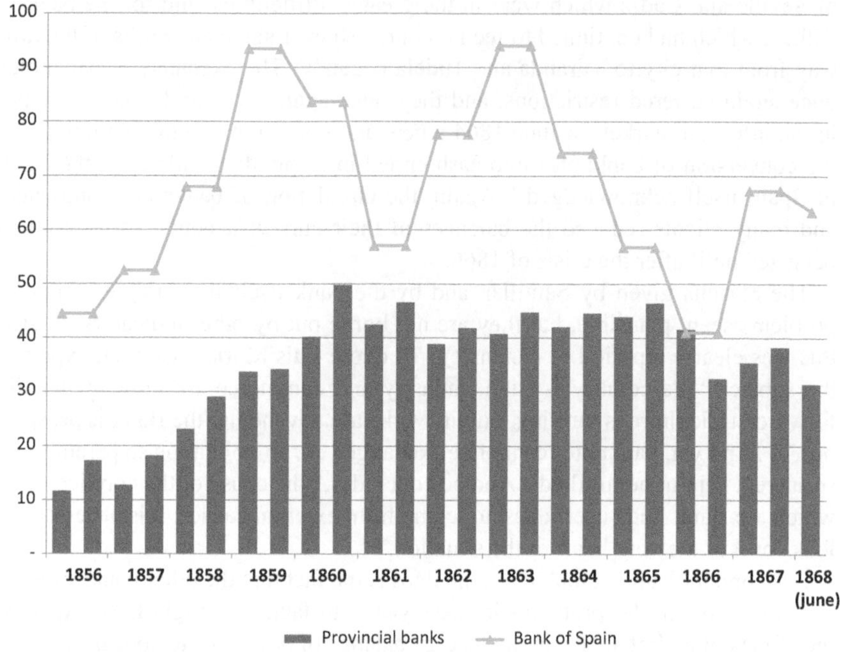

Figure 5.11 Money created by the banks of issue (million pesetas)

Note: Sources for banks' data from statements published in the *Gazeta de Madrid* and banks' reports. See Chapter 4.

The comparison with the Bank of Spain is striking. While the provincial banks maintained a notable degree of stability in terms of the money created, the Bank of Spain fluctuated wildly: between 1858 and 1866 two complete cycles of expansion and contraction were observed, with highs close to 100 million pesetas and lows around 50 million. Clearly, these movements were related to the financing needs of the state, which was practically the Bank of Spain's sole client, and they had little to do with the general financial climate of the time.

These figures confirm the relative importance of the Spanish provincial banks in comparison with other countries in which there were a number of banks of issue in operation, but also an "official" (though private) bank operating under state control. During the decade before the crisis of 1866, provincial banks contributed around a third of the fiat money created in Spain; this figure rose to around a half in the years in which the Bank of Spain created less money, such as 1861 and 1865–1866.

Of course, the defining feature of the provincial banks was their local character and their dedication to a specific business community. For this reason, it is interesting to compare the sum total of the notes issued and the money created by each bank with the estimated income of the province in which they were based (Table 5.7).

Table 5.7 Banknotes in circulation and money created, 1864

Province	*Banknotes per 1,000 inhab.*	*Province*	*Banknotes per 1,000 pts of GDP*	*Province*	*Money created per 1,000 pts of GDP*
	Pesetas		Pesetas		Pesetas
Cádiz	30.5	Biscay (Bilbao)	67.2	Biscay (Bilbao)	69.1
Biscay (Bilbao)	25.0	Cádiz	45.7	Santander	55.9
Barcelona	17.7	Santander	38.0	Cádiz	33.0
Seville	15.0	Barcelona	32.0	Valladolid	29.9
Málaga	13.9	Valladolid	30.7	Barcelona	24.6
Valladolid	12.4	Seville	28.1	Seville	24.1
Santander	11.5	Málaga	24.1	Málaga	18.6
Gipuzkoa (San Sebastián)	7.5	Gipuzkoa (San Sebastián)	23.1	Gipuzkoa (San Sebastián)	18.5
Zaragoza	3.5	Zaragoza	8.5	A Coruña	7.9
Tarragona*	2.7	Tarragona*	7.7	Balearic Isl.	6.0
Balearic Isl.	2.3	A Coruña	7.2	Zaragoza	5.5
A Coruña	2.0	Balearic Isl.	6.0	Álava (Vitoria)	3.2
Álava (Vitoria)	1.5	Álava (Vitoria)	4.6	Navarre (Pamplona)	2.4
Burgos	1.1	Burgos	3.8	Burgos	2.2
	0.6	Oviedo	3.1	Oviedo	–0.2
Oviedo	0.6	Navarre (Pamplona)	1.7	Palencia	–0.5
Palencia	0.3	Palencia	0.9	arragona/Reus*	–1.1/2.3

* The Bank of Tarragona had in circulation banknotes for 119,000 pts and destroyed money for 386,000 pts; the Bank of Reus had in circulation 750,000 pts in notes and created money for 261,000 pts. (in parentheses, provincial capital)

Source: *Anuario Estadístico de España* and GDP data kindly provided by Julio Martínez Galarraga (see Rosés et al. 2010)

The figures suggest the presence of two groups, one comprising eight provinces and other nine. The provinces with the highest rates of banknote issue and money creation did not fully coincide with those designated by law to be the first recipients of new banks: the Bank of San Sebastián, for example, was created in June 1862 and within two years its banknotes had achieved a high relative level of penetration; while at the other extreme the issuing activity of the banks of Zaragoza and A Coruña was lower than might have been expected in view of the economic activity of their respective provinces.

Within the first group there were also some notable differences. In terms of both banknotes in circulation and money created, the Bank of Bilbao was the institution that achieved the strongest presence or, more precisely, the one that made the most intensive use of the means of payment it offered. Bilbao was followed by Santander and Cádiz. The only province in this group without access to the sea was Valladolid, a key railway hub and a strategic centre of the transport network of north-central Spain. As for the group of provinces with lower levels of banking, the recently created banks of Oviedo, Navarre and Tarragona were particularly weak, with minimal issuing activity and a negative contribution to the creation of money.

This quantitative analysis of the activity of the banks of issue during this expansionary phase should also mention their function as lenders. The regulatory norms of the banks of issue did not explicitly stipulate the uses authorised for their funds, except that a third of the amount corresponding to the banknotes issued had to be kept in the bank in coin or bullion.

Figure 5.12 reflects the evolution of the portfolio of banks of issue and that of the private discounting of the Bank of Spain. In general terms, they follow the same trend that we have already seen for other variables: a strongly ascendant phase until 1861, followed by a stagnation that turned into a slight contraction after the crisis of 1866. The benchmark we propose on this occasion is not the total portfolio of the Bank of Spain, but the part of the portfolio that corresponded

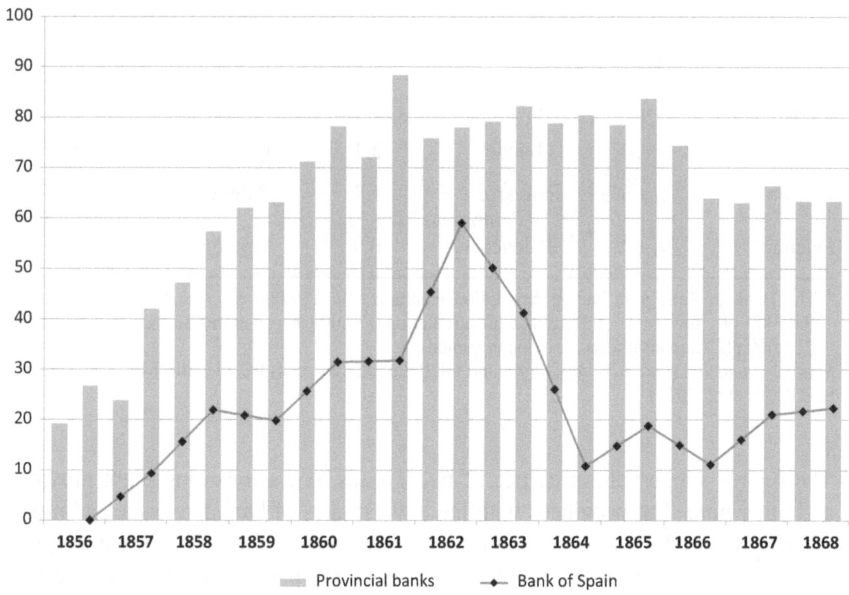

Figure 5.12 Banks of issue: credit granted to private sector (million pesetas)

Note: Sources for banks' data from statements published in the *Gazeta de Madrid* and banks' reports. See Chapter 4.

to private credit. Transactions with the Treasury were among the Bank of Spain's main activities, a situation that often led to complaints from the business community and the financial press. The weakness of credit to individuals is reflected in the figure, which shows that the provincial banks of issue granted twice as much in discounts and loans as the Bank of Spain. Equally noteworthy is the profound collapse after 1862, undoubtedly aggravated by the fact that one of Madrid's major credit companies went into receivership. In any case, it is clear that the Bank of Spain could do little to alleviate the situation of companies and individuals either before or during the crisis that would culminate in the spring of 1866.

5.4. The crisis of 1866 and its aftermath

The financial crisis in Spain between 1864 and 1866 had a decisive effect on the future of issue plurality. Although the establishment of the monopoly in 1874 was due to political interests, the fact is that the weaknesses that propitiated the decision were created in those turbulent years by an investment boom inevitably followed by a crisis. As we will see, the provincial banks of issue bore the brunt of the downturn but, with a few exceptions, they managed to stay afloat and even played their part in the later return to financial stability.

The crisis has an extensive bibliography, inaugurated more than 40 years ago by Nicolás Sánchez-Albornoz and Gabriel Tortella. These scholars' studies are still seminal today, although in recent years the fear of new crises has served as a stimulus for new research.[27] The Spanish crisis of 1866 occurred against the backdrop of a generalised financial imbalance in the economies of Europe; however, neither the immediately preceding tensions nor the crisis itself can be attributed to a simple contagion from Britain and other countries. As we will see, external factors played a role in the process, but they were far from being the cause: rather, they compounded a highly dangerous dynamic already at work in Spain, linked to the financial problems of the state and the evolution of railway investments.

As far as public accounts were concerned, the key factor was the state's growing deficit. The conservative governments in power since 1856 adopted a series of measures that significantly pushed up expenditure without a parallel increase in revenue: intervention in military campaigns abroad, in Morocco, Latin America and Cochinchina (in present-day Vietnam); the granting of subsidies to the battered railway companies; the halting of further confiscations of church properties and so on. All this inevitably multiplied the state's deficit, increased public debt and exacerbated the government's chronic insolvency. The situation became desperate in mid-1864, forcing successive finance ministers to formulate increasingly unorthodox plans to try to meet their most pressing obligations.

The key issue was known as the *floating debt*, that is, the debt that was not consolidated in issues approved by parliament. It was made up of debts owed to suppliers and also short-term loans requested by the state to meet its most urgent needs, and which had not gone through the legal procedures required for the issue of consolidated debt. In this period, most of the mounting deficit was covered not by issues but by loans obtained from the Bank of Spain or directly from the public through the *Caja de Depósitos*, a state body set up in 1852 to attract savings from private individuals for investment in the government's short-term financing. The aim was to avoid the constant recourse to private lenders, who often imposed highly burdensome conditions; however, a measure initially designed to deal with temporary imbalances soon became a permanent resource.

Deposits in the *Caja de Depósitos* rose from 50 to 250 million pesetas between 1858 and 1860 and climbed still further between 1860 and 1863, reaching the sum of 420 million pesetas. This was a huge amount, if we consider that the ordinary annual income of the state in those years was around 500 million pesetas.[28] It should be borne in mind that the bulk of these deposits were to be repaid on demand or were payable at six months or one year. So the situation was very dangerous, with a state that had no surplus liquidity but owed money to thousands of individuals who could demand it at any time or at very short notice.

Pedro Salaverría, finance minister in Alejandro Mon's government, presented a proposal to solve the problem in the spring of 1864, but the operation was unsuccessful: the depositors of the *Caja* did not accept the offer of conversion and the government's liquidity problems persisted. Several governments followed, each more short-lived than the last. Distrust in the public finances multiplied. The low price on the market made the issuing of debt very difficult and it made the ordinary placement of new mortgage bonds impossible, while the interest paid by the *Caja de Depósitos* had to be raised to stop the rising demands for reimbursement. There was no other option than to place more mortgage bonds on the market at 12% below its nominal value, and to issue consolidated debt through auction at whatever rate could be obtained.

In June 1865 a new government took power with Leopoldo O'Donnell as prime minister and Manuel Alonso Martínez as finance minister. The change was received with relief in financial circles, but the problems of the Treasury persisted. In the following months, the resources provided by the previous government's measures allowed some respite, but at the cost of a notable fall in the price levels of public debt. In any case, the new government was considering a longer-term arrangement, which would have to involve the restoration of credit abroad. The negotiations at an international level were kept secret and only became known at the beginning of April 1866 when a bill was presented to the Cortes that would fundamentally alter the banking system. We will return to this new legislation later.

Alongside the state's financial problems, the other decisive factor in the crisis was the failure of the railways. The studies available on the subject show how the cost overrun of the construction, together with a rate of traffic that was below the forecasts, landed the companies in dire straits and had an immediate effect on the credit companies that had facilitated their financing.[29] The best indicator of the process was the sharp fall in the prices of Spanish rail stocks on the Paris Stock Exchange, where the shares of the two main companies saw their valuation drop by 70% between 1863 and early 1866.[30] As regards the three large French credit companies associated with the process, the General Credit Company went into receivership in October 1864, while the other two hit serious trouble due to the devaluation of their portfolios, made up essentially of railway bonds.

In Catalonia, where the railway network had been built with local capital, the situation was quite similar.[31] The most important Catalan company, which ran the line from Barcelona to Zaragoza, noted at the end of 1864 (when all the connections had already been made) that revenue was little more than half what had been forecast and that the gross profits were only 40% of the expected figure. The company could not even pay the interest on its obligations, and any attempt to meet the repayment schedule was out of the question. The inevitable conversion of the debt was going to cause serious difficulties in the Barcelona financial market, incapable of absorbing more paper. The company was finally obliged to merge with the one that operated the Zaragoza-Pamplona line, which was in a slightly better financial position, although its yields were lower.[32] The situation of other companies with local capital was similar.

The fall in the value of the railway stocks occurred before the banking crisis, although the crisis aggravated the bearish trend. In February 1866, the Catalan General Credit Corporation – directly involved in the railway business – informed its shareholders of the formation of a committee composed of railway companies, credit companies and discount houses to request the intervention of the state in aid of the railway companies: "We are overwhelmed by the thought of the scale of the conflict that would ensue if the state did not intervene in some form or other to remedy the ills."[33] This appeal to the state, however, sat uneasily alongside the criticisms of the government's excessive spending and deficit.

The low profitability of the railways and the state's squeeze on financing were not the only factors that contributed to the crisis. For contemporaries, one of the most striking manifestations of the financial turmoil in the country was the massive outflow of metal currency, especially silver. The problem was a long-standing one: the increase in the relative price of silver with respect to gold had seriously affected countries with bimetallic systems, in which the parity fixed between the two metals stimulated the outflow of silver.

However, the problem was not only monetary: it was also due to the progressive reduction of inflows of foreign capital. In these circumstances, the monetary reform adopted in mid-1864 in an attempt to stop the outflow of silver failed to yield the expected results. The aim was to convert all fractional silver coins into fiat money (their exchange value would be much higher than their intrinsic value) and leave only the larger coins at a value equivalent to their content. These measures did not succeed in stopping the cash outflow, which was driven essentially (according to most observers) by the persistent deficit in the trade balance. Indeed, the exchange rate in Barcelona with respect to the franc began to fall in 1863 and continued to spiral downwards from the beginning of 1864.[34] The dishoarding and capital inflows, which had made possible the expansion of the early 1860s and had offset the foreign trade deficit, were now too weak to maintain the old equilibrium.

In any case, in the first months of 1866 the economic and financial situation was extremely unstable. Everywhere, voices were heard announcing impending disaster: in a report sent in March, the British ambassador to Madrid described the situation in no uncertain terms:

> The country is going through a monetary and commercial crisis which, if swift measures are not taken, will result in a great national calamity and will ruin it. The cause of this crisis lies in the absorption and dislocation of the available capital, both because of the excessive exports abroad and its exclusive and simultaneous dedication to speculative initiatives at home; that is to say that the capital invested in the country, wherever it has come from, has been sunk into investments that have no intrinsic value and that are represented by paper. . . . Coin is sent to Bayonne, Marseille and Paris and this simple operation produces a profit of between 1.5 and 2.5 per cent, while the cost of payments to be made in France reaches 6.25 per cent.[35]

The finance minister, Manuel Alonso Martínez, offered a similar analysis in presenting his draft bill for a National Bank to the Spanish parliament:

> With the immobilisation of a large part of the capital that was previously given over to banking operations and the movement of business, as a result of the large mass of national goods on the market and the development of urban constructions, and with the absorption of another large part as a result of the last issues, which obtained for the Treasury perhaps greater sums than those available in our mercantile centres, the shortage of cash is keenly noted. The most serious symptom of the crisis is the irregularity of the exchange rates, caused, among other reasons, by the clear imbalance between imports and exports and the collapse of our credit which makes it very difficult and expensive to acquire capital abroad.[36]

Against this background of uncertainty for the state and for the country in general, the finance minister Alonso Martínez introduced the proposal that he had been negotiating frantically over the previous months. It consisted of two groups of measures. The first was aimed at balancing the state's accounts in the short term, and the second was intended to lift the blockade that Spain suffered in the international markets and to ensure a more stable and more potent mechanism for financing the state.

On 7 May, the first set of measures was made public. The government was now authorised to collect the contributions even if the budget was not approved in time, and also to issue 300 million pesetas in debt. The negotiation of a settlement of the foreign debt was also proposed. The news of the proposal met with an immediate response. On the very same day, 7 May, the price of public debt plummeted: in the first days of the month the consolidated debt had already fallen from 37.5% to 35.5%, but it dropped further to 31.5% on the 7th and to 30.5% on the 9th. Since the beginning of the worst phase of the crisis, in the spring of 1864, the consolidated debt had seen its valuation decrease by more than 20 points (a 40% fall), but half of this loss had occurred in the last six months. This evolution had a marked effect on the financial system since the public debt, together with the railway bonds (also in free fall), was the main guarantee of the loans granted by the banks.

The second block of Alonso Martínez's programme had an even more direct impact on the functioning banks. The idea was to establish a new National Bank, the only one with the right to issue, with 300 million pesetas in capital (at that time the Bank of Spain had 50 million in capital) which would absorb the banks of issue still in existence. The new bank had the backing of a London banking syndicate. Its constitution would ensure the financing of the accumulated deficit and would be coupled with a settlement of the dispute with foreign holders of Spanish securities and the placement of a new issue of foreign debt in the British capital. This part of the government's programme seemed well founded and it was well received in the markets, despite, as was to be expected, the fierce opposition of the existing banks of issue.[37]

The international crisis now deepened the crisis in Spain. Financial markets throughout Europe had begun to experience difficulties at the end of 1863. In London, the Bank of England's base rate rose from 4% at the end of October 1863 to 9% in May and September of the following year. The increase was attributed to the rising prices of raw cotton at the height of the American civil war, and to the war between Prussia and Denmark. After this the situation stabilised for almost a year until the end of 1865, when a new downward turn began that would last until May 1866.

Indeed, on 10 May 1866, to the great surprise of the general public (though not of those who know the market well), Overend, Gurney & Co. of London went into receivership. Overend & Gurney was the most important discount bank in London, and enjoyed a prestige comparable only to that of the Bank of England itself. The ultimate reason for its bankruptcy was an excessively permissive discount policy which led to heavy losses, especially in operations related to railway contractors.

The financial situation of the British capital had worsened in the immediately preceding weeks. The base rate had risen again from 5% in October 1865 to 8% just before the outbreak of the banking crisis. This second increase was due to the bankruptcy of several relatively large railway companies and, as a result, the receivership of discount houses that held their commercial paper. The withdrawal of Italian and Austrian funds as a result of the military tension between the two powers was also cited, as was the high demand for capital arising from the creation of new companies under the aegis of the limited liability laws of 1855 and 1856.

Overend, Gurney & Co. was one of the companies that had changed its legal status from a general partnership to a joint-stock company. In its case it seems that the objective was to obtain more capital to offset losses already accumulated. The strain in the credit market and the bankruptcies of several of the bank's clients led to a massive withdrawal of deposits. The bank requested help from the Bank of England by rediscounting part of its securities portfolio, but the bank of issue refused. Receivership became inevitable and caused widespread panic: the impact of 'Black Friday' was only mitigated by the government's decision to suspend the Peel Banking Act of 1844, authorising the Bank of England to issue banknotes above the established limit. In any case, the effect was not immediate: the Bank of England's discount rate remained at 10% until August and did not return to normal levels until the end of the year.[38]

One might have thought that this situation would have little if any effect on Spain, but it so happened that Overend & Gurney was one of the main stakeholders in the consortium negotiating with the Spanish government over the creation of the new National Bank which was to replace the Bank of Spain and the other issuers, and which was a fundamental part of the minister Alonso Martínez's corrective plan. Criticised by some for his fiscal policies and by others for seeking the cancellation of legally held privileges, and seeing his attempts to attract foreign support frustrated, Alonso Martínez resigned a few days later.

All these events had a devastating effect on the Spanish financial system. There were two decisive moments: the first was a limited crisis in 1864, and the second, which was much more widespread, was linked to the events of 1866. Between 1865 and 1868, 6 of the 20 banks of issue in operation at the end of 1864 disappeared – a total of 30%. In terms of paid-in capital the impact was smaller, as these banks were relatively small: but it was nonetheless significant, amounting to a 21% fall from 36.6 million pesetas in 1864 to 28.9 million in 1869.

As to how and why they closed their doors, the six banks that went out of business can be classified into two groups: those that were dragged down by their association with credit companies in the midst of scandals, and those that closed voluntarily at the behest of their own shareholders in view of the low volume of business obtained and the few prospects of increasing it. The first group comprised the banks of Valladolid, Seville and Cádiz, and the second those of Burgos, Palencia and Santiago.

The two biggest scandals suffered by the provincial banks of issue in the three decades of their history involved the banks of Valladolid and Seville. Both episodes have been the subject of several studies.[39] On both occasions, the underlying problem was the relationship between the banks of issue and credit companies, and more specifically the use of the banks to conceal the losses that the credit companies incurred. In principle, there is nothing wrong in banks of issue lending to other banks or financial intermediaries. Quite the opposite, in fact: it seems quite reasonable that a bank of issue should act as the main financial agent, distributing part of the funds it created through other intermediaries which were better informed about certain sectors, or were equipped with more flexible instruments that the banks of issue were not allowed to use. This was a policy followed by the Bank of Barcelona in these same years, when it signed two rediscounting agreements with the *Crédito Mercantil* and the credit firm *El Comercio*.[40] However, the situations that arose in Valladolid and later in Seville were quite different.

In Valladolid, the directors of the credit companies, some of whom were also directors of the bank, took control of the bank and transferred to it the portfolio of devalued assets held by the companies. The operation was carried out over the objection of the Royal Commissioner. Non-operating shareholders managed to regain control of the bank shortly afterwards and denounced those responsible for the move, but in the end the bank had to suspend the convertibility of its notes and cease operations, although it was not officially dissolved until April 1870. After the final acquittal of the defendants, in 1869, neither holders of its banknotes nor its creditors were able to recover all their money, and the shareholders were even less fortunate.

Broadly speaking, these circumstances were repeated a year and a half later, in Seville. On this occasion, it was the *Crédito Comercial* that dragged down the city's other financial entities. The fateful deed was the agreement signed between the *Crédito Comercial* and the Bank of Seville in June 1866, by which the bank of issue took over the company's assets and liabilities. The argument put forward by those behind the operation was that the imminent fall of the *Crédito Comercial* would have triggered a wave of panic that would have pulled all the other local credit institutions down with it. The agreement was nullified by the finance ministry, which then took the bank under its wing and tried to recover the guarantees provided by the company. The convertibility of banknotes remained tightly restricted until 1870. In that year, an agreement was finally signed according to which the participants in the original operation agreed to pay back a much lower sum than the total defrauded, in order to bring the case to a close. The bank's directors thought that this would be enough to return things to normal, but in fact the difficulties continued, and the entity remained unable to meet its obligations. An offer of a merger with the Bank of Castile came to nothing when the monopoly of issue was decreed in March 1874. The Bank of Spain initially opposed the absorption of the Seville bank of issue because of its demonstrable inefficiency, but the government forced it to accept.

The case of the Bank of Cádiz is not as well known. By 1860, it was already in difficulties: its current accounts halved between 1859 and 1860 and continued to decline in the following years. In 1863 it began to restrict the exchange of notes and the government obliged it to adjust its portfolio and reduce its circulation of fiat money. At the end of 1866 its balance sheet presented a situation of total illiquidity and its activities were paralysed. The government agreed to its dissolution in January 1870, which was ratified in March of the same year.[41]

In contrast to these cases of mismanagement or fraud, other banks decided to close when their shareholders considered that the money invested in them could be better placed elsewhere. In fact, this occurred in three cities where trade still followed traditional patterns of organisation and which, significantly, were all located inland. The cases of Palencia and Burgos present many similarities.[42] In Burgos, the disagreements within the board of directors over the company's continuation were reflected in the call for a general meeting by a group of shareholders, at which the motion to dissolve the bank was passed by a narrow margin. Apparently, those advocating closure were mainly from other regions, especially the Basque Country. There were several attempts to stop the process, and it was even debated by the Council of State, which ruled that the dissolution should proceed, adding an interesting reflection:

> It should also be ensured that the issuing and discounting banks and the credit companies established in the provinces that have not corresponded to the expectations at the time of their creation are dissolved; due to their poor situation, they are a permanent cause of the persistence of the crisis afflicting trade and industry.[43]

In Palencia, the liquidation of the company was far less traumatic. At the general meeting held on 30 November 1867, the closure was approved by a large majority of those present. The representation to the government requesting the ratification of the agreement indicated that the reason for the closure was "the limited scale at which the Bank has been able to operate in the three years of its existence, with profits that are not enough to cover the expenses of its administration."[44]

Finally, in the case of the Bank of Santiago, the decision to liquidate the company seemed to have been related to an internal conflict between the bank's executive officer and its board of directors, which led to the former's dismissal and the beginning of a long legal dispute. This confrontation began at a time when the most critical moments of the financial crisis had passed. Whatever the possible impact of the director's dismissal on the decision to liquidate, we should not forget that the Bank of Santiago had the lowest nominal capital of all Spanish banks, at only 750,000 pesetas, and the lowest volume of banknotes issued, between 160,000 and 200,000 pesetas.

In addition to the banks that went out of business, the financial crisis also had an impact on the banks that survived. Figures 5.14 and 5.15 show the comparative evolution of the fiat circulation provided by the Bank of Spain and by the remaining provincial banks of issue. As can be seen, the provincial banks of issue maintained a highly stable supply in comparison to the Bank of Spain's strongly pro-cyclical movement. The differences in policy cannot be attributed to the lesser intensity of the crisis in the commercial cities of the provinces. Barcelona was the first to suffer; the widespread panic that took hold of the city eventually dragged down most of its financial businesses. Both in Bilbao and in Santander the local credit companies faced major difficulties, closely linked to the promotion of the railways, and many of them went into liquidation.[45] If the banks in these cities were able to overcome the situation, it was undoubtedly due to their prudent attitude toward the country's railway and financial boom, which was now coming to an end. Many of the bank's directors and major shareholders participated actively in the railway business but did so privately or as partners of credit companies and did not irreversibly involve their banks with these other companies. But this is not to say that the banks of issue did not participate in the financing of the railways, or that there were no cases of operations that gave clear signs of insider lending.[46]

After the crisis, the evolution of the remaining provincial banks presents some interesting features. In this case, however, we should distinguish between the Bank of Barcelona and the other banks, in view of the differences in their

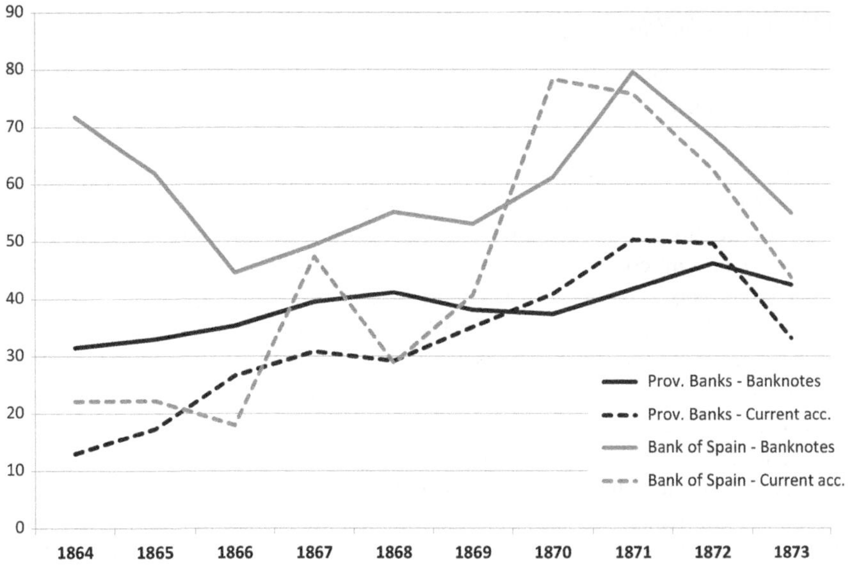

Figure 5.13 Banks of issue: banknotes and current accounts, banks in operation in 1870 (million pesetas)

Note: Sources for banks' data from statements published in the *Gazeta de Madrid* and banks' reports. See Chapter 4.

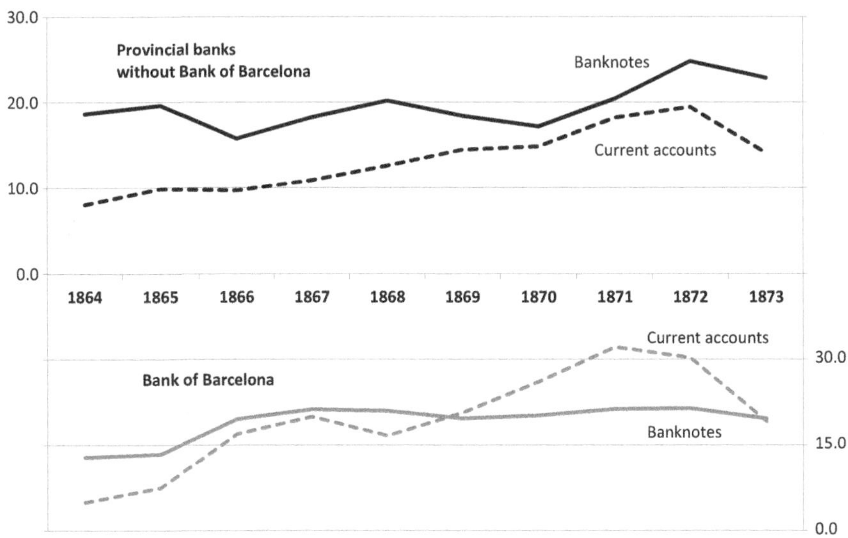

Figure 5.14 Provincial banks in operation in 1870: banknotes and current accounts, 1864–1873 (million pesetas)

Note: Sources for banks' data from statements published in the *Gazeta de Madrid* and banks' reports. See Chapter 4.

respective approaches. First of all, while the banks as a whole reduced monetary circulation during the crisis, the Bank of Barcelona expanded it (Figure 5.14), due to its decision to withdraw the banknotes issued by the local credit companies and banks from the market and to replace them with its own. The unusual behaviour of the Catalan bank in the following years is even more striking. As can be seen, the amount corresponding to banknotes in circulation remained stable, while the amount corresponding to current accounts increased significantly; this reflects the bank's intention of not increasing its effective capital above the figure of 7.5 million pesetas reached in 1866, which in turn left the maximum limit of issue set at 22.5 million. This amount was probably lower than the needs of the local market, which meant that companies and individuals were encouraged to use current accounts as a means of payment. What is more, the bank maintained a very restrictive credit policy in these years, to the point of keeping more money in its coffers than the resources contributed through banknotes and current accounts. The result was that over several years the Bank of Barcelona, which held a monopoly of issue in the city and the province, drained net resources from the money supply (Figure 5.15).[47]

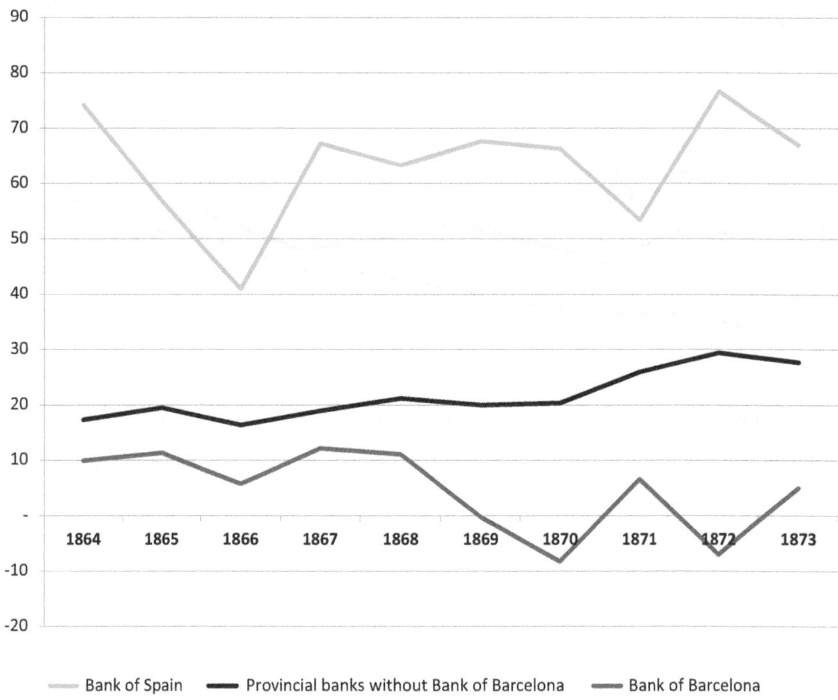

Figure 5.15 Money created by the banks of issue, 1864–1873 (million pesetas)

Note: Sources for banks' data from statements published in the *Gazeta de Madrid* and banks' reports. See Chapter 4.

After the crisis, in contrast to the erratic movements of the monetary accounts of the Bank of Spain and the Bank of Barcelona, the evolution of the rest of the banks of issue was stable and slightly expansionary – much more in line with the progress of the economy as a whole. According to the most recent GDP estimates, economic growth was moderate but robust from 1868 onwards and by 1871 had returned to the levels reached before the crisis.[48]

The effect of this situation on the granting of credit is shown in Figure 5.16. As can be observed, the Bank of Spain and the Bank of Barcelona immediately rebounded to their pre-crisis portfolio levels, although in the case of the Bank of Barcelona this was compatible with the maintenance of an exorbitant level of reserves in its coffers. It must also be borne in mind that in these years the Bank of Barcelona carried out a number of large-scale operations with the Treasury, especially one involving the acquisition of gold bullion to the value of 20 million pesetas. Without counting this extraordinary operation, the evolution of the Bank of Barcelona's credit at year-end would have been very similar to that of the Bank of Spain's private credit, with a downward trend after the peak recorded in 1868.

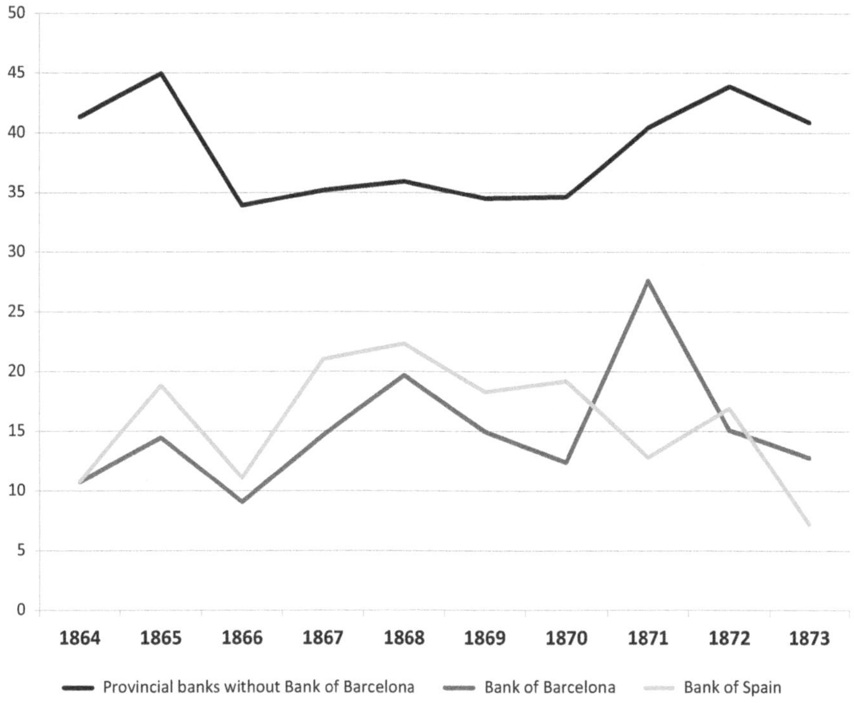

Figure 5.16 Total credit granted by provincial banks, and by the Bank of Spain to the private sector (million pesetas)

Note: Sources for banks' data from statements published in the *Gazeta de Madrid* and banks' reports. See Chapter 4.

On this occasion as well, the trends in the other banks of issue were practically the opposite: after the crisis, the credit level remained low and only began to recover after 1871.

In general, we conclude that the provincial banks of issue had a stabilising effect during these difficult years. According to Tortella, between 1864 and 1873, 60% (21 out of 34) of the existing credit companies disappeared and many of those which survived were operational only on a very limited scale. Among the banks, only 3 (out of 20) went out of business, and even in these cases the bankruptcy was more the result of clearly criminal abuses than the result of their normal operations. Three other banks withdrew from the market, in an orderly fashion. The decision in Spain to replace a system of plurality of issue with a monopoly cannot be attributed to a supposed instability of the plural system or its possible destabilising effects on the economy; rather, it appears to have been due to the permanently precarious state of the country's finances throughout the period.

Notes

1 On the creation and operation of the Bank of Isabel II, see Tedde (1999, p. 155ff.).

2 Explanatory memorandum of R.D. 25 January 1844, creating the Bank of Isabel II: *Gaceta de Madrid*, 30 January 1844.

3 This is the idea defended by Tortella (1973, pp. 30–34). Pedro Tedde is less critical of the management of the Bank of San Fernando: see Tedde (1999, pp. 159–160).

4 Tedde (1999, pp. 188, 200).

5 Explanatory memorandum of R.D. 25 February 1847 ordering the merger of the Bank of Isabel II and the Bank of San Fernando: *Gaceta de Madrid*, 26 February 1847.

6 On Ramón Santillán, a key figure in the financial development of nineteenth-century Spain, see Tedde (2015, electronic resource) and Vallejo (2006); and his own memoirs: Santillán (1996).

7 Figures from J. Maluquer and C. Sudrià collected in Nadal et al. (2012, II.1.3 and II.2.15). Other indicators in Blasco-Martel and Sudrià (2010, p. 120).

8 *De los bancos de Cádiz*, an anonymous pamphlet published by the printing press of the Revista Médica, Cádiz, 1847, pp. 1–2.

9 "Report written by Mr. José Fariñas regarding the visit made to the credit societies of Barcelona" (12 July 1859). *National Historical Archive*, Treasury, bundle 429/1. Fariñas's report is an exaggeration: in 1859 the bank had more than twice as many banknotes in circulation as at the beginning of 1856.

10 The reluctance to accept banknotes to pay debts or loans persisted for decades, as is witnessed by the persistence of clauses prohibiting payment "in paper" in contracts of all kinds. See Pascual and Sudrià (2004).

11 In the case of the Bank of Barcelona, the first directors – traders and bankers with extensive experience themselves – sought the assistance of a first administrator, Jaime Badía, who had expert knowledge of the US banking system. See Blasco-Martel (2007).

12 *Crowding out:* when private individuals are forced out of the credit market because the state increases its borrowing.

13 Tortella (1970, p. 27).

14 "Report of the Sociedad de Credito Mobiliario Español", May 1857, published by the *Gazette of the Iron Roads*, on 7 June 1857. Cited by Tortella (1970, pp. 45–46). Ramón Santillán, governor of the Bank of Spain and a staunch enemy of the proliferation of issuing banks (and, even more so, of the granting of issue to a foreign company), was

pleased that "the public foresaw what the government did not. . . [and] no one was willing to take the shares . . . that were issued". Santillán (1982 [1865], II, pp. 102–103).

15 Apparently at least three proposals did not receive the government's approval: the proposals from Murcia, Logroño and Almería (Tortella, 1970, p. 32n).

16 Data for the Crédito Mobiliario Español in Tortella (1973, p. 347). For the Barcelona credit societies, data for 1865 in Blasco-Martel and Sudrià (2010, p. 211).

17 On the credit companies, the key references are still the works of Gabriel Tortella (1970, 1973) and Nicolás Sánchez-Albornoz (1967, 1977). On the Catalan credit companies, additional information can be found in Navas and Sudrià (2007) and in Pascual and Sudrià (2008). For Santander, see Hoyo (1988); for Valladolid, Pérez García (1991); for Andalusia, Titos (2003); for Valencia, Ródenas (1978).

18 Tortella (1973, pp. 63–64).

19 Blasco-Martel and Sudrià (2010, ch. 8); Navas and Sudrià (2007); Pascual and Sudrià (2008); Pascual (2006).

20 Blasco-Martel and Sudrià (2010, pp. 270–272).

21 Tedde (2015, pp. 171–175); Moro et al. (2015); Sudrià (2018).

22 After welcoming the decision to increase capital, the *Gaceta de los Caminos de Hierro* advised the bank to dedicate the capital increase to ensuring the convertibility of the banknotes: ". . . to keep the doors of the establishment open and to eliminate the loss suffered by the banknotes. . . [is] all that can honourably done with that money" (11 December 1864).

23 Santillán (1865, vol. II, pp. 217–226). The destabilising factors of a macroeconomic nature that were apparently unrelated to the bank's responsibilities were compounded by others, such as counterfeiting attempts and internal irregularities, which led to complaints and dismissals.

24 Santillán (1865, II, p. 251).

25 *Memoria leída . . . Bank of España*, 4 March 1865, p. 12.

26 Pastor (1865, p. 75).

27 Sánchez-Albornoz (1963, 1967, 1968, 1977); Tortella (1973); Sudrià and Pascual (1999); Navas and Sudrià (2007); Martín Aceña and Nogués-Marco (2013) and Sudrià (2013).

28 L. Gonzalo (1981, pp. 453–471); on the *Caja de Depósitos*, see also M. Titos (1979).

29 Tortella (1973, pp. 183–200, 254–262); Tedde (1978, pp. 106–158).

30 N. Sánchez-Albornoz (1966).

31 For an exhaustive study of the saga of the Catalan railways, see Pascual (1999).

32 Pascual (1999, pp. 263–279).

33 *Memoria de la Sociedad Catalana General de Crédito leída en junta general de accionistas en Febrero de 1866*. See in this regard the *Memorandum* produced by the Catalan railway and credit companies around the same dates and published in the *Gaceta de los Caminos de Hierro* (vol. IX, 1866, pp. 67–70, 87–89 and 102–104).

34 Sudrià and Pascual (1999).

35 *Parliamentary Papers. Accounts & Papers. Reports. Secretaries of Embassy*, vol. LXXI (1866, pp. 446–447).

36 *Diario de las sesiones de Cortes. Congreso de los Diputados*. Apéndice 1°, n. 39, 4 April 1866.

37 The project was well received: see *Almanaque del Diario de Barcelona para el año 1867*, 90–93. See also Tortella (1973, pp. 277–278), and López Morell (2005, p. 214). For the opposition of the Bank of Spain see Tortella (1973, p. 278), and for the opposition of the Bank of Barcelona see Blasco-Martel and Sudrià (2010, pp. 472–475).

38 On the crisis of Overend, Gurney & Co. see the classic works by Macleod (1889); Clapham (1944, vol. II, pp. 263–270), and W.T.C. King (1936, pp. 238–256). For a summary, see R.A. Batchelor (1986). A fuller and more detailed account (though from a more journalistic perspective) is provided by G. Elliott (2006).

39 A very well-documented initial study can be found in Tortella (1973, pp. 262–292). For a more thorough-going study with a summary of the case of the Bank of Valladolid, see M. Pilar Pérez García (1991, 2016). On the Bank of Seville, see Barrera and Romero (2003) and Sánchez Casado (2016).
40 Blasco-Martel and Sudrià (2010, pp. 270–272).
41 For a recent review of the evolution of the Andalusian issuing banks, see Tedde (2018), and also Titos (2003, pp. 96–105).
42 Pérez García (2016, pp. 560–578, 505–523).
43 Archives of the Consejo de Estado, file 37713.
44 *Archives of the Consejo de Estado,* File 38185.
45 On the crisis in these cities, see the references in Tortella (1973, pp. 279–284) and, more specifically for Barcelona, Navas and Sudrià (2007); for Santander, see Hoyo (1988) *Ferrocarriles y banca: la crisis de la década de 1860 en Santander*, Cámara de Comercio, Industria y Navegación de Cantabria.
46 On the Bank of Barcelona and its special relationship with the Zaragoza Rail Company, controlled by the Girona family, see Blasco-Martel and Sudrià (2010, pp. 281–287).
47 On the unusual trajectory of the Bank of Barcelona over these years, see Blasco-Martel and Sudrià (2010, ch. 13).
48 Prados (2003).

Sources

Archives of the Consejo de Estado (Madrid)
National Historical Archive (Madrid)
Parliamentary Papers
Banks' Reports
Gaceta de los Caminos de Hierro
Gazeta de Madrid

Bibliography

Barrera, L., and Romero, R., 2003. *El Banco de Sevilla: 1857–1874. Temas Libres*. Ayuntamiento de Sevilla. Servicio de Publicaciones, Sevilla.

Batchelor, R. A., 1986. The avoidance of catastrophe: Two nineteenth century banking crises. In F. Capie and G. E. Wood (Eds.), *Financial Crises and the World Banking System*. Macmillan, London, 41–76.

Blasco-Martel, Y., 2007. 'Retornos' de América, Banca y Capital Humano: El Caso de Jaime Badía. *Historia Social*, 125–150.

Blasco-Martel, Yolanda and Sudrià, Carles, 2010. *El Banco de Barcelona (1844–1874), Historia de Un Banco Emisor*. LID Editorial, Madrid.

Clapham, J.H., 1944. *The bank of England, a history*. The University Press, Cambridge, England.

Elliott, G., 2006. *The Mystery of Overend & Gurney: A financial Scandal in Victorian.* Methuen, London.

Gonzalo, L., 1981. *El Tesoro Público y La Caja General de Depósitos (1852–1868): Un Estudio Sobre La Deuda Flotante En España a Mediados Del Siglo XIX*. Instituto de Estudios Fiscales. Ministerio de Hacienda, Madrid.

Hoyo Aparicio, Andrés, 1988. *Ferrocarriles y Banca: La Crisis de La Década de 1860 En Santander*. Cámara Oficial de Comercio, Industria y Navegación de Cantabria, Santander.

King, Wilfred Thomas C., 1936 [1972]. *History of the London Discount Market*. Frank Cass, London.

López-Morell, Miguel Á., 2005. *La Casa Rothschild En España (1812–1941). Memorias y Biografías*. Marcial Pons, Madrid.

Macleod, Henry Dunning, 1889. *The theory of credit*. Longmans Green and Co, London NV – 2.

Martín Aceña, Pablo and Nogués Marco, Pilar, 2013. Crisis Bancarias En La Historia de España Del Antiguo Régimen a Los Orígenes Del Capitalismo Moderno. In Comín, Francisco and Hernández Benítez, Mauro (Eds.), *Crisis Económicas En España, 1300–2012: Lecciones de La Historia*. Alianza, Madrid, pp. 141–168.

Moro, A., Nuño, G., and Tedde, P., 2015. A twin crisis with multiple banks of issue: Spain in the 1860s. *European Review of Economic History*, 19 (2). Oxford University Press, 171–194. doi:10.1093/ereh/heu025

Nadal, J., Benaul, J.M., and Sudrià, C., 2012. *Atles de La Industrialització de Catalunya, 1750–2010*, Vicens Vives, Barcelona.

Navas, M. y Sudrià, C., 2007. La crisi financera de 1866 a Barcelona. Una revisió. *Recerques*, 55, 35–72.

Pastor, L.M. 1865. *La libertad de bancos y cola del de España*. B. Carranza, Madrid.

Pascual, P, 1999. *Los Caminos de La Era Industrial: La Construcción y Financiación de La Red Ferroviaria Catalana (1843–1898)*, vol. 1. Edicions Universitat de Barcelona, Barcelona.

Pascual, P. and Sudrià, C., 2008. Industrialización, Desarrollo Financiero y Oferta Monetaria En Barcelona a Mediados Del Siglo XIX. *Investigaciones de Historia Económica*, 12 (12), 45–76. doi:10.1016/S1698-6989(08)70169-3

———, 2004. El temor davant del diner paper a la Catalunya del segle XIX. In *Josep Fontana : Historia y proyecto social*. Crítica, UPF, Barcelona.

———, 2006. El "Free Banking" Barcelonés de Mitjan Segle XIX: Una Nota. *Miscel Lània Ernest Lluch i Martín*, 1, 267–280.

Pérez García, María Pilar, 2016. "El Banco de Valladolid (1857–1874)"; "El Banco de Palencia (1864–1874)" y "El Banco de Burgos (1863–1874)". En Sudrià, C., Blasco-Martel (Eds.), *La pluralidad de emisión en España, 1844–1874*. Fundación BBVA, Bilbao, pp. 358–379, 505–525, 560–578.

———, 1991. *La Bancarrota de Un Banco Emisor: El Banco de Valladolid*. Instituto de Contabilidad y Autoría de Cuentas. Ministerio de Economia y Hacienda, Madrid.

Prados, L., 2003. *El Progreso Económico de España 1850–2000*. Fundación BBVA, Bilbao.

Ródenas, C., 1978. *Banca i Industrialització: El Cas Valenciá 1840–1880. Biblioteca d'estudis i Investigacions*. Tres i Quatre, Valencia.

Rosés, J.R., Martinez-Galarraga, J., and Tirado, D.A., 2010. The upswing of regional income inequality in Spain (1860–1930). *Explorations in Economic History*, 47 (2), 244–257.

Sanchez Albornoz, N., 1977. *España hace un siglo. Una economía dual*. Alianza Editorial, Madrid.

———, 1968. Los bancos y las sociedades de crédito en provincias. *Moneda y Crédito*, 104, 39–67.

———, 1967. La Crisis de 1866 En Madrid: La Caja de Depósitos, Las Sociedades de Crédito y La Bolsa. *Moneda y Crédito*, 100, 3–40.

———, 1966. De los orígenes del capital financiero: la sociedad general de crédito mobiliario español, 1856-1902. *Moneda y Crédito*, 97, 29–68.

———, 1963. *La Crisis de 1866 En Barcelona:(Notas Para Su Estudio)*. Sociedad de Estudios y Publicaciones, Madrid.

Sánchez, J.L., 2016. El Banco de Sevilla (1856–1874). In Sudrià, C. and Blasco-Martel, Y. (Eds.), *La pluralidad de emisión en España, 1844–1874*. Fundación BBVA, Bilbao, pp. 312–339.

Santillán, R. 1996. *Memorias 1808–1856*. Edición de P. Tedde, Banco de España, Madrid.

———, 1865. *Memoria Histórica Sobre Los Bancos Nacionales de San Carlos, Español de San Fernando, Isabel II, Nuevo Banco de San Fernando y de España*. Banco de España, Madrid.

Sudrià, C., 2018. Emptying the coffers: Old money to build new railways, Spain 1850–1874. *European Review of Economic History*, 22 (2). Oxford University Press, 210–232. doi:10.1093/ereh/hex016

———, 2013. La crisis de 1866. El Estado, los ferrocarriles y los bancos. In Gutiérrez Sebares, J.A. y Javier Martínez García, Francisco (Eds.), *Cinco estudios sobre crisis económicas en la historia de España. Cuadernos de investigación UCEIF, 10*. Editorial de la Universidad de Cantabria, Santander, pp. 129–164.

Sudrià, C. and Pascual, P., 1999. Financing a railway Mania: Capital formation and the demand for money in Catalonia, 1840–1866. *Financial History Review*, 6, 127–145.

Tedde, P. 1978. "Las compañías ferroviarias en España (1855–1935)", In Artola, M. (Ed.) *Los Ferrocarriles en España, 1844–1943*. Servicio de Estudios del Banco de España, Madrid.

———, 1999. *El Banco de San Fernando*. Alianza Editorial, Madrid.

———, 2015. *El Banco de España y El Estado Liberal (1847–1874)*. Banco de España y Gadir Editorial, Madrid.

———, 2015. *Ramón Santillán González* (Lerma, 1791-Madrid 1863). www.aehe.es/wp-content/uploads/2015/09/ramon_santillan.pdf

———, 2018. La Banca de Emisión Andaluza En Perspectiva Nacional (1856–1914). *Revista de Historia Económica/Journal of Iberian and Latin American Economic History*, June. Cambridge University Press, 1–33. doi:10.1017/S0212610918000095

Titos, M., 2003. *El Sistema Financiero En Andalucía: Tres Siglos de Historia, (1740–2000)*. Instituto de Estadística de Andalucía, Sevilla.

———, 1979. La Caja General de Depósitos (1852–1874). *Moneda y Crédito*, 151, 79–104.

Tortella, G., 1973. *Los Orígenes Del Capitalismo En España : Banca, Industria y Ferrocarriles En El Siglo XIX*. Tecnos, Madrid.

———, 1970. La evolución del sistema financiero en España de 1856 a 1868. En AA.VV. (Eds.), *Ensayos sobre la economía española a mediados del siglo XIX*. Ariel, Madrid, pp. 17–147.

Vallejo, R., 2006. Ramón Santillán González, reformador de la Hacienda liberal. En Comín, F., Martín Aceña, P. and Vallejo, R. (Eds.), *La Hacienda por sus Ministros: La etapa liberal de 1845 a 1899*. Prensas Universitarias de Zaragoza, Zaragoza, pp. 91–131.

6 The unexpected end of monetary plurality

A premature demise?

Lluís Castañeda

The plurality of banknote issue effective in Spain since 1844 was brought to an end in 1874, when it was replaced by a single issuer system. The decision was taken by a provisional government in power under extraordinary circumstances. Indeed, the decree was drafted and implemented by liberal politicians opposed to any state interference in the economy, including the issue of banknotes. These men were aware of the contradiction between the doctrine they defended and the decisions they made, and they left a record of the circumstances that compelled them to go against their ideas.

This chapter looks at the substance of the decree, examines the circumstances of its adoption and the role played by the Bank of Spain and the provincial banks themselves in the drafting process, and concludes with an analysis of the various choices made by the banks that were stripped of their power to issue. A more detailed approach can be found elsewhere (Castañeda, 2001).

6.1. The coming of the monopoly of issue and its circumstances

The decree of 19 March 1874 on unified fiduciary circulation was issued by the finance ministry under the leadership of José Echegaray and ratified by the head of the provisional government, General Francisco Serrano. The content of the decree can be boiled down to four points:

1 Establishment of unified fiduciary circulation

   The Bank of Spain undertook the issue of banknotes on an exclusive basis with the status of a National Bank (art. 1). The notes of provincial banks would cease to be legal tender within three months. The banks' own liquidation committees would be responsible for withdrawing their notes from circulation (art. 5). The Bank of Spain would be permitted to issue banknotes up to a value of five times its capital and it would be required to keep holdings in metallic money worth at least a quarter of its banknotes in circulation (art. 2). The Bank of Spain would be granted these privileges for a period of 30 years. Provisionally, banknotes would not be redeemable at all branches of the bank, only at the branch that had issued the note and at the bank's central offices (art. 7 and 8).

2 Reorganisation of the Bank of Spain

The bank's share capital would be increased to 100 million pesetas (it was 50 million at the time) and its capital reserve requirement would be set at 10%. Until the capital reserve reached this level, half of the bank's profits would be allocated to its increase. Shareholders would receive 6% as 'ordinary interest', accounted for as a cost, and the portion of the profits that the general assembly awarded to them (art. 1, 12 and 13).

To ensure the circulation of its banknotes, the Bank of Spain undertook to open branches in the country's primary marketplaces (art. 6).

The articles in the bank's statutes that referred to its operations with the government and the private sector were retained. This meant that the Bank of Spain was to act as a bank of issue, the government's bank and a commercial bank.

3 Liquidation or transformation of the provincial banks of issue

The provincial banks of issue were declared in liquidation. They were given an opportunity to transfer their capital and reserve funds to the Bank of Spain in exchange for Bank of Spain shares at par. They were required to decide whether they would accept the offer within 30 days (art. 4).

Though the decree did not specify it, any banks that rejected the merger offer would be permitted to remain in operation, but only by surrendering their prerogative to issue banknotes.

4 Bank of Spain loan to the government

"In consideration of the powers granted to the Bank of Spain to increase its capital and issue, extend its privilege and merge with the provincial banks, the Bank shall advance 125 million pesetas to the Treasury" (art. 17).

The decree's content ratifies what the finance minister had indicated when the decree was first presented, namely that its sole purpose was to obtain funds to confront the severe problems that beset the government. Nonetheless, the new legislation did not merely replace one issue regime with another. It also sought to bolster the role of the Bank of Spain as much as possible within the financial system as a whole. As shall be seen below, the precise wording of the sections that were most advantageous to the Bank of Spain was, in effect, proposed to the government by the bank itself. The final text was more the result of a negotiation between the bank and the government than a decision taken freely by the authorities. The Bank of Spain, it must be recalled, was a private entity acting under the auspices of the state. Most of its capital was in the hands of individuals and institutional investors. The government appointed its senior leadership, though the shareholders also had a presence on its governing bodies.

The Bank of Spain's attempt to achieve a position of practical monopoly in this way did not become fully realised because some of the banks of issue opted to continue as commercial banks. From 1875, however, its position in the Spanish financial system was clearly dominant. In addition to holding a near-monopoly on public credit, it also rose to a dominant position in the field of private credit. A modest estimate indicates that the Bank of Spain's market share of private-sector lending rose from roughly 10–20% prior to unified circulation to nearly 50% in 1878–1879 and to 60% 20 years later. The decree of 1874 turned the Spanish financial system into a quasi-monopoly of the Bank of Spain.[1]

The circumstances that surrounded the proclamation of the decree of 19 March 1874, which established unified fiduciary circulation, were genuinely extraordinary for two reasons: first, because of the precarious legitimacy of the government that issued the decree; and second, because of the state's dire for liquidity need at the time. The acting government had been formed after the effective dissolution of the First Spanish Republic by a faction of the armed forces earlier that year on 3 January. Faced with the power vacuum that ensued, a group of eminent figures put forward a proposal for General Francisco Serrano to take over the presidency of the executive branch in the name of the republic and the constitution of 1869, but acting under martial law after having dissolved the parliament. The new government had to face enormous difficulties at once, most notably a Carlist uprising and the first Cuban revolt.

The progressive revolution of 1868 had sparked a backlash from groups opposed to the liberal regime and in favour of the traditional monarchy. These groups had already led several uprisings in the previous decades, calling for the Spanish Crown to pass to the descendants of the Infante Carlos, the younger brother of Ferdinand VII. On this occasion, the revolt was led by his grandson, Carlos, Duke of Madrid. The first clashes took place in 1872. By early 1874, the situation had turned desperate for the government of the republic, especially in the Basque Country and Navarre. After several victories, the Carlist forces had taken up firm positions and were posing a grave threat to the city of Bilbao.

While these events were occurring on the Iberian Peninsula, the Spanish government also had to cope with another conflict that was just as serious or even more so: the first uprising for Cuban independence in the wake of the 1868 declaration from Carlos Manuel de Céspedes, the so-called *Grito de Yara* or Cry of Yara. After an initial phase of intermittent skirmishing, the clashes became widespread and the casualties among the peninsular soldiers began to mount.

Together, these serious armed conflicts led to a growing demand for economic resources that the government was unable to supply. Between 1870 and 1873, the state's annual deficit climbed to over 250 million pesetas a year. To finance the deficit, it was necessary to resort to strategies of all sorts, especially loans negotiated abroad and brokered through the Rothschilds and other international bankers. The public debt in circulation in those years rose from 7.3 to 11.4 billion pesetas.

These circumstances impelled the authorities to enter into highly controversial transactions, such as the signing of a contract to lease the Almadén mines to the Rothschild Bank (1870) and the sale of the Rio Tinto mines (1873). In each and every case, the transaction was concluded on very burdensome terms for the public purse, which was forced to accept them in the face of urgent needs for liquidity.[2]

When General Serrano and his ministers took charge of the government in January 1874, they encountered an economic situation that was genuinely distressing. With no possibility of further raising the tax burden and no hope of finding credit abroad, their room for manoeuvre was very limited. The man who had to tackle the challenge as finance minister was none other than José Echegaray, who had discharged ministerial duties in governments prior to the proclamation of the First Spanish Republic, having held the Development and Finance portfolios.

In his earlier ministerial duties, Echegaray had given ample demonstration of his liberal beliefs on several occasions. In the case of the subject here, the most telling example was his participation in the debate and final approval of the law of 19 October 1869 on the freedom to create joint-stock companies and credit companies. Before he was appointed minister again, Echegaray had served as a member of the lower house in the Spanish parliament and, in that capacity, had presided over the parliamentary committee that examined the draft bill submitted by the minister Ruiz Zorrilla. The committee's report went beyond the government's intentions on the freedom to create banks, going so far as to remove the precautionary measure in the draft bill that impeded the creation of banks of issue in any cities in which one had already been granted the right to issue by the government as long as that right remained in force. The report from Echegaray and the other committee members stated that it was not fair "to prohibit the establishment of new banks where there already existed one or more with an exclusive privilege, because not having acquired said privilege for good and fair consideration, there was no reason whatsoever of justice, and even less of fairness, to deny the benefit of this bill to places that are precisely of greatest importance and have a need to experience the great results of freedom on a larger scale". The immediate reaction of the parliamentarians connected to the Bank of Spain and other banks of issue forced the deleted article to be reinstated. The final text, signed by Echegaray as the minister responsible, included the banking exception on the terms indicated.[3]

The undeniably liberal leanings of José Echegaray gave credence to his claim that unavoidable factors of an extraordinary nature compelled him to decree the unified circulation of banknotes only five years after he had argued for the free establishment of banks of issue. The explanatory memorandum of the decree of 19 March 1874 touched on the state's diminishing credit and the costs incurred in the war and pointed out that it was "under such critical circumstances [and] yielding to the demands of the present reality and to the urgent needs of the fighting [that] the undersigning minister, in accord with the Council of Ministers, proposes to create on the basis of the Bank of Spain, with the assistance of the provincial Banks, a National Bank [. . .] to come to the aid of the public Treasury". A monopoly of issue was instituted, but the forced tender of banknotes was flatly rejected in the following terms: "it would be the greatest of disasters and the worst of economic calamities". The urgency of the circumstances did not blind the minister to the importance or the consequences of the decision that he was taking: "[. . .] replacing multiple fiduciary circulation [with] unified fiduciary circulation [. . .] is a far-reaching reform that the future shall judge [. . .]."[4] It should be noted, however, that the adoption of unified issue did not spell the immediate reshaping of the Bank of Spain as a central bank. Indeed, the process did not reach its conclusion until the passage of the Spanish Banking Act (Ley de Ordenación Bancaria) in 1946, which required the Bank of Spain to act as a lender of last resort. Rather, the period initiated by Echegaray's decree witnessed only the gradual spread of unified banknotes and the consolidation of a national bank (Martín-Aceña et al., 2013). It is worth remembering that the Bank of Spain remained privately owned until 1962 (Martín Aceña, 2017).

6.2. The making of a decision: the government and the Bank of Spain

Despite it would seem a precipitate measure, the decree had been discussed for several months, since the formation of the provisional government and the appointment of José Echegaray as finance minister. Echegaray was confronted with an untenable situation. The government had no creditworthiness either at home or abroad and the civil war was swallowing up vast resources. As a result, he had no choice but to turn to the Bank of Spain, requesting its economic support in exchange for a prerogative that it could not refuse: becoming the sole issuer of banknotes.

The first contact on the matter between Echegaray and the Bank of Spain appears to have taken place on 23 January, when the minister sent a draft of the proposed decree to the bank. According to the draft, the Bank of Spain was to be awarded the sole right to issue in those provinces where there was no established bank of issue, but not in the remaining provinces. Some days later, however, the government appears to have accepted the granting of a complete monopoly.

The first time that the Bank of Spain addressed the matter in depth was at a meeting of its board of directors on 26 January 1874. In the meeting, the draft decree was well received and the board of directors set up a special committee for further investigation. The new committee, which was called the "committee for the creation of a national bank", was made up of seven board members and two deputy governors. It met first on 4 February 1874 and soon took charge of overseeing the entire process of absorbing the provincial banks of issue. When the process was complete on 21 April 1875, the committee was disbanded and replaced with one that focused on "branches."[5]

The first task of the new committee was to analyse the draft decree submitted by the government. After doing so, it proposed the board of directors to request the government to introduce several amendments. The changes were aimed at strengthening the Bank of Spain's bargaining position vis-a-vis the provincial banks. Three points were particularly important. The first was related to the duration of the bank's exclusive privilege of banknote issue. According to the government's draft, the period in question would be for 30 years in the province of Madrid, but for only 10 years in the other provinces. The committee took the view that this clause would leave the door open to an eventual return of issue plurality. The amendment formulated by the bank proposed that the length of the "exclusive privilege" should be set at 30 years for all intents and purposes throughout the entire mainland territory of Spain and its adjacent islands.

The second amendment put forward by the committee related to the fourth point in the draft and was surely the most important one for the bank. In its original version, the proposed decree established that "every effort shall be made so that the other banks that exist on the Peninsula and adjacent Islands merge with the Bank of Spain with all or part of their effective capital and their reserve funds in metallic money". The ambiguity of the wording did not like committee members, who proposed new one. Their suggestion was approved in an extraordinary session of the bank's board of directors on 6 February 1874 and submitted to the ministry. The first sentence of their version could not have been more categorical: "All Banks of issue and discounting that exist today on the peninsula and adjacent islands shall be declared in liquidation". This was the demand that would lead to the complete dissolution of the provincial banks of issue. For the sake of prudence, the minister accepted the language proposed by the Bank of Spain, but he added a point to the decree's preamble that put some limits on the bank's intentions: "If [the provincial banks of issue] do not accede to the merger, they will certainly lose their right to issue; but at heart this is not a cause for their forced liquidation, for as a credit establishment, they can continue operating with all or part of their capital under one of the thousand forms to which they are authorised by the law on freedom of association". This was what actually happened, frustrating the Bank of Spain's attempt to dissolve the provincial banks by any means and to leave them no other alternative.[6]

The third key amendment proposed by the Bank of Spain was related to the effective implementation of the unified circulation of banknotes. The language suggested by the bank introduced caveats and limitations of all sorts and illustrated the bank's discomfort with the free circulation of banknotes. This can be seen in the final wording of the decree: "given that, in the situation through which the nation is now going, it is not possible to verify the material movements of wealth with the speed that would be required to redeem the notes of the Bank of Spain on their presentation in the Branches, there shall be deposited in each one, for the time being, the amount of notes that are required by the importance of its operations, the notes being distinguished by a stamp that indicates the Branch to which they pertain". In this manner, one of the major innovations of the financial system that had been used to justify a monopoly – unified circulation – was curtailed and limited. Indeed, everything would remain the same as before. The branches' banknotes could not be used to make payments in other provinces and the circulation would stay local as it had been with the former provincial banks. Unified banknotes would not arrive until 1883 and, even then, their circulation would be affected by the slowness with which the Bank of Spain complied with one of the other provisions set forth in the decree: the erection of branches in every important commercial centre (art. 6). Indeed, this point did not become a reality in terms of the provincial capitals until 1887.

After sending proposals back and forth between the finance ministry and the bank's leadership, the bank convened an extraordinary general meeting of the shareholders for 19 February 1874. The idea was to present a proposal that was so clearly favourable to the bank that it would be adopted rapidly by the assembly. That, however, was not what happened. A portion of the shareholders spoke out against the proposed operation and put up strong resistance, citing legal and financial arguments. There were lively discussions interspersed with relatively more fraught exchanges. The shareholders in opposition were convinced that the problems involved in the project would lead to the bank's ruin. They foresaw legal problems from the interminable lawsuits that would be brought by the provincial banks of issue whose contracts and rights were to be violated. There would be financial problems arising from a potential excess of banknotes in circulation that the Spanish economy did not need and that would ultimately lead to forced tender, and there would be problems with the government itself, whose capacity to meet its payment commitments on its debt and interest seemed more than doubtful in the midst of a civil war. Ultimately, the assembly went on for four sessions and concluded on 25 February.

In the end, the assembly voted to approve the proposal from the bank's leadership and the government by 88 votes in favour to 29 votes against. Some days later, the decree of 19 March 1874 established unified circulation and set in motion the liquidation of the provincial banks of issue on terms that gave the Bank of Spain a strong bargaining position.

6.3. The reaction of the provincial banks of issue

As expected, the contacts between the finance ministry and the provincial banks of issue over the draft decree were different in character and tone. The first news of the matter to reach the provincial banks came on 9 February, a few days after the draft was sent to the Bank of Spain but before the ministry received the bank's formal counter-proposal. The notification arrived via a letter sent by the director of the Treasury to each bank of issue:

> The Government has resolved to create a National Bank on the basis on the Bank of Spain, with which the provincial banks can merge on the following conditions: within thirty days from the 15th of the current month during which they can request merging, the notes of the banks shall cease to be legal tender. The provincial banks shall be permitted to contribute to the National Bank all or part of their effective capital that can be liquidated and of their reserve fund. If they contribute only their effective capital, they shall receive shares of the National Bank at par and if they add their reserve fund, they shall receive shares at 110 percent.[7]

The government's letter ended by demanding a response within one week and calling representatives from all the banks to a meeting in Madrid to establish the rules for the decree's application.

Unsurprisingly, the reaction of most banks of issue was highly critical of the government's plan, though there were also marked differences of nuance. Broadly, the banks that had developed more robustly and maintained a high level of turnover were the most resistant, while the banks that were struggling and, in some cases, facing serious problems saw the offer as a potentially dignified and beneficial way out of their difficulties.

In the weeks that followed the government's announcement, many meetings and contacts occurred between the various banks and the ministry and among the banks themselves. While there is not a record of all of these dealings, information is available on some in which the Bank of Barcelona took part.[8] After receiving formal notification from the finance ministry, the board of directors of the Bank of Barcelona took the decision to reject the offer, arguing that the period for which it had been granted the privilege to issue banknotes did not end until 7 August 1875 and that there was no legal basis for early cancellation. The bank sent its decision in writing to the ministry and received a personal reply from Echegaray, whose lengthy letter denoted the importance he attached to the position that the Bank of Barcelona might adopt as the doyen and most senior of Spain's provincial banks. In essence, his letter was a call to patriotism in the face of the country's deplorable situation, beset by Carlist insurrection on the home front and by the pro-independence uprising in Cuba:

> To reassure the country by once again re-establishing the material and moral order of this shaken society, to bring back its past esteem through courageous and necessary reforms, and to end the civil war no matter what the cost, here you have the intent of the government in general and of the finance ministry insofar as it is concerned. But this work, which would always be commendable and which is today of the utmost patriotism, requires the cooperation of every financial grouping. At crowning moments, other peoples have risen to the stature of their challenges, with the aid of the Banks and the assistance of the interests they represent. Recent examples we have on display, and goodwill and self-sacrifice will save, will almost always save the Nations in their economic order as it saves them in their political order. A proof of economic manhood is required to normalise our Treasury and our budget and this proof shall not be at the cost of forced liquidations or spurious interventions in the provincial Banks.
>
> The merger of the privileged credit establishments has been studied thoughtfully and with such a spirit of impartiality that it shall, far from resulting in losses for anybody, produce benefits for all [. . .]. The merger is not the absorption of all the Banks in one at the cost and to the harm of all the rest. The merger is the condensation of forces and capital to save the country economically, while also preserving as far as possible, which shall be much, these establishments and the particular and provincial features that characterise them. No, Sirs, do not fear that the particular character of this Bank shall disappear.[9]

After receiving Echegaray's amicable and conciliatory letter, the board of directors of the Bank of Barcelona agreed that three of its directors should travel to Madrid to talk with the minister. Their meetings took place on 7 and 9 March and proved fruitless. Echegaray remained adamant on the substance of the matter and refused to accept any delay to his plans.

Even with the publication of the decree in the government gazette on 23 March, the more belligerent banks did not relent in their opposition strategy. Some of them agreed to lodge a joint appeal against the decree within the month established by the law. In addition, nearly all the provincial banks that were still active continued with their operations without making any move to withdraw their banknotes in circulation. The resulting deadlock in the process forced the finance ministry to take more drastic measures. On 11 June, the new minister, Juan Francisco Camacho, approved an order that granted an additional period of three months to comply with the decree, while also noting his full support for its content. A few days later, the president of the executive branch, General Serrano, delivered his ruling on the appeal lodged by the banks of issue, ordering them to comply with the order of 11 June from the finance ministry and thereby rejecting their submitted requests.

Despite his ratification of the decree of 19 March, the new minister seemed much more inclined to look for a negotiated settlement. According to Jaume Girona, representative of the Bank of Barcelona in Madrid, Camacho did not conceal his total "non-conformance" with the procedure followed by his predecessor, but he did feel obligated to abide by what had already been done as a fait accompli. In the case of the Bank of Barcelona, his greater willingness resulted in a new round of talks that again concluded without agreement. In any event, the debate now revolved around the conditions under which the Bank of Barcelona would agree to a merger, not around the effectiveness of the monopoly of issue as such. A final decree, on 20 October 1874, granted a further period of 30 days to permit the ongoing negotiations to reach a conclusion. In the case of the banks in Barcelona and Bilbao, there was one last skirmish after the installation of the first government of the Bourbon Restoration, but it had no significant effect on the outcome.

The decree of 19 March 1874 became law under the restored monarchy when Alfonso XII ratified it on 17 July 1876, closing the final legal loophole that might have had an effect on the chequered process by which note-issue monopoly was established in Spain. For the banks that decided to carry on without the privilege to issue, one phase in their history had come to an end and another very different one began. As for the banks that agreed to the merger offer, the road ahead was winding and not always smooth.

6.4. The merger processes[10]

According to article 4 of the decree of 19 March 1874, the provincial banks of issue had 30 days to merge with the Bank of Spain and they could do so only up to the amount of their effective capital and reserve funds, in exchange for shares in the Bank of Spain at nominal (par) value. In practice, the process of absorption was not very rigorously enforced. As noted earlier, the period was extended twice and negotiations continued even after the third and final deadline with some of the banks that were resistant to the merger and would ultimately become commercial banks, such as those of Barcelona, Santander and Bilbao. First, however, it is important to look at the way followed by the banks that did indeed merge with the Bank of Spain.

The merger or absorption operations were associated with an increase in Bank of Spain's share capital from 50 to 100 million pesetas as set out in the decree. A portion of the increase was earmarked for shareholders of the absorbed banks. In each case, the Bank of Spain was to award its shares at par for the nominal value of the shares in the acquired bank plus 10% for the reserve fund. This amount was supposed to be furnished in metallic money by the provincial banks or by their respective shareholders. The winding-up of each provincial bank was to be carried out at its own shareholders' expense. The Bank of Spain had no plans to retain the clients, liabilities or assets of the absorbed banks; at the most, it might purchase the furnishings and negotiate the transfer or acquisition of premises. No bank was going to be appraised on the basis of its share price or financial value.

The committee dealing with the matter summed the situation up clearly at its first deliberative meeting to lay out the process. Plainly, the Bank of Spain was not willing to carry out any full-fledged mergers or absorptions. The main working principles adopted by the committee were: 1) "The Bank of Spain cannot undertake to realise the securities that make up the holdings of the provincial establishments being annexed, nor to admit in the merger more than coin for the sum-total of the effective value of the shares that they have issued and the reserve fund that they have created [. . .]"; 2) "that in any locale where the existing Bank has been annexed, a branch shall be established as early as possible under the terms prescribed by the Regulations that currently govern the branches created in Alicante and Valencia"; and 3) "that the premises in which the annexed Banks are located and that are the property of said Banks, as well as the furnishings of their offices, shall be acquired by the Bank of Spain if the price conditions and other circumstances are suitable."[11] The points laid out by the committee were later discussed and ratified in an extraordinary session of the Bank of Spain's board of the governors on 30 April 1874. Under the circumstances, the bank's position is understandable. The main objection that might be raised is that all the provincial banks received an excessively uniform treatment, when in fact the position of each was very different. It should be mentioned here, however, that something similar had occurred in France in 1848 when the banks of issue in the French departments were absorbed by the Bank of France in a homogeneous manner.

In short, the planned operation was neither an absorption nor a merger as they have subsequently come to be understood. Rather, it involved the sale of Bank of Spain shares on highly favourable price conditions for an amount equal to the nominal capital and reserves of each bank being wound up. The difference between the nominal value at which the shares were sold and the traded price of the shares on the stock market generated a net capital gain for the provincial banks' shareholders, provided that they succeeded in liquidating their respective bank's assets without losses. It was more about compensation for losing the privilege to issue banknotes than about a merger or absorption. The amount of the compensation can be estimated for each case and time by looking at the share price for the Bank of Spain.

On this basis, the process of winding up the provincial banks of issue and adding their shareholders to those of the Bank of Spain was slower and more complex than desired. Of the 15 banks in existence in 1874, 10 merged with the Bank of Spain and 5 carried on as banks without the right to issue. The five banks that did not merge were the ones located in Barcelona, Bilbao, Santander, Tarragona and Reus. Indeed, the process played out in three stages demarcated by the initial decree of 19 March and the successive extensions granted in the decrees of 11 June and 20 October later in the same year.

Within the time period set by the initial decree, only three merger requests were received. They corresponded to the banks in Vitoria, Pamplona and Oviedo. The Bank of Pamplona notified the Bank of Spain in a letter dated 9 April 1874, stating that an agreement had been reached in an extraordinary general meeting of its shareholders to merge with the Bank of Spain in accordance with the decree of 19 March. The notification was received and debated by the Bank of Spain's board of directors on 20 April and their sole response was to acknowledge receipt of the letter. The first merger to be analysed in depth pertained to the Bank of Vitoria, which submitted a formal request dated 22 April to negotiate a merger. Almost at the same time, the Bank of Oviedo's request was received as well. However, it was the proposal from the Bank of Vitoria that spurred the Bank of Spain's committee for the creation of a national bank to establish the abovementioned general conditions at a meeting on 25 April. Agreement was reached on 5 May to merge with the banks in Oviedo and Vitoria, and the bank in Pamplona was added in an extension agreed on 16 May. Though the Bank of Spain was under no obligation to do so, it agreed in all three cases to take on the former directors and staff of the three banks and to use the same premises. The plan was to start operating as the Bank of Spain in the new branches on 1 July, though in practice there were minor delays.

In view of the limited success and the ongoing conversations with other entities, the finance ministry decreed a 90-day extension to the process on 11 June. This second phase brought the absorption of Bank Balear and the banks in Málaga, Seville and San Sebastián. The mergers of Bank Balear and the Bank of San Sebastián were approved with few problems at a meeting of the Bank of Spain's board of directors on 18 September, though they did not accept everything requested by the pair. The representatives of the banks in Málaga and Seville, however, found the going more difficult. A committee of shareholders that represented the interests of the Bank of Málaga, including Manuel Larios and the Marquis of Casa Loring, very prominent and wealthy businessmen, sought a significant improvement in the merger conditions and the transfer of the building where the bank was located. The Bank of Spain held firm and the merger ultimately took place on its terms, limiting recognition strictly to a bank's paid-in capital and reserves. Even more unfortunate was the committee representing the interests of the Bank of Seville's shareholders, though in this case the bank's committee knew that the negotiation would be complicated because the bank had not been active for years. In fact, the Bank of Spain refused for some time to accept that the Bank of Seville was entitled in any way to merge with it. Doubtless to avoid legal problems, however, it did ultimately accede to selling 2,000 shares at 550 pesetas each to the Seville shareholders in lieu of the 8,000 shares that they had originally sought and that corresponded to the bank's original capital.

Lastly, an additional extension of 30 days was issued by decree on 20 October 1874 in order to try to complete the process. During this third and final period, the banks in Zaragoza, A Coruña, Jerez and Santander entered into the exchange of shares. In the cases of Zaragoza and A Coruña, the shareholders decided to create another banking entity that took the form of a credit company in accordance with the legislation of 1856, without the right to issue banknotes, but in competition with any branches that the Bank of Spain was to open in their cities. This eventuality is precisely what the Bank of Spain wanted to avoid, but it was not always able to do so. Nor, however, did the predictions of some shareholders come to pass: that the new entities would compete with a local Bank of Spain branch by issuing securities payable on demand to the bearer (similar to banknotes) in direct competition with the Bank of Spain's banknotes.

In general, the shareholders of the banks of issue that accepted the merger conditions obtained a return from the operation that was not small. In March 1874, shares in the Bank of Spain traded at 150%, but the price was trending downward just at the time when the legislation required a capital increase. During the months of the share swaps, the Bank of Spain's shares traded between 130% and 140% (Table 6.1). Under these conditions, the shareholders of the banks whose shares were valued at par in the market obtained a net profit of between 17% and 26% on their invested capital. Given the design of the operation, their returns were greater, the lower the market value of the shares of the merging banks. Unsurprisingly, therefore, the banks that were more resistant to merging were the ones that had acquired greater size and had a higher market valuation.

Of the five banks that finally rejected the merger, there is precise information on the three that had the largest amount of business: the banks in Santander, Bilbao and Barcelona. The case of the Bank of Santander is unusual. While staunchly opposed to the merger at first, the position of its leadership softened as other banks took the offer. Finally, they decided to propose their own terms of exchange to the Bank of Spain, putting a price tag on their shares in excess of face value. The proposal likely reflected the fact that the bank's market value was effectively

Table 6.1 Bank of Spain share price quotation (par = 100)

January 1874	168
July 1874	138
December 1874	138
December 1875	174
December 1876	199
December 1880	299

higher than the nominal value of its capital. When the Bank of Spain rejected the conditions, the Bank of Santander withdrew its request and transformed the entity into a credit company without the right to issue banknotes.[12]

Finally, in the months of February and April 1875, after all three time periods had elapsed, the Bank of Spain received requests from the Bank of Barcelona and the Bank of Bilbao. For these entities, the design of the merger likely did not offer any convincing short-term returns from a financial standpoint. While it was true that the Bank of Spain's shares were trading at higher prices than the shares of the two latecomers up to March 1874, the compulsory planned capital increase had caused the price to fall. Indeed, on the day of 19 March when the decree on monetary unification came out, the Bank of Spain's shares were trading at 154% and the Bank of Barcelona's shares stood at 118%. Four months later, on 19 July, the former had fallen to 125%, while the latter had held steady. At this time and under the conditions established by the decree, the operation would have resulted in losses for the Bank of Barcelona's shareholders.[13]

The limited appeal of the government's offer for the banks in Barcelona and Bilbao at the time did not preclude the possibility that matters in the longer run might be different. Losing the privilege of note issue also led to a relative loss of value in the shares of the Bank of Barcelona and, probably, in the shares of the Bank of Bilbao. At the close of 1874, the Barcelona bank's shares were holding steady around 120%, while the Bank of Spain's shares had rebounded to 138%. A year later, in late 1875, the two banks' share prices stood at 140% and 174%, respectively. By 1880, the gap was even greater: 300% for the Bank of Spain and 165% for the Bank of Barcelona.

Against this backdrop, the request submitted by the Bank of Barcelona in February 1875 must be understood as an attempt to recoup the loss in value stemming from the withdrawal of the right to issue banknotes. In fact, the Catalan bank took literally the language in the initial decree of March 1874, which referred in article 4 to the transfer of Bank of Spain shares to the shareholders of the provincial banks "as compensation for the lapsing of their respective privileges", to claim its right to purchase 15,000 Bank of Spain shares at 110%, which was equivalent to the capital of the Bank of Barcelona plus 10% for its reserves (which totalled 8.25 million pesetas). The Bank of Barcelona would then carry on operating as a credit company "perfectly compatible with the new establishment".

In the opinion of the members of the Bank of Spain's committee for the creation of a national bank, the request was outrageous. They flatly rejected it at their meeting of 23 February 1875: "When the floor was open for discussion, all the gentlemen took part, commenting unanimously that the previously stated proposals were inadmissible and that they appear to want to belittle the board of directors of this Bank [. . .]. It is easy to see the utilitarian object, according to their own words, in the premium that their shares would earn and that would yield them a profit of ten million *reales*, approximately, without any compensation whatsoever for the Bank of Spain (to which the Bank of Barcelona has been openly and tenaciously hostile), in order to found or strengthen the new company into which it has transformed itself, without liquidating as required [. . .]. The committee resolved to notify the board of directors of its views and urged that a confidential letter be sent by the governor to the finance minister stating additionally that there appeared to be no reasonable terms that would permit the union of the Bank of Barcelona and the Bank of Spain [. . .]". The Bank of Barcelona saw its request rejected.

Lastly, on 21 April 1875, the committee for the creation of a national bank discussed a merger proposal with a delegation from the Bank of Bilbao. It is important to recall that the city of Bilbao had been encircled by Carlist rebels for some months and it had not been completely liberated until the beginning of May 1874. At the meeting, the Bank of Spain asked the Bilbao representatives to make a commitment that, if the merger were accepted, the Bank of Bilbao would transfer its headquarters to the Bank of Spain and not set up another credit company of the same name to operate in the city. In the ensuing discussion, a Bilbao representative did not accede to the Bank of Spain's request, given that only the shareholders' general meeting could take such a decision, but he did seize on the opportunity to highlight the excellent financial health of the bank, which was better even than that of the Bank of Barcelona. When the discussion between the two groups had finished, the Bank of Spain members met in closed session and agreed that they would only give 3,868 shares at 110% to the Bank of Bilbao's shareholders. According to the committee, all of the merger deadlines had passed and the increase in capital had already been completed, so there was no more leeway except for shares that had not yet been placed among the Bank of Spain's own shareholders by December 1874. It was agreed to give this limited number of shares at par value to the Bank of Bilbao's shareholders as corresponded to them, provided that the bank was wound up, the premises that it occupied were handed over and its banknotes were gathered in.

These conditions proved wholly unacceptable to the Bank of Bilbao. At an extraordinary general meeting of the shareholders in Bilbao on 2 July 1875, it was decided that the bank should ignore the decree of 1874 giving the Bank of Spain a monopoly on banknote issue. Consequently, the Basque bank's notes were to remain in circulation and a legal battle was initiated to neutralise the original decree of 19 March 1874.[14] The legal battle dragged on for nearly four years and only when it had ended were the Bank of Bilbao's notes withdrawn from circulation.

When viewed altogether, the process of monetary unification launched in March 1874 cannot be described as fair or efficient. It was not fair because many of the banks of issue were stripped of a privilege – the right to issue banknotes – that they had obtained legally. The 'compensation' that was intended for the banks' shareholders proved especially beneficial for the least sound entities, including some that were bankrupt. By contrast, the banks that had succeeded in adding value to their balance sheets suffered direct harm and received no compensation whatsoever. The damage caused could be inferred from the very large and widening difference between the market value of the shares of the banks that remained in business and that of the shares of the Bank of Spain.

The decision against merging that was made by the five banks mentioned above has also been analysed from a strategic perspective, especially in the case of the Bank of Barcelona. Critics point out that the bank's leadership, if the merger had been accepted, would have exerted a great deal of influence over the management of the Bank of Spain. The issue, however, is more complex. An internal group within the leadership of the Bank of Barcelona headed by the founder himself, Manuel Girona, was always in favour of reaching an agreement with the Bank of Spain if the agreement would, in exchange for accepting the merger, allow the resulting Barcelona branch of the issuing bank to be granted its own statute and permit its leadership to maintain an independent policy. However, they were defeated by others opposed to the merger, who were perhaps holding out for a better deal based on the valuation of the bank's shares. This would account for the change of heart over the offer conveyed via the finance minister in early 1875 and ultimately rejected by the Bank of Spain.[15]

Notes

1 For more on the evolution of Spanish banking from 1874 onwards, see Tortella (1974). For more on private-sector lending by Spanish banks, see Martín Aceña and Pons (2005).

2 For more on the operations of the Rothschild family and the financial straits of the governments of the *Sexenio Demócratico*, see Nadal (1975), pp. 106–115); López-Morell (2005, chapter 6); Martín Niño (1972); Comín (1988, vol. I, chapter 3). For more on the relations between the Bank of Spain and the governments, see Tedde (2015).

3 Echegaray was an engineer and mathematician who, in addition to his work as a politician and economist, was also a very popular dramatist. He was awarded the Nobel Prize in Literature in 1904. On his economic ideas, see Tedde (2006); Pascual (2000); Martín Rodríguez (2009, pp. 411–421, 473–476).

4 *Gaceta de Madrid*, no. 82, 23 March 1874, p. 714.

5 Archive of the Bank of Spain, Secretariat, box 673.

6 The bank leadership's dislike of the preamble was made clear at the meetings of the board of directors on 23 and 26 March. After receiving a request from the government for an advance on the loan of 125 million pesetas established in the decree, the board of governors "informed the governor that it was not possible to take the decision [to deliver the advance requested by the government] before learning of the assent of the Provincial Banks and having the Bank of Spain constituted with its new organisation, for which there would be difficulties because of the terms in the preamble of the Decree, whose fulfilment could be eluded by said Provincial Banks in order to continue functioning as credit companies, deprived of the power to issue banknotes, but able to make up for the loss by means of other mercantile securities, nullifying in their respective locales [the securities] of the National Bank, which would circulate as hitherto without the necessary breadth". ABE, book 27107.

7 Compiled in Blasco-Martel and Sudrià (2010, p. 346).

8 Blasco-Martel and Sudrià (2010, pp. 345ff.).

9 Reproduced in Blasco-Martel and Sudrià (2010, pp. 362–363).

10 Additional details on the subject in Castañeda (2001, pp. 40–45).

11 Archive of the Bank of Spain, Secretariat, box 673. Minutes of the Committee for the Creation of a National Bank.

12 Martín Aceña (2007, pp. 34–36).

13 For 100 Bank of Barcelona shares whose market value stood in the region of 600 pesetas, the Bank of Spain would have to deliver 90 Bank of Spain shares at 562 pesetas to the Catalan bank's shareholders.
14 Castañeda (2001, pp. 44–45).
15 For more on the subject, see Castañeda (2001, pp. 42–44), and Blasco-Martel and Sudrià (2010, pp. 353–360).

Sources

Archive of the Bank of Spain, Madrid.

Bibliography

Castañeda, L., 2001, *El Banco de España (1874-1900). La red de sucursales y los nuevos servicios financieros*. Banco de España, Madrid.

Blasco-Martel, Y., and Sudrià, C., 2010. *El Banco de Barcelona (1844-1874). Historia de un banco emisor*. LID, Madrid

Comín, F., 1988. *Hacienda y economía en la España contemporánea: 1800–1936*. Ministerio de Economía y Hacienda. Instituto de Estudios Fiscales, Madrid.

López-Morell, M.Á., 2005. *La Casa Rothschild en España (1812–1941), Memorias y biografías*. Marcial Pons, Madrid.

Martín Aceña, P., 2017. *The Banco de España, 1782–2017 the history of a central bank*. Banco de España, Madrid.

Martín Aceña, P. and Pons, A., 2005. Sistema monetario y financiero. In Carreras, A., and Tafunell, X. (Eds.), *Estadísticas Históricas de España: siglos XIX-XX*, 2nd Edition. Fundación BBVA, Bilbao.

Martín-Aceña, P., Martínez-Ruíz, E., and Nogués-Marco, P., 2013. The bank of Spain: A national financial institution. *J. Eur. Econ. Hist*., 42, 11–46.

Martín Niño, J., 1972. *La Hacienda española y la revolución de 1868*. Instituto de Estudios Fiscales. Ministerio de Hacienda, Madrid.

Martín Rodríguez, M., 2009. *Análisis económico y revolución liberal en España. Economistas académicos en las Cortes liberales, 1834–1874*. Civitas, Cizur Menor, Navarra.

Nadal, J., 1975. *El fracaso de la revolución industrial en España, 1814–1913*. Editorial Ariel, Barcelona.

Pascual, J., 2000. Algunas notas sobre la figura de José Echegaray como economista. *Econ. y Econ. Españoles*, 4, 535–542.

Tedde, P., 2006. José Echegaray, economista. In Comin, F., Martín Aceña, P., and Vallejo Pousada, R. (Eds.), *La Hacienda Por Sus Ministros: La Etapa Liberal de 1845 a 1899*. Prensas Universitarias de Zaragoza, Zaragoza, pp. 339–368.

Tedde, P., 2015. *El Banco de España y el Estado liberal (1847-1874)*. Gadir/Banco de España, Madrid.

Tortella, G. (Ed). 1974. *La banca española en la Restauración*. 2 vols. Banco de España, Madrid.

7 A final assessment: Spanish banking development in nineteenth-century Europe

Carles Sudrià

The aim of the book has been to present a new perspective on the early stages of Spain's financial development, giving special attention to the role played by banks of issue. This final chapter brings together the most salient features addressed in previous chapters and sets out to evaluate the process as a whole, putting the Spanish case into the European context.

From a comparative perspective, the first element to bear in mind must be the relative time lag in the introduction of issue plurality in Spain, in 1844. In the early years of the 1840s, the first Carlist revolt came to end, bringing to a close nearly five decades of chronic internal and external warfare and intense political instability. In the financial realm, these circumstances had two crucial consequences: first, the early appearance of a major 'state' bank – the Bank of San Carlos, founded in 1782 – was not accompanied by other banking institutions aimed at satisfying the private sector's financial demands; and second, the state, which needed funds to cope with the country's various conflicts, monopolised nearly all of the lending activity of the Bank of San Carlos and its successor, the Bank of San Fernando. The figures in Table 7.1 show the gap between the Spanish bank and its European counterparts in terms of the capital that supported their activities.

Given this situation, the banknotes put out by Spain's sole bank of issue circulated only in Madrid and only among merchants and state contractors. The financial services provided to all other sectors came from money-changers and private bankers. Their function, however, was confined to facilitating the purchase and sale of securities and the circulation of bills of exchange, because they had limited resources for the effective granting of credit, either through commercial discounting or through loans against securities or merchandise. The weakness of their own capital constrained the guarantee that they could offer to prospective depositors, who were logically few in number.

The appearance of new banks of issue in Spain in the mid-1840s, therefore, must be seen against a backdrop of economic normalisation and recovering trade, which soon made evident the need for new ways to furnish credit and means of payment to the economy's private sector. Nevertheless, the authorisation and launch of new banking entities with a right to issue banknotes was not the result of a deliberate policy arising out of debate in political or academic forums. Quite the contrary, it was a unilateral decision taken by a transitional government in response to requests from specific groups of merchants: one based in Madrid, with

Table 7.1 Financial development indicators

	Spain	*England*	*France*	*Germany*	*Italy*
	1843	***1843***	***1847***	***1846***	***1850***
Capital of 'state' bank (million pesetas)	10	363	68	42*	8**
Number of other banks of issue	0	279	9	4	9
Total GDP (million G-K$ 1990)	15,094	51,886	58,806	48,178	33,019
GDP per capita (G-K$ 1990)	1,062	1,886	1,635	1,428	1,350

* Bank of Prussia ** National Bank of the Sardinian States (Banca Nazionale degli Stati Sardi)
Sources: Noël (1888, pp. 20, 34, 113, 247, 261), Spinelli and Frantianni (1991, pp. 137–151) and Maddison (2003).

the Marquis of Salamanca as the principal party concerned (Bank of Isabel II); and the other organised in Barcelona around the figure of Manuel Girona (Bank of Barcelona). In the case of Cádiz, competing interests among different groups gave rise simultaneously to three banks of issue, which ultimately shrank to one in 1847 (Bank of Cádiz).

That it was a political decision that had not previously been debated is not to say that it lacked a strong rationale or did not respond to a real need. The decision to give authorisation to independent banks also has its logic. It does not appear that the then Bank of San Fernando was in a position to expand its activities even within Madrid, where the finance minister himself understood that "[. . .] the high price of interest on money [. . .], the sad state of exchange rates in the various centres of the kingdom [and] the unprecedented difficulty of commercial transactions [were] a sure symptom of the inadequacy of [the bank] as the sole credit establishment."[1]

When the Bank of Isabel II opened for business, a period of competition began between the notes issued by the old Bank of San Fernando and the new bank's notes. The experience of plurality with competition failed, though it is not certain that the failure should be put down to competition itself. While there were episodes of malicious confrontation between the two establishments, all indications are that the essential factors of the problem were, on the one hand, the impact of the crisis of 1847 and, on the other, the imprudent management of the recently created bank, which was much more dynamic but also overly dependent on the private interests of its leaders, particularly José de Salamanca.

The banks in Barcelona and Cádiz were the only new banks to survive until 1856. But did they live up to the expectations placed on them during the period? We do not believe that the response can be straightforward. The available information on the Bank of Cádiz is far from satisfactory and the information referring to the Bank of Barcelona, though better, is hardly complete.

Table 7.2, which has been prepared for 1847 (the last year prior to the establishment of note-issue monopoly in France), allows for some comparisons. First, the

Table 7.2 Banks of issue in France, the UK and Spain in 1847

	Capital	*Banknotes in circulation*	*Banknotes in circulation per capita*		*Capital*	*Banknotes in circulation*	*Banknotes in circulation per capita*
	Million pesetas	*Million pesetas*	*pesetas*		*Million pesetas*	*Million pesetas*	*pesetas*
France				United Kingdom			
Bordeaux	3.2	20.9	210.1	England			
Rouen	3.0	12.0	132.6	Bank of England	364.1	478.0	31.5*
Nantes	3.0	4.3	51.6	Provincial banks (254)		184.0	12.2*
Lyon	2.0	19.8	137.5	**Total for England**		**662.0**	**43.7***
Marseille	4.0	16.3	110.7				
Le Havre	4.0	4.4	166.7	**Scotland (19)**	**281.0**	**88.8**	**32.5***
Lille	2.0	4.5	70.5	– average per bank	14.8	4.7	
Toulouse	1.2	4.8	62.3				
Orléans	1.0	3.0	76.9	**Ireland (6)**	**105.0**	**150.2**	**20.5***
				– average per bank	17.5	25.0	
Average for departmental banks	2.6	10.0	116.8	Spain			
Total for departmental banks	23.4	90.1		Barcelona	2.5	4.5	26.2
Bank of France	67.9	247.1	6.9*	Cádiz**	2.6	2.2	33.1
Total for France	**91.3**	**337.2**	**9.4***	Total for provincial banks	5.1	6.7	
				Bank of San Fernando	50.0	142.5	–
				Total for Spain	**55.1**	**149.2**	**10.2***

* The figures that refer to national totals are not comparable with other entries in the same column, which are calculated based on municipal population.

** The figures for Cádiz refer to the year 1848.

Source: *Annuaire de l'économie politique et de la statistique, 1849; Statistics for Great Britain, Germany and France; National Monetary Commission (US)*, (1910, pp. 123–125), Tedde (1999, p. 212) and Sudrià i Triay and Blasco-Martel (2016, appendix)

data show a large gap between the British and Irish provincial banks and those of France and Spain. Clearly the levels of financial development differed widely between the two pairs of countries.

The banks in Barcelona and Cádiz resemble the French banks in the size of their equity capital, but they clearly rank lower in terms of banknote issue. In the case of equity capital, it is necessary to take into account the unusual policy pursued by the Bank of Barcelona. The figure of 2.5 million pesetas that appears in the table corresponds to paid-in capital, but the bank's nominal capital was actually 5 million pesetas. Also, the unpaid capital was not exempt from the bank's liabilities. By means of a notarial deed, the shareholders committed to paying in the outstanding amount in a very short period of time if requested to do so by the bank's board of directors. It was a system designed to increase the bank's solvency, while keeping the ratio of shareholders' equity to total assets very low, with a corresponding effect on profitability.

As for the amount of banknotes in circulation, two points of clarification are necessary. First, the French banks had been open to the public for much longer than their Spanish counterparts. The first three French departmental banks were founded in 1817–1818, followed by the six remaining ones between 1835 and 1838. This means that by the early 1840s, some had 30 years behind them and others had 10, whereas the Spanish banks had barely completed 2 years in business. Introducing modern financial habits in new areas was a slow process, even in cities with a deep-rooted mercantile tradition like Cádiz and Barcelona. Second, the regulatory policy adopted by Spain's moderate governments was highly adverse to financial development.

When the moderate party came to power in May 1844, it ushered in a ten-year period governed entirely by the most conservative segment of liberalism. In the economic sphere, the moderates' policy was dominated by a deep distrust of new tools for lending and business development. The party's leading economic figures were staunch supporters of strict control over banks of issue, resolute opponents of the free formation of joint-stock companies, and of course extremely reluctant to accept the proliferation of banks of any type, but especially banks of issue.

Their timorous view of economic reality lay at the foundation of a series of regulatory measures that would seriously constrain the country's economic development. In the lending arena, two laws enacted in 1849 and 1851 dramatically restricted the issue capacity of the Bank of San Fernando and reduced its capital in an equally dramatic fashion. The consequence was an extremely tight squeeze on the supply of fiat money, which fell from 53 million pesetas to 33 million, a decline that doubtless had important effects on the financial market (Table 7.3). It is also true, however, that these contractionary effects were partly mitigated by the increased lending that could be done by the banks thanks to the increased balances in their customers' current accounts. Indeed, all indications are that current accounts were used as a means of payment in light of the scarcity of banknotes. The use of current accounts, however, was only available to interested parties who had been taken on as clients by the banks and their number was very small even in relation to the minuscule world of business in the period. By 1854, the Bank of

Table 7.3 Banknotes, current accounts and credit: banks of issue, 1848 and 1853 (million pesetas)

	1848	*1853*
Banknotes in circulation		
Bank of San Fernando	45.1	29.8
Bank of Barcelona	5.4	1.2
Bank of Cádiz	2.2	1.9
TOTAL	**52.7**	**32.9**
Current accounts		
Bank of San Fernando	1.1	17.3
Bank of Barcelona	1.0	14.2
Bank of Cádiz	0.7	5.7
TOTAL	**2.8**	**37.2**
Credit to the private sector		
Bank of San Fernando	10.0	37.6
Bank of Barcelona	7.0	8.5
Bank of Cádiz	2.0	5.4
TOTAL	**19.0**	**51.5**

Sources: Tedde (1999); Blasco-Martel and Sudrià (2010); Titos (2003).

Barcelona had opened only 338 current accounts, a total that was lower than the number of its own shareholders. At any rate, it is a fact that the gap in financial development between Spain and other countries undoubtedly widened in these years.

In the closing years of the decade under the rule of the moderate party, the Spanish economy showed increasing symptoms of financial suffocation. The signs included higher interest rates,[2] the public's acceptance of private receipts and promissory notes as payment instruments[3] and requests submitted to the government for the authorisation of new banks.[4] The Bank of San Fernando itself, through its governor Ramón Santillán, who was mindful of the situation, sent a request to the government in 1853 to seek authorisation for an increase in monetary circulation and the opening of branches provided for in the law of 1851[5].

Neither of Santillán's demands was met, which helps to explain what happened after July 1854, the time at which the progressive party returned to power on the back of a military revolt. The requests for authorisation of new banks were reiterated and the new parliament faced legislative initiatives to draft a specific banking act that was extremely liberal in nature. In response, the government felt compelled to manoeuvre to ensure that a much more moderate bill prevailed.

These parliamentary wrangling reflected a fundamental conflict over the preferable banking structure for Spain, with the debate over issue plurality at the forefront. Pedro Tedde (1999, pp. 270–276) has rightly pointed out that the positions in the debate did not line up on ideological or party political terms. Leading figures in the new progressive ascendancy, like Manuel Collado, the Duke of Sevillano and Francisco Santa Cruz, were also shareholders or directors in the Bank of San Fernando and defended its interests, while groups of merchants and bankers in the provinces urged their local parliamentary representatives to fight for the granting of independent banks of issue.

In our view, the crux of the problem lay in the scant credibility of the Bank of San Fernando and its leaders when they announced their interest in opening branches in Spain's major cities. Though some sectors within the bank held that "abandoning the privilege of establishing branches in the important centres of the kingdom is to doom the establishment to stagnation and death,"[6] the truth is the bank's directors and shareholders had strong misgivings about expanding too fast or too far afield. Under government urging, the bank agreed to promote the creation of branches in the nine cities that would later figure in the law, but when the draft bill presented by the executive to parliament specified that this would have to be done within a year, the bank's governor Ramón Santillán went to the ministry to express the inconvenience of the deadline on logistical and financial grounds. Specifically, he laid out his misgivings over obtaining the resources needed to cover the consequent capital increase "in a country so lacking in available capital". None of these purported difficulties, however, impeded the creation of new independent banks after the approval of the law.[7]

As we know, the final decision of Spain's parliament came down in favour of the plurality of banknote issue with exclusive territorial privileges. This meant following the French model with its defunct departmental banks and not the model in force in other countries that accepted direct competition between banks of issue. This hybrid position can be explained in large part by the memory of confrontations between the Bank of San Fernando and the Bank of Isabel II in the period 1844–1847, which had ended in a state-mandated merger.[8]

The confused endpoint of the parliamentary debate and the contradictory language in the text itself have encouraged a critical view of the new law on banks of issue, which has also been ascribed some responsibility for the financial crisis of 1866. In our opinion, a properly balanced assessment needs to consider three questions that are formally distinct, but closely related:

a Was a change in banking regulations necessary in the mid-1850s?
b Which of the three alternatives was most appropriate: total freedom with some minimum reserve requirements; a system like the one that was actually adopted, with independent banks that enjoyed exclusive rights to issue in their province; or a single bank with branches?
c Was the role of the provincial banks important? What were the main obstacles that prevented them from making a greater contribution?

In our view, the answer to the first question is an unequivocal yes. We have referred above to the irrefutable symptoms of financial strain appearing in the country. The opinion of scholars of the history of Spanish finance – in contrast to the view of contemporaries at the time – is almost unanimous in support of the need for reform and of the positive effects of the measures adopted. In a recent overview, Tortella and García Ruiz state:

> There is no doubt the economic policy of the Progressive party was a shot in the arm to the lethargic Spanish economy [. . .]. It provoked an injection of foreign investment and entrepreneurial initiative which obviously had a contagious effect on the rather inert local economic agents.[9]

The second question, namely which alternative was most appropriate, proves more complex to elucidate. The possibility of introducing a fully liberalised system was not, nor could it be, the aim of the reform that was undertaken. Competition required the establishment of a system of oversight to safeguard the rights of customers. A state still in the process of formation was not in a position to organise services of such scope. In addition, all the cases of free banking in existence at the time had arisen spontaneously and not as the product of permissive or specific laws. In this respect, Spain was a latecomer.

The choice between a system of local monopolies managed by independent companies or a centralised system lay at the heart of the discussions at the time and it must similarly be pivotal in the historical assessment that we are tackling. The first option has the advantages of flexibility in adapting to each locale and market, the ease of obtaining local financial support to open the new establishments and the possibility of undertaking the opening of several branches at the same time, a task that would be more complicated for a single entity however large it might be. The second option has the advantages of potentially greater size and stability and the facilities that a single bank could offer to large clients (including the state itself), for whom the size of the partner is a substantive concern.

As indicated above, a key factor for decision-makers was to determine whether the Bank of Spain was genuinely determined to give an impetus to territorial banking expansion or it simply intended to keep hold of the prerogatives that it had obtained in previous years. We have already noted that some of the attitudes and decisions adopted by the Bank of San Fernando (the future Bank of Spain) immediately before the political shift that heralded the new legislation led many observers to doubt the bank's interest in establishing a branch network to meet the overall demand for means of payment. A small comparison a posteriori can shed light on the debate.

As we know, after giving enforced priority to local entrepreneurs, only two of the locales in the Bank of Spain's original plans were still open to receiving a branch of the bank: Valencia and Alicante. A comparison of the trajectories of the Bank of Spain's branches and the independent banks offers useful information on the attitudes of the leaders of the "official" Spanish bank.

Table 7.4 above sets out the results presented in Chapter 5 (Table 5.7), but now also including the Bank of Spain's branches in Valencia and Alicante. The figures correspond to an average over four years, from 1860 to 1863.[10] As the table shows, the level of banknotes in circulation reached by the two branches in relation to the number of inhabitants and to GDP is clearly below the level attained by the local

Table 7.4 Banknotes in circulation at 31 December 1864

Provinces	*Banknotes per 1,000 inhabitants*	*Provinces*	*Banknotes per 1,000 pesetas of GDP*
	Pesetas		*Pesetas*
Cádiz	30.5	Biscay (Bilbao)	67.2
Biscay (Bilbao)	25.0	Cádiz	45.7
Barcelona	17.7	Santander	38.0
Seville	15.0	Barcelona	32.0
Málaga	13.9	Valladolid	30.7
Valladolid	12.4	Seville	28.1
Santander	11.5	Málaga	24.1
Gipuzkoa (San Sebastián)	7.5	Gipuzkoa (San Sebastián)	23.1
Zaragoza	3.5	Zaragoza	8.5
Tarragona*	2.7	Tarragona*	7.7
Alicante	**2.7**	**Alicante**	**7.6**
Balearic Isl.	2.3	A Coruña	7.2
A Coruña	2.0	Balearic Isl.	6.0
Valencia	**1.9**	Álava (Vitoria)	4.6
Araba/Álava	1.5	**Valencia**	**4.5**
Burgos	1.1	Burgos	3.8
Navarre (Pamplona)	0.6	Oviedo	3.1
Oviedo	0.6	Navarre (Pamplona)	1.7
Palencia	0.3	Palencia	0.9

Source: See Table 5.7 in Chapter 5 (in parentheses, provincial capital)

banks in locales of similar rank and size. While the evidence is not conclusive, it does show a limited interest in territorial expansion among the Bank of Spain's directors. This is also similar to what is found again after 1874 and has been discussed earlier. A comparison between the issue dynamic of the branches and that of the independent banks shows more volatility in the branches' fluctuations, which appears contradictory given the larger size of the parent bank (Figure 7.1). In short, we can conclude that the independent provincial banks maintained significantly higher and more stable activity than the Bank of Spain's branches, indicating that the choice to establish independent banks proved more effective than relying on the Bank of Spain, at least for the spread of credit and modern means of payment.

The third and final question concerns the importance of the activity of the banks of issue with respect to the economy of the country as a whole. Joan Sardà, though he regards the contribution of fiduciary circulation to be positive for the growth of the Spanish economy at the time, adds a note of caution:

> Of course, it must be noted that the growth of the Spanish economy in those years is not based on the fact of paper money, but rather primarily on the minting of gold coinage that had been made possible by the reform of 1854.[11]

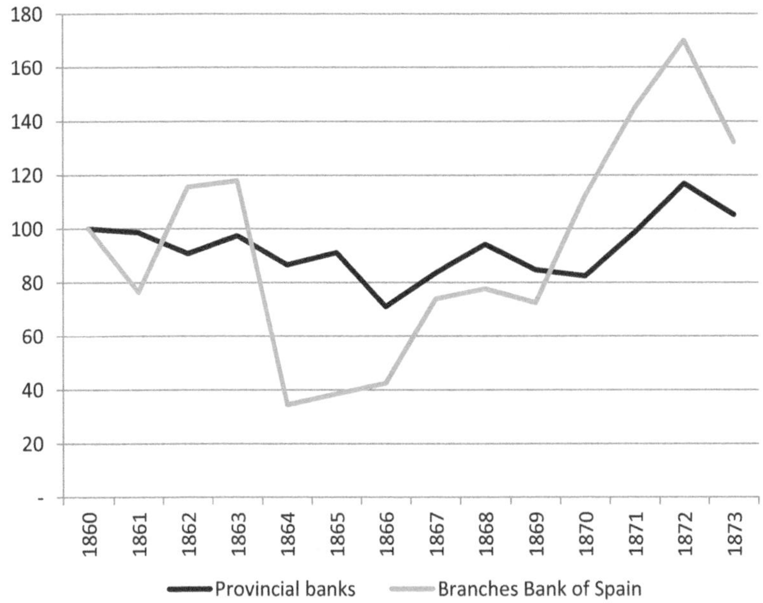

Figure 7.1 Banknotes in circulation: provincial banks and Bank of Spain branches (index 1860=100)

Note: Provincial banks on operation without Bank of Barcelona, and branches of Bank of Spain.

Indeed, there is no doubt that the share of paper money in transactions taken as a whole was still very modest in this initial period. Though there are still serious doubts about the amount of metallic money in circulation, it does not seem plausible that the amount of fiat money should represent more than 10% of the total money supply. If we look at the situation in 1864 and accept the estimates proposed in his day by Gabriel Tortella, the net share of paper money in the total money supply would not reach 9% and the share corresponding to the provincial banks would hover in the region of 4%.[12]

However, if we assume that the money supply was distributed territorially according to the estimates of GDP by province, a few calculations enable us to state that, for some provinces, the contribution of their respective banks was genuinely significant. Figure 7.2 shows the results of this speculation. For provinces like Biscay and Santander, the increase due to their respective provincial banks reaches levels as high as 20–30%.

Therefore, while it is not possible to refute the merely modest contribution attributed to the banks of issue with respect to total money supply, it is worth pointing out that for the country's more dynamic provinces this contribution was surely much greater and perhaps, in some cases, pivotal to accounting for the growth in these years.

A second strand to pursue in assessing the role played by provincial banks of issue is the international comparison. In this case, the exercise only makes sense

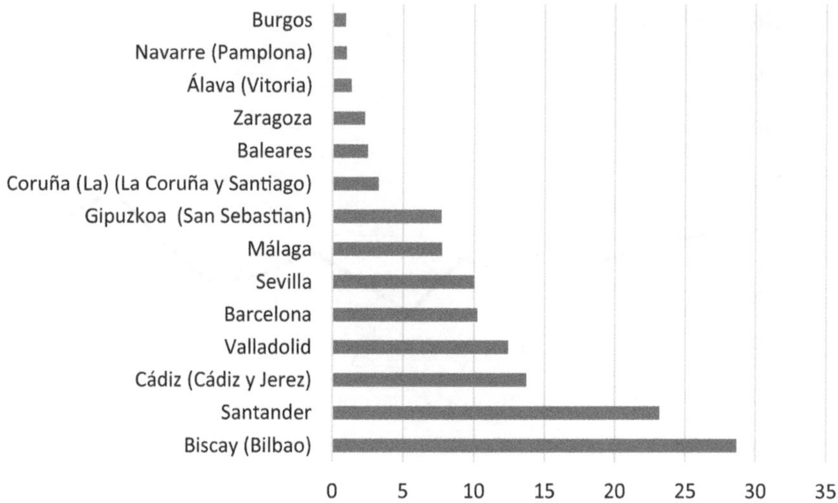

Figure 7.2 Share of bank money in the total money supply, 1862 (%)

Note: This assumes that money supply was distributed among provinces according to GDP.

Source: Martín Aceña and Pons (2005, p. 678). GDP data provided by Martínez Galarraga (see Rosés et al. (2010))

in relation to the countries that had a system of issue plurality. The aim is to determine the weight of "non-official" banks and their relative sizes. To this end, we have used banknote issue as a baseline variable.

Table 7.5 shows the result of the comparative exercise. Making use of different years has been unavoidable, but we do not believe that this has diminished the validity of the reflections that the comparison elicits. The first element to underline is that Spain is the country with the greatest relative weight of non-official banks in the circulation of fiat money. This does not mean that the banks in question were larger in size than other European banks. However, it is worth mentioning that, while the Bank of Spain circulated banknotes in amounts that were clearly lower than their European counterparts, the most active Spanish provincial banks were at the same level of issue as Scotland's and England's non-privileged banks. The figures in Table 7.5 below also make clear the special nature of the case of Scotland, where competition among banks with a similar amount of banknotes in circulation proved to be positive for the spread of credit.

In comparative terms, we can conclude that the role of Spain's provincial banks of issue was not under any circumstances anecdotal and that despite their belated establishment and the uncertainty of the regulatory framework, they attained a considerable size and succeeded in introducing modern financial habits more efficiently than the Bank of Spain where it had the opportunity to do so.

In spite of their upward trend, however, it is true that the crisis of 1866 had very negative effects on the provincial banks of issue, as it did more generally

Table 7.5 Comparative banking structure: banknotes in circulation (million pesetas and %)

	Million pesetas	*(%)*		*Million pesetas*	*(%)*
Italy – 31/12/1879			***England and Wales – 4/12/1869***		
National Bank of the Kingdom of Italy	**441**	**60.2**	**Bank of England**	**563**	**81.9**
Other banks	**292**	**39.8**	**Private banks (125)**	**67**	**9.7**
National Bank of Tuscany	*59*	8.1	**Joint-stock banks (56)**	**58**	**8.4**
Tuscan Bank of Credit	*14*	1.9	- *Stuckey's Banking Co.*	*8*	1.1
Bank of Rome	*44*	5.9	- *Gloucestershire Banking Co.*	*3*	0.5
Bank of Naples	*145*	19.8	- *Yorkshire Banking Co.*	*3*	0.4
Bank of Sicily	*30*	4.1	- *Other joint-stock banks (53)*	*44*	6.3
Germany – 31/12/1869			***Ireland – 3/12/1869***		
Bank of Prussia	**571**	**65.3**	**Bank of Ireland**	**77**	**43.0**
Other banks	**303**	**34.7**	**Other banks**	**102**	**57.0**
Bank of Frankfurt	*62*	7.1	*National Bank*	*34*	18.7
Bank of Saxony, Dresden	*53*	6.1	*Provincial Bank of Ireland*	*28*	15.6
Bank of Bavaria	*25*	2.9	*Ulster Bank*	*15*	8.6
Remaining banks (15)	*163*	18.6	*Belfast Bank*	*13*	7.4
			Northern Bank	*12*	6.7
Spain – 31/12/1865			***Scotland – 4/12/1869***		
Bank of Spain	**62**	**54.0**	**Bank of Scotland**	**16**	**12.3**
Provincial banks	**53**	**46.0**	**Royal Bank of Scotland**	**16**	**12.3**
Bank of Barcelona	*14*	12.2	**Commercial Bank of Scotland**	**18**	**13.8**
Bank of Cádiz	*12*	10.3	**Union Bank of Scotland**	**16**	**12.3**
Bank of Bilbao	*6*	5.5	**Other banks (7)**	**64**	**49.2**
Remaining banks (17)	*21*	18.0			

Source: Italy (Canovai and Ferraris, 1911); Germany (Noël, 1888, p. 199); the UK, *Bankers Magazine*.

on the banking system that emerged after the legislation of 1856. However, there is a need for some nuance. As we saw in earlier chapters, distinctions must be drawn between three different types of situation in relation to the crisis. The first situation concerns the banks that suffered the most serious impacts, which were in some cases directly attributable to improper or even criminal management. The second relates to banks that did not experience such problems, but did see their activity seriously diminished, while the third set of banks managed to withstand the buffeting and stayed on course.

The general causes of the crisis and its effects on the various banks of issue has already been noted. An additional element, however, is worth adding to these final considerations. As mentioned earlier, the state's actions and specifically the public deficit played a distortionary role in the financial market at the time. The crowding out of private-sector lending was not only the result of issuing government debt at increasingly higher prices, but also took the form of openly capturing resources from the public in direct competition with the banks and, more broadly, with all financial intermediaries.

The latter activity was carried out by a public entity created in 1852: the *Caja General de Depósitos*. The purpose of the entity was to attract deposits directly from the public and use them for the short-term financing of the state, the so-called floating debt that was not covered by the regular issues approved by the Spanish parliament.

As shown in Figure 7.3, the *Caja*, which operated through the provincial delegations of the finance ministry, took on major importance from 1859, when it launched an aggressive policy of high returns. The potential effect of the policy is evident from the parallel fall in the deposits of the Bank of Spain and the provincial banks. The policy drew harsh criticism for two reasons: first, it promoted the maintenance of the deficit by facilitating its financing and, second, it turned the

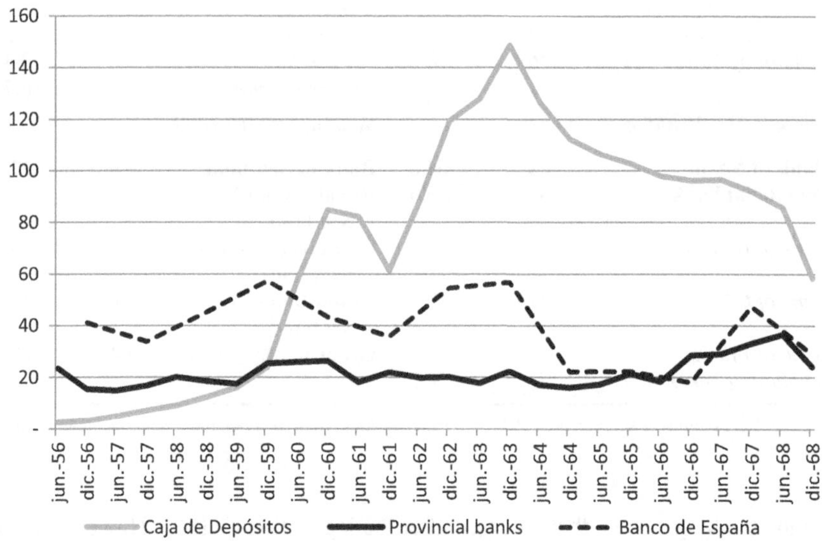

Figure 7.3 Current accounts in the provincial banks and the Bank of Spain and voluntary deposits in the *Caja de Depósitos*, 1856–1868 (million pesetas)

Source: Gonzalo (1981)

state into a direct debtor of the *Caja*'s depositors, with the attendant risk that this entailed for the state itself.

The problems arising from the creation of the *Caja General de Depósitos* did not occur solely at the general level. There were also specific versions in each province. Table 7.6 above shows the amount of voluntary deposits kept by the delegations of the finance ministry on behalf of the *Caja* in the provinces that had a bank of issue. The last column shows the ratio of the banks' total assets to the *Caja*'s voluntary deposits. As can be observed, there is no easy relationship between the two magnitudes. In any case the bigger banks seemed to be the more successful competitors as well. Nor can there be any doubt of the intense crowding-out effect in the capital market and directly on the banks of issue as a result of the *Caja*'s activity.[13]

Logically, our final considerations must turn to analysing the introduction of note-issue monopoly and its consequences. At the time that the decision was taken to eliminate issue plurality in Spain, it was still in place in most European countries, though France and the Austro-Hungarian Empire were important exceptions. It is also true, however, that several of these countries had witnessed the introduction of reforms that entailed a *de facto* progressive adoption of the principle of

Table 7.6 Voluntary deposits in the *Caja de Depósitos* and current accounts in the provincial banks, 1865

	Caja de Depósitos	*Provincial banks*	*Bank assets over Caja deposits*
Province (Provincial capital)	*Deposits 1,000 pesetas*	*Total assets 1,000 pesetas*	
Málaga	1,840.8	11,906.6	6.5
Zaragoza	3,952.5	12,480.3	3.2
Valladolid	1,832.5	5,402.3	2.9
Cádiz	9,012.5	22,404.0	2.5
Seville	6,265.0	13,654.1	2.2
Santander	5,087.5	6,785.9	1.3
Biscay (Bilbao)	8,342.5	9,962.1	1.2
Palencia	1,095.0	1,114.2	1.0
Barcelona	26,292.5	24,341.2	0.9
Tarragona	3,785.0	3,184.8	0.8
Burgos	3,365.0	1,604.5	0.5
Gipuzkoa (San Sebastián)	7,267.5	3,317.4	0.5
A Coruña	10,220.0	4,509.6	0.4
Navarre (Pamplona)	4,888.3	1,986.4	0.4
Álava (Vitoria)	4,175.0	1,395.1	0.3
Oviedo	4,587.8	1,508.5	0.3
Balearic Isl.	6,507.5	1,963.5	0.3
Total 17 provinces	108,517	127,521	1.2

Source: *Memoria dirigida al Sr. Ministro de Hacienda por el director de la caja general de depósitos de las operaciones ejecutadas en el año económico de 1865 a 1866*, Madrid, Imprenta Nacional, August 1866

fiduciary unity. This was the case with England and Ireland and it would shortly become the case with Germany as well. Though the advantages of a hypothetical system of widespread competition can be defended from a theoretical standpoint, the fact is that the actual experience at the time attests to an inexorable march toward the introduction of unified fiduciary money for each country or even for a common currency across several countries. Contemporaries who took an interest in such matters were aware of this fact and accepted it to some degree. An outstanding example of this way of thinking comes from Manual Girona, founder and director of the Bank of Barcelona and ultimately the first to be harmed by the eventual reform in favour of fiduciary unity.[14] Girona, in an open discussion within the Bank of Barcelona's board of governors on the stance that should be taken toward the decree of monetary unification, issued a warning to his colleagues:

> [. . .] the principles that science has erected with respect to credit and the issuance of paper, having been given practical demonstration in France, England and other countries, are all in agreement that there must exist only one Bank of issue and that this must naturally and inevitably come to pass in our country.[15]

Ultimately, the problem raised by the government's decision in 1874 was not about the adoption of a monopoly on banknote issue *per se*, but rather about how and when. The how was obviously affected negatively by the urgency with which the government was compelled to act and by the evident legal fragility of the decision, especially a decision of such magnitude.

In view of the experience of other countries, it can be argued that a formula that combined the effective control of banknote issue with a plurality of banks of issue – along the lines of England's Peel Banking Act or the German reorganisation of 1875 – would have had the advantage of making full use of the momentum of the most well-established banks, while at the same time avoiding the concentration of power and market dominance that the new system accorded to the Bank of Spain. This alternative appears *a posteriori* particularly desirable, if we take into account the Bank of Spain's reluctance in subsequent years to expand the use of its banknotes and to open branches.

In conclusion, while a greater control over fiduciary circulation by the authorities was probably convenient, there was no reason for such a move to be associated with the introduction of a banking monopoly like the one that was instituted, particularly if we look at the low level of integration that was still apparent in the Spanish financial market. It is doubtful that the Bank of Spain exerted its monopoly in the best way for the country as a whole, especially if we take into account that in addition to its monopoly of issue, the Bank of Spain also held a quasi-monopolistic position in both the public and the private credit markets. In some sense, the Spanish Banking Act of 1921 (the Ley de Ordenación Bancaria) had to arrive 50 years later to correct the enormously concentrated system created in 1874 by converting the Bank of Spain into a bank of banks that would no longer be engaged in commercial banking.

Notes

1 Preamble to the royal decree of 25 January 1844 establishing the Bank of Isabel II in Madrid, signed by Juan José García Carrasco, *Gaceta de Madrid*, 30 January.
2 Between 1852 and 1854, interest rates in the Barcelona market rose from 5% to 6.6%, a level that had not been reached since the height of the crisis of 1847–1848 (figures prepared by L. Castañeda and X. Tafunell and compiled in Blasco-Martel and Sudrià, 2010, p. 185).
3 In October 1855, the royal commissioner of the Bank of Barcelona referred to the local circulation of "bearer orders" (*órdenes al portador*) and "simulated deposits" (*depósitos simulados*) in his response to the government's query on the draft banking act (*Archivo de Congreso de los Diputados*, file 100, no. 36, folder 1). In 1859 an expert informant stated that, before the legislation of 1856 came into force, many merchants accepted as money some promissory notes issued by "simple money-changers without any more liability or other furniture or furnishings than a few pine tables set up in the public squares" according to a memoir written by D. José Fariñas on a tour of the credit companies in Barcelona (entry for 12 July 1859). *Archivo Histórico Nacional*, Hacienda, file 429/1.
4 For additional examples, see Tedde (1999, p. 270).
5 Tedde (1999, pp. 270–271).
6 Report of the Executive Committee to the Bank's Board of Governors, 24 May 1855. Cited by Tedde (1999, p. 271).
7 For detailed information on the reaction of the Bank of San Fernando to the drafting of the new banking act, see Tedde (1999, pp. 269–276).
8 This precedent was explicitly raised by Miguel Cantero, a member of Spain's lower house and a director of the Bank of San Fernando, in defence of local monopolies rather than the total freedom of issue proposed by Camilo Labrador, who attributed the disaster of 1847 to criminal wrongdoing by the leadership of the Bank of Isabel II (Diary of the sessions of the Cortes, Congreso de los Diputados.).
9 Tortella and García Ruiz (2013, p. 57); see other favourable opinions in Canosa (1945, pp. 40–41) and Sardà (1948, p. 126).
10 We use this particular four-year average to avoid consideration of the year 1864, when the activity of the two branches fell sharply. Consequently, the ratios are the highest possible.
11 Sardà (1948, p. 143).
12 We use the data supplied by Martín Aceña and Pons (2005, p. 678).
13 Titos (1979).
14 Girona had already expressed his conviction in 1865 that the banks of issue "those factories of paper money [. . .] must come under State oversight, as the only way [. . .] that it will be possible to avoid the conflicts that the freedom to issue inevitably brings and must bring" and, to that end, he proposed the establishment of a kind of federation of banks of issue (Girona, 1865, p. 29).
15 Minutes of the bank's board of governors cited by Blasco-Martel and Sudrià (2010, p. 346).

Sources

Archive of the Congreso de los Diputados
Archive Histórico Nacional
Diary of the sessions of the Cortes, Congreso de los Diputados.
Gazeta de Madrid

Bibliography

Blasco-Martel, Y. and Sudrià, C., 2010. *El Banco de Barcelona (1844–1874), Historia de Un Banco Emisor*. LID Editorial, Madrid.

Canosa, R., 1945. *Un siglo de banca privada 1845–1945. Apuntes para la Historia de las finanzas españolas*. Nuevas Gráficas, Madrid.

Canovai, T. and Francesco Ferraris, C, 1911. *The banks of issue in Italy*. United States National Monetary Commission, Washington, DC.

Girona, M., 1865. *Ensayos para mejorar el crédito y arreglar la situación de España*. Est. Tip. de Narciso Ramirez y Rialp, Barcelona.

Gonzalo L. 1982. *El Tesoro Público y la Caja General de Depósitos* (1852–1868). Instituto de Estudios Fiscales, Madrid.

Maddison, A., 2003. *The world economy: Historical statistics*. OECD, Paris.

Martín-Aceña, P. and Pons, M.A., 2005. Sistema monetario y financiero. In Carreras, A. and Tafunell, X. (Eds.), *Estadísticas históricas de España: Siglo XIX–XX*. Fundación BBVA, Bilbao, 645–706.

Noël, Octave, 1888. *Les banques d'émission en Europe*. Berger-Levrault, París.

Rosés, J.R., Martinez-Galarraga, J., and Tirado, D.A., 2010. The upswing of regional income inequality in Spain (1860–1930). *Explorations in Economic History*, 47 (2), 244–257.

Sardà, J., 1948. *La Política Monetaria y Las Fluctuaciones de La Economía Española En El Siglo XIX*. CSIC, Madrid.

Spinelli, F. and Frantianni, M., 1991. *Storia monetaria d'Italia : l'evoluzione del sistema monetario e bancario. La storia*. A. Mondadori, Milano.

Sudrià, C. and Blasco-Martel, Y. (Eds.), 2016. *La Pluralidad de Emisión En España, 1844–1874*. Fundación BBVA, Bilbao.

Tedde, P. 1999. *El Banco de San Fernando*. Alianza Editorial/Bnaco de Españal, Madrid.

Titos, M., 1979. El Sector Financiero En Andalucía. Una Aproximación Bibliográfica. *Revista de Estudios Regionales*, 3, 253–268

Titos, M., 2003. El sistema financiero en Andalucía: tres siglos de historia (1740-2000. Instituto de Estadística de Andalucía, Sevilla.

Tortella, G. and García Ruiz, J.L., 2013. *Spanish Money and Banking: A History*. Palgrave Macmillan, Basingstoke.

Index

Note: Page numbers in *italics* indicate figures, in **bold** indicate tables.